the Nine Lives of Charlotte Taylor

the Nine Lives of
CHARLOTTE TAYLOR

THE FIRST WOMAN SETTLER
OF THE MIRAMICHI

SALLY ARMSTRONG

RANDOM HOUSE CANADA

www.randomhouse.ca

Random House Canada and colophon are trademarks.

Library and Archives Canada Cataloguing in Publication

Armstrong, Sally
    The nine lives of Charlotte Taylor : the first woman settler of the
Miramichi / Sally Armstrong.

ISBN 978-0-679-31404-2

    1. Taylor, Charlotte, b. 1754 or 5. 2. Women immigrants—New
Brunswick—Miramichi River Valley—Biography. 3. British—New
Brunswick—Miramichi River Valley—Biography. 4. Miramichi River Valley
(N.B.)—Biography. I. Title.

FC2495.M57Z49 2006   971.5'2102'092   C2005-906079-4

Text design by Kelly Hill

Printed and bound in United States of America

10 9 8 7 6 5 4 3 2 1

For Sigrid Anna Stephenson Taylor
Intrepid, incorrigible, intelligent—like Charlotte

Charlotte's World

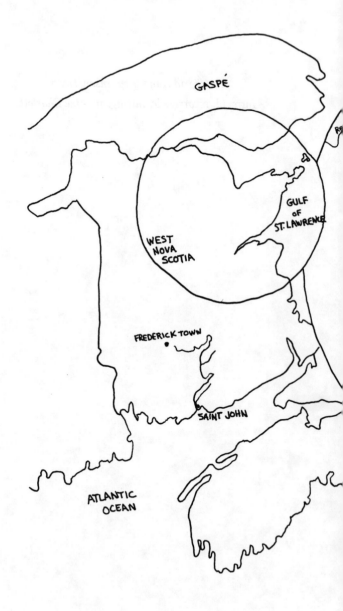

The Bay

2004

*L*ike an unfinished symphony, her story played on my mind for most of my life. It would rock to the tune of the passage of time, an adagio of high notes, low notes and illusive movements. Then when I least expected it, I happened upon the missing notes in the life of Charlotte Howe Taylor.

The rising sun is stretching out over Alston Point as I cycle along the boardwalk on the Baie de Chaleur in northern New Brunswick. A glint catches my eye and I glance sideways, trying to keep the bike upright on the narrow path. The morning rays are bouncing off a newly installed bronze plaque. Curious, I leave the bike and wade through knee-high shimmering seagrass to find out what warrants a marker at the end of Youghall Beach.

The inscription sends shivers up my spine. Line by line it spills out details I've been searching for. Recently erected government plaques do not usually resolve historical mysteries. But seeing this one, I realize that while I was toiling away in the archives and searching for birth and death dates in family Bibles trying to piece the Charlotte Taylor story together, an archaeologist had discovered a connection I'd overlooked.

More than two hundred years ago, this point of land, not much more than the end of a sand dune really, had been the site of the only trading post in the vast northeast. The proprietor, Commodore George Walker, ran a brisk trading business between England, the West Indies and this place, Nepisiguit. One of the men he worked with was Captain John Blake, who would become Charlotte Taylor's first husband.

Charlotte was a woman who upset many preconceptions. Her descendants say she fled her home in England with the family's black butler, bound for the West Indies. Historians claim she was the first woman settler on the Miramichi River. How she got from what was supposed to be sanctuary in Jamaica to John Blake's tilt on the Miramichi was a mystery. George Walker seems the likely shepherd, the man who not only brought her to these shores, but also the one who arranged her marriage to Blake, ten months after she arrived. This spot, memorialized in bronze, is where Charlotte Taylor began her life in Canada in 1775. I'm certain of it.

She is far from me in time and circumstance but connected to me by the ties that bind. Her often remarkable, sometimes questionable and certainly redoubtable story is told every time my family gathers.

Charlotte Taylor lived most of her life just one hundred kilometres south of this beach. Every summer during my youth, we would travel from the family cottage at Youghall to visit my mother's extended clan at Wishart's Point and Tabusintac near the Miramichi. And at every gathering, the aunts and uncles, my parents and grandparents would sit around the kitchen table of the old farmhouse—the very house Charlotte herself had built in 1798—telling tales of the woman who first baked bread at this hearth.

She was a woman with a past. Not exactly a gentlewoman. It was said that she came from an aristocratic family in England, although there wasn't much that seemed genteel about the settler my elders always referred to as "that old Charlotte." Words like *lover* and *land grabber* drifted down from the table to where we kids sat on the floor, but the family also had a powerful respect for her, as if their own fortitude and guile were family traits passed down from the ancestral matriarch. For as long as I can remember, I've tried to imagine the real life she lived and how she ever survived it.

The family house we return to today is where she raised her many children and plotted her next step in the survival stakes of settling in the New World. Land grants could make or break a family's fortunes. Immense forests thick with spruce were both enemies and friends to settlers who desperately needed to clear the land and plant a crop so they'd have enough food to survive the winters, and to trade the tall timbers in the region's burgeoning lumber business. The Tabusintac River, which loops around three sides of Wishart's Point, was the waterway Charlotte depended on for news and for material goods. It was also her route back to the rough-hewn world that was the Miramichi River, where she had first settled in 1776. The relentless coastal winds that blow from the northeast and the northwest, whipping up storms from the sea as well as brutal winter blizzards, are as much a part of life around the old homestead today as they were when Charlotte struggled with the elements.

The geese that flock to the fields in spring, and gather again for their autumn flight, still stop to feed on her land.

As a child, one of the rituals of my summertime visits was a trip to the Riverside Cemetery for a prayer service. The time-worn grave markers of Charlotte Taylor and her offspring are mixed in with the new marble tombstones in this peaceful place perched on a cliff overlooking the Tabusintac River. Her marker, a moss-covered, pock-marked stone that measured a foot by six inches and lay flat in the green grass, was simply labelled "Charlotte Taylor, 1755–1841." The magnitude of the memory versus the size of the marker troubled me as a child. What had she done to warrant such minimalist treatment at the grave and such nonpareil biography at the dinner table?

From the riverbank beside the burial ground, you can see her homestead at Wishart's Point in the distance and gaze over the uncluttered wilderness she would have confronted every day. Standing here, you can imagine her struggles and triumphs, from the time she staggered to the shore until a canoe, paddled by the Mi'kmaq, carried her to this resting place.

On dark winter nights back home in Montreal, my siblings and I would beg for more stories of the "olden days" and ask our mother endless questions about Charlotte Taylor, our great-great-great-grandmother.

"She came to this country with nothing but a trunk full of clothes that suited a lady more than a pioneer," she'd tell us. Her own father (my grandfather) was born just forty-five years after Charlotte died. "He told us the stories about burying food in a pit by the river so they'd have something to eat in the winter. We stored food in the same pit when I was a girl," my mother said. But like my grandfather, she used to raise her eyebrows and make remarks about the unbecoming behaviour of a woman who had three husbands. My Uncle Burt used to wink at the gathered family and say, "Sly old Charlotte had her way with men and with their land as well." What *had* happened to her husbands? I once asked whether she had killed them. My question was met with hoots of laughter that only served to heighten my fascination.

She was a woman whom historian William Ganong called "a remarkable early settler." Her obituary in the *Royal Gazette of Newcastle* described her as "a respected woman who was the third British settler" in the region. But hers is not a story of a woman in starched white petticoats and a beribboned bonnet, displaced from the Old World and trying to re-create it in the new one. She managed to keep her ten children alive through the American Revolution that was fought on her doorstep, the Indian raids that burned out her neighbours and the droughts and floods and endless winters that challenged her wit and tenacity. She was of this place.

I have spent ten years on and off searching for hooks to this elusive woman and became hooked myself—on shipping schedules from 1775, on Mi'kmaq history, on settler survival skills and the clash of Acadian, Loyalist and pre-Loyalist personalities.

In 1980, during the Old Home Week celebrations that are held every five years in Tabusintac, the memorial service at the cemetery featured the unveiling of a prepossessing new headstone for Charlotte that heralded her as "The Mother of Tabusintac," a fitting epitaph since almost every family from here can trace its roots to her. The stone stands first in the cemetery as you enter by the main gate. It is made out of granite, tough enough to withstand the storm of time—just like the woman herself. And it also has an error, rendering her death date as 1840 when, in fact, she died in 1841. There's nothing inscribed that speaks of the compassion and grace in her rugged life, or hints at the rogue in her.

After Old Home Week in 1995, when I got back to my desk as editor-in-chief of *Homemaker's Magazine* in Toronto, I decided to write my editorial letter about her, wanting to share the story of one of the earliest settlers in Eastern Canada with my readers. As a result, the magazine received letters from her descendants from all over the world. They came from England and Saudi Arabia, from the United States and Kenya, and expressed the same passion and pride I'd known since childhood. I wrote to each of these far-flung branches of Charlotte's family tree and asked for their memories and memorabilia. In return I learned of her winter trek by snowshoe from the Miramichi to Fredericton, more than two hundred miles away, and of her bitter quarrels with the Loyalists who came to the river after the American Revolution. Almost all of my correspondents mentioned a liaison with a Mi'kmaq man.

The archives in New Brunswick provided facts about births, marriages and deaths, and also handwritten, sometimes desperate petitions for land titles. Historians such as Ganong, and before him the explorer and erstwhile entrepreneur Nicolas Denys, faithfully recorded the details of those early days in what would become northern New Brunswick.

It wasn't yet a province when Charlotte set foot there. Canada was still ninety-two years short of its official birthday. All of the territory east of Quebec was called Nova Scotia except for the tiny Isle Saint-John, which was renamed Prince Edward Island in 1799. The Mi'kmaq (called Micmac by the settlers) were considered mentors by the Acadians, wily traders by men like Commodore Walker and savage enemies by the British military. When Charlotte arrived, the Acadians who hadn't taken refuge from the expulsion in Mi'kmaq camps were staggering back to the land after twenty years in exile. Tabusintac, the Miramichi and Nepisiguit (present-day Bathurst, New Brunswick) were part of a vast wilderness that claimed the lives of many soldiers, settlers and traders.

Charlotte Taylor lived in the front row of history, walking the same path as the Mi'kmaq, the Acadians, the privateers of the British-American War and the Loyalists. Her story is shaped by the howling nor'easters, the isolating winters, the grind of daily survival and the devastating circumstances that stalked her growing family.

Her adventurous spirit is what's on my mind as I stare at the marker on Youghall Beach on a July morning before the rest of the world is awake. At this wondrous time of day, you can leave your footprints like first tracks on the sandbars. You can watch, at a silent distance, a great blue heron pausing to feed on the shoreline. Sun dapples the water of the Baie de Chaleur, creating dazzling mirrors of light. It strikes me that Charlotte could have seen this too.

Did she walk these sandbars before paddling south to the Miramichi? Was she a runaway frightened by her new surroundings or thrilled by her sudden bolt from home? I know only one other thing about her life before she landed here, a secret that she carried with her from England.

CHAPTER I

The Ocean

1775

*I*t's just an hour after dawn on the first Monday in May 1775 when the *Anton* lurches its bulk away from the docks at Bristol and sets sail for the West Indies. Charlotte Taylor is at the rail, rivetted to the huge square sails puffing out like bullies in the wind and bucking the ship into the open sea. A tall woman with flame-red hair tied in a knot at her neck, she keeps her eye to the bow as if setting her own course and her back to the land she has left behind. Standing beside her at the rail is Pad Willisams, her lover and co-conspirator in the hurried exit from Charlotte's family, Pad's job as butler in the Taylor household and a truth they each had only a part of.

A hastily packed trunk is stowed with the cargo. The calico sack she'd prepared for the voyage, and now realizes is pathetically inadequate since the trunk cannot be opened again until they reach shore six to eight weeks from now, is slung over her back.

A scrofulous man of indiscriminate age eyes her repeatedly from his place by the forward capstan. He's one of the woebegone collection of humanity she's travelling with—mostly men in their twenties and thirties and one young boy with freckles on his nose who seems to be in the employ of the haughty Captain Skinner. They all stare shamelessly at the white woman and the black man by her side. Pad has pulled together all the stiff dignity of the butler he had been just days earlier, but she can feel the anxiety that thrums through him. She is somewhat surprised to realize that she isn't daunted by the stares, the days ahead or the consequences of leaving her family's country home outside of London. Standing in the brisk wind on the deck of a sailing ship just a week after her twentieth birthday, Charlotte Taylor is unafraid—maybe even elated.

She's still leaning on the portside, watching the water, letting the wind blow on her face when she allows herself to cast her thoughts to what she has run away from. The terrible row with her father when he learned she'd been "consorting," as he called it, with Pad. The endless rounds of tea, the suffocating rules and her mother's predictable attacks of the vapours whenever there was a hint of excitement in the household. She smiles in anticipation of the life ahead. A marriage to the dashing Pad, a home in the tropics. She's grinning at the prospects when Pad interrupts her reverie to suggest they go below and secure their living quarters.

The quarters are cramped; the ceiling is so low they have to duck their heads. The bunks are arranged in two rows, one on each side of the dreary lower deck with damp curtains hanging between them to lend an illusion of privacy. There are hooks on which to hang their possessions and a lopsided stove in the centre. The only light and fresh air is from the hatch to the upper deck; the quarters smell of mildew and rotten wood. Indeed, the black streaks of rot crawling up the legs of the cots speak of the months at sea, the flourishing business of carrying human and other cargo across the ocean as many times as the weather will allow between May and October, never stopping long enough to refit or repair.

They pick a bunk at the end of the row and tie their sacks to the hooks before exploring the rest of the lower deck. There are stalls toward the stern filled with animals—two steers, four sheep, a ragged flock of chickens and three fat pigs. Charlotte looks at each and lingers on the soft, uncomprehending eyes of the steers that will become meals for the passengers and crew. Tucked under the bow in a wedge-shaped hold are the ship's stores—burlap sacks of flour, sugar and grain, cases of biscuits, salt and limes. Charlotte and Pad walk back to midship, where a wide hatch is battened shut on the deck.

"What's down there?" Charlotte asks a stocky sailor who is hurrying aft.

"Cargo, madam," he says. "Plenty a' cotton cloth and wool. That's what makes 'em rich, madam, shippin' the likes a' that."

My trunk is down there too, Charlotte thinks ruefully.

THE YOUNG LAD who'd caught her eye when they left the dock is friendly, puppyish and not too shy to tell her his name is Tommy Yates when she finds him exploring the lower deck.

"Me dad was the one who got me on board," the boy confides gravely. "He brought me to the dock and hired me out to the captain. He told him I was sixteen, an' I'm but thirteen."

"Thirteen?" Charlotte looks at him closely. "Are you even that?"

"Oh yes, madam. Honest, I am."

She had thought him no more than a scrawny eleven.

When he is not scrambling up the rigging at the captain's orders or crawling through the hold below the sleeping quarters to fetch something the captain needs from the cargo, Tommy finds his way to Charlotte's side. In the first week at sea, she heard about his fourteen brothers and sisters, the drink that made his father what he was and the mother who was so sickly she could hardly manage to stagger from her bed.

Charlotte shares her own story with him—putting a more varnished spin on her departure than is the case. She tells Tommy that she and Pad are married and that her father, General Taylor, doesn't approve of the relationship so they decided to leave home for the West Indies and start a new life.

She entertains the winsome boy with details of the world she left behind, imitating her nanny's priggish etiquette. "She insisted I sit like this all day long," says Charlotte, perching herself on a bench and exaggerating the pose—her back ramrod straight, her legs bent at the knee and turned slightly sideways and her hands folded together in her lap. She makes him laugh when she describes her antics in the straitlaced household—refusing to marry the man her mother had chosen for her, looking contrite when her father admonished her, galloping around the estate on her horse and lingering at the stable with Pad. Tommy thinks it's a blissful life she's left, but even this boy can see the rebel in the woman he has befriended.

Throughout those days Pad often lies marooned in his cot. The seasickness is terrible for him, while Charlotte hardly feels the transition from land to water. Sometimes she wonders if Pad's real sickness is the knowledge of what he has done, leaving all he knew behind, and worry about what might lie ahead.

"They're such little waves," she pleads, but he only turns his head and is silent. At night, by a guttering candle, she makes entries in her diary with her best quill, dipping ink from the biggest bottle she'd dared carry.

*I wonder what Papa and Mama are thinking. They must
suspect that I have run off with Pad. Papa has always liked
Pad—had hopes for him to become something more than a
butler—and perhaps thought a stern speech to me might
prevent any "foolishness" as he called it. But while he
lectured me, I felt as though the ceiling in his study had
dropped to inches over my head.*

She flips back the pages of her diary to read the entry made
that fateful night after her father had dismissed her and she'd
bolted to her bedroom, then scribbles another line onto today's
entry . . . *The pitched battle I've been in for as long as I can remember
over the seemliness of my behaviour is behind me now* . . . and closes
the diary.

As one week stretches into two, then to three, then a month,
Charlotte is determined to insulate her exhilaration from Pad's
continuing illness, the monotony of the voyage, the worry about
the future. The rations begin to diminish in the fifth week and
ambitious weevils and fuzzy blue mould appear in the flour and
biscuits. She feels as grimy and bedraggled as the gloomy men
around her, but her joy is dimmed only a little sitting by the ships
rail where, wind and water offering refreshing relief, she takes
her diary from her pocket and glances through the entries.

A BLACK HORIZON. They'd had squalls and days of grey skies
and rain, but Charlotte had seen nothing like the storm clouds
that lie ahead, as though the sky is disfigured by bruises, black,
yellow and purple. Standing at her usual spot at the rail she's
astonished by the sudden change. The jagged edges of storm
clouds ahead meet the white-capped water as though one could
become the other at any moment.

"Shorten sails!" the captain calls. "Stiggs, get below with three men and fasten loose cargo!"

"Aye, sir," the first mate shouts.

"Have the passengers go below now!"

"Aye, sir!"

Salt spray stings her eyes and soaks her cloak as Charlotte struggles to the hatch and steps her way down the wet rungs. She hurries to Pad and is surprised to find him sitting up.

"It must be the little waves that bother me," he says with a smile. "I feel right enough now."

Charlotte stuffs their few possessions into her calico bag and ties it securely to the hook on the wall. The stomping of boots plays like a drumbeat on the deck overhead while the livestock squeal and mewl their terror. Anxiety is as thick as fog. She and Pad settle by the stovepipe in the centre of the double row of berths, rubbing their hands together for consoling warmth. She looks back to her berth as though there might be some comfort hanging there in the calico bag. Her keepsakes are so few—a volume of poetry, her well-worn copy of *Clarissa,* her diary, the combs she'd worn in her hair when she'd been presented to the county magistrate on her recent birthday, her sketch of the garden she could see from her childhood bedroom window—flotsam of a life far from the bowels of the creaking ship. A man vomits onto the floor beside her and the latrines tip as the ship rolls and their contents ease out accordingly. She gathers her skirts around her, trying to keep them out of the slop.

Half the night passes. She may have dozed. She opens her eyes to find Pad crouched beside her, his eyes wide. She places a hand on his brow: he's not right enough now. There is a fever there perhaps. Small wonder. Confined to his bunk since they came aboard, and, with the vomit and night soil sloshing about, contagion might well spread to everyone. She wipes his brow with her kerchief, he leans his head on her shoulder gratefully. Pad is not himself, she knows. When she'd fallen in love with him, she saw him as a man who knew what to do in any circumstance, who calmed the household by his very presence.

The ship lurches forward. The wind grows louder. Tommy must have escaped his duty with the captain because he appears on the ladder, clutching at the rungs. At the bottom, he stumbles over and huddles on the other side of her for a time without speaking.

"Will we die?" he finally whispers.

"No, we will not." Charlotte makes her voice sharp, impatient, but she is not entirely certain he is wrong. The permanent frown on Tommy's brow reminds her of the stable boy, Jack, who helped with her father's horses. Jack's grimace disappeared when he was with the animals, and Charlotte would sometimes find him curled up against the haunches of a cow, asleep, his face as tranquil as that of a baby.

"Let's go and visit the livestock," she proposes to Tommy, then whispers to Pad, "I'm going to go with the boy, to see the cows. It may calm him."

In the holding pen, they find trembling animals that look as if they might stampede into the raging sea if they weren't confined by the barrier leading to the main deck. A sound comes from a heap of straw, hard to hear over the roar of water and the screech of the ship's timbers—a litter of newborn kittens, meowing for their absent mother.

"Where's Lucifer?" Charlotte shouts. She had believed the ship's black cat to be a male, but this was not the case.

"She's not here," Tommy calls, kneeling beside the kittens.

"Look!" Charlotte kneels beside him. "Look. They're as frightened as we are."

She could imagine the captain would not look kindly on more cats. But here was a cause that could distract a frightened, lonely boy.

"Help me, Tommy! We must hide these kittens or the captain will surely toss them overboard."

Together they carry the litter into a dark recess of the stalls, where their mother would easily find them later. Tommy would have to occupy his mind with finding a way to keep them out of the captain's sight.

Charlotte returns to her post by the stove, leaving Tommy to tend to the kittens. Save for the few men whose job is to steer the vessel through the storm, the rest of the passengers and crew have taken refuge in the living quarters—a euphemism for this collection of stacked wooden cots, she thinks.

The rain is pounding the ship now, splashing into the lower deck through the leaky hatch and sending all the passengers to the centre where Charlotte has staked out her spot by the stove. The wind picks up, howling like nothing she had ever heard. Huddled by the stove with men she would rather not talk to, she takes her diary from her pocket, looks through her recent entries.

May 25—I was awakened last night by the most awful noise. It sounded as though someone or something was crying for help outside the so-called living quarters. The wailing went on for several minutes. Then it was quiet, save the sound of a few men busy with a chore. When I got up this morning and went on deck, I found out it was the slaughter of a sheep—the poor thing bleated so pathetically. Pad thinks I'm being spoiled and dramatic.

June 2—One can't very well celebrate the halfway point when one doesn't have a way of knowing where in the middle of all this water the ship is—but Captain Skinner says we're moving very well.

Suddenly, as if an explosion had ripped across the bow, the storm strikes the ship and the souls on board with such punishment Charlotte wonders if they will survive. She certainly cannot write in the diary now—it's all she can do to stay upright. The fire goes out in the stove. The oil lamps in the hold dim and die, leaving them all in darkness. She clings to the pole the stove is lashed to and Pad clings to her. The ship heaves and pitches. Someone near her vomits. Someone else is crying. Most of them are praying. This is as close to hell as she can imagine. The waiting feels like an eternity—hovering in the dark, clinging to anything that is tied down. Waiting, waiting for the abatement.

Then—silence, quickly followed by the sound of boots beating across the upper deck. The captain's voice calls down into the lower deck: "We're in the eye of the storm. Quickly, make tea, get the biscuits and jam. It may be a long time before you eat again." Everyone rushes to comply. Pad manages to reignite the stove as well as the lamps, and Charlotte yanks the biscuits from the storeroom shelves and passes them around. Then she wraps a fistful of broken biscuits into the folds of her skirt, fills a vessel with water and goes to check on Tommy and the kittens who are, all of them, fast asleep. The rocking motion that terrified the others had soothed boy and cats to a blessed slumber.

The calm doesn't last long. Once across the eye of the storm, the winds roar into action buffeting the ship again, sucking it up a monstrous wave and dropping it in free-fall until it pounds into the trough below. Charlotte listens to the people huddled around her at the stove who alternately plea for mercy and try to second-guess the captain. She nods off from time to time, they all do. No one moves. They are shivering, damp, frightened and thoroughly mesmerized until one by one, they give in to exhaustion.

Charlotte isn't sure whether she is dreaming or waking when she sees light streaming in around the hatch to the upper deck. All is quiet. They are at an odd collection of angles, leaning into one another, bent forward, lolling back against a plank. The light becomes brighter. Charlotte wonders whether they have sailed out of this purgatory. When she rises to see for herself, she upsets the pyramid of bodies gathered around her. They shake the long night's damage from their aching backs and stand to follow Charlotte to the ladder. As she lifts her head above the hatch, she stops. The brilliance of the sky, the radiance of the morning, the sun already halfway to the zenith, the charged thrill of the fresh breeze—she can neither exclaim nor form any thought but steps on the deck and lets the pleasure of it wash over her.

Captain Skinner beckons them to join him on deck and announces, with the flourish she'd come to expect of him, "By the grace of God and the skills of the good men who are my crew, we have weathered a mid-Atlantic storm."

Charlotte studies the man. She had thought him aloof, arrogant. But he had stood on the main deck while she and most others on board had huddled like frightened children in the dark. Who was to say what qualities made some good ship's masters and some good butlers.

Below, sailors are mopping up the filthy water and checking the hull for damage. Charlotte slips away to the stalls and finds Tommy rubbing the sleep from his eyes.

"Get up," she whispers. "No one has missed you yet."

—

By mid-afternoon, they are fed, dried out and gathered on the upper deck for a reckoning of the ship's condition conducted by the purser, Watkins, a stout man of perhaps forty who looks to Charlotte as though he'd be better suited to minding a haberdasher in Whitechapel. Food supplies, cargo, health status and injuries are to be determined. The captain announces, "The storm has mercifully pushed us ahead. We have passed the halfway point in my considered judgment and will find the shore in four more weeks." Then the inspection begins. They hadn't seen anything resembling fresh fruit or vegetables since the end of the first week at sea. The oatmeal, although damp and sticky, is still in ample supply, so are the dried peas. The biscuits are spotted with mould, as is the quickly diminishing supply of cheese, but the barrels of thick, sweet molasses will suffice. Potatoes, so filling, so easy to prepare, are still in abundance, but it is only a matter of time before their softening skins will rot and the supply is lost to vermin. The head count of livestock has suffered more loss during the storm than anyone had counted on. Two of the remaining three sheep and a dozen chickens suffocated and one of the steers, bawling and sick, has to be shot and thrown overboard. It is the water they worry about most.

Two sailors emerge from below decks to whisper to Watkins, who looks concerned. He hurries forward to where the captain has resumed conversation with the first mate. The crew members arch their necks as the officers speak together in low tones. Man whispers to man that the storm had breached the water barrels. Watkins comes back, clears his throat.

"Water is to be rationed," he says. He pokes nervously and repeatedly at the bridge of his spectacles with one finger. "Any fresh water lost or befouled will mean a shortage. Henceforth, the captain orders that there will be no use of water for any such purposes as washing."

"What about the passengers?" a young man in a battered felt hat calls out.

Watkins sets his small face with determination.

"No one is to use water for any purpose but that set out by the captain, which is drinking only and the boiling of potatoes and meat and such."

"You know what happens?" All eyes turned to a weathered sailor at the back. "You know what happens when a ship runs out of water in them south Caribbean waters? You know how they go, them aboard? Like animals, they do, fightin' for each ladle."

There is a buzz of agreement from the crew, who turn ominous eyes on the twenty passengers, who meet their gaze with shrinking confidence.

"Not before they been in terrible awful torments," another sailor adds, wagging his head gravely.

Charlotte thinks there is a certain malicious twinkle in the eyes of both men, but the truth of the warning is not lost on her.

"Yates!" Watkins barks at the boy, who had edged near Charlotte. "Why ain't you countin' candles in the hold?"

"Didn't know to do it, sir."

"You did, Yates. You're a lazy rascal, you are. Get below."

"Yes, sir,"

Other men emerge from the hatch to report on the state of the cargo, the tallow, the ropes, the barrels of pitch and oakum and salt. During these proceedings, young Tommy emerges to report ten boxes of candles.

"Ten?" Watkins frowns. "What's become o' the others?"

"I ain't counted them yet, sir."

"Why not, boy?" Watkins stabs at his spectacles.

"I ain't got but ten fingers, sir."

The crew roars with delight.

"Count all those boxes, Yates, or you'll have a finger less!"

Tommy scampers down the hatch.

"It's not candles we want," Charlotte whispers to Pad. "It's water. Why did they not store it securely?"

When the job is finished, every man and the one woman on board have to give an accounting of their own health and injuries. There isn't one among them without scrapes and bruises from the beating they had taken during the storm. Life below decks has exacted a physical and spiritual toll they are all paying. Charlotte wants to tell Watkins that the fact they present themselves as reasonably healthy this day is a testament to their toughness or perhaps desperation, not to any care offered by the crew of this ship. But she remains silent.

By now Charlotte has bits and pieces of the backgrounds of the passengers. Most of these men, she came to realize, were running away from something, some from the police or debt and others, she assumes from their grumbling at meals and cries in the night, from any manner of misfortune. Several bought their passage by agreeing to sling the ship's cargo at one end or the other. Some were being delivered as workers to the islands. "Is that what 'indentured' means?" she asks Pad. She bets they have stories to tell, stories that for their own good are better kept secret. Like skeletons dangling on their backs, the unrevealed dramas sail along with the human cargo.

The voyage is finally starting to sap Charlotte's enthusiasm. On July 5, she writes in her diary:

Will this voyage never end? The only excitement is when someone calls out "Portside" or "Starboard" and we get to see

some huge fish swimming by the ship. At least there's some-
thing out there other than the soggy people on this boring
boat. When fair winds blow, everyone cheers our progress, but
when the sails slacken and the ship is becalmed, we sit, some-
times for days at a time. That's when the arguments begin.
Every perceived slight threatens physical violence.

The only pleasure I have is talking to Tommy. He has
an odd way of talking, as though he's trying to imitate a
grand gentleman, when he greets me on the deck with a
slight bow and says, "A fine day to yerself, Miss Charlotte."
I'm going to ask Pad if we can take him with us when we
get off this boat. As for Pad, I'm beginning to wonder about
the family ties he says he has in Jamaica. He feels I'm
criticizing him when I ask questions about who it is we
will meet once we land. But I can't imagine walking onto
the shore and asking for Willisams, just like that, which is
I think what he has planned.

THE SEA IS SPREAD around her, the horizon as wide and featureless as it has remained for seven weeks. Tommy is scraping pots by the gunwale.

"Are you well this morning, Tom?"

He looks up. "Yes, madam. Well enough at least."

Later in the day she finds him feeding the livestock. Such a runt of a child, she thinks. Run ragged with chores from dawn to dusk.

"Did you get your share of water to drink?" she asks.

"Not 'til I'm done entirely."

Water is divvied up in portions so precise the passengers have begun to hoard what they can. But the boy seems to be every sailor's scapegoat. His grimy face is flushed, but she forbears to touch his brow for fear he is contagious. Even from six paces, she can sense fever.

"I'll fetch you some of mine," she says and goes back to the bunks where Pad lies asleep. She fills a small cup from the vessel they keep beneath their bedding. On the way forward, she sees Captain Skinner and the bo's'n emerge from a storeroom. She is surprised to encounter Skinner below decks. He is a man to delegate most tasks. The bo's'n hurries off.

"Mrs. Willisams."

Skinner is of moderate height and some forty years, impressively broad across the chest, his face permanently burnished by years of weather. His eyes are brown and intelligent, or penetrating at least, but a heavy chin and high-bridged nose give the impression of rather too much character.

"Captain Skinner."

"How are you faring, Mrs. Willisams?"

"Well enough, captain. We must all bear up as best we can."

"Yes. Well, you bear up well. Your husband"—and here he hesitates just a little too long for true civility—"seems . . . not as well."

"He may have a fever."

"Parsons is our man in charge of illnesses here."

"I've spoken to Mr. Parsons, captain, but he has nothing more to offer."

"If you should need to rest a little from your tasks, Mrs. Willisams, may I suggest you join me some evening at table. I find a change of setting a cheering thing."

"Thank you, captain. But I must attend my husband."

"Of course you must. But should he be sleeping well and you would perhaps enjoy some conversation, please speak to me."

The flicker of a glance the captain tosses her way tells Charlotte that she will not soon be joining this man for supper.

She brings the water back to Tommy. He guzzles it, wiping his mouth and licking the drops from his fingers. Then he shivers, though the hold is stifling. She takes the scarf she's wearing and wraps it around his neck. "Try to rest some," she tells him and heads back to the sleeping quarters.

To pass the time, the men often gather on the upper deck to listen to the captain tell stories about crossings past. On the evening of July 6, Charlotte joins them, staying well back of the men. She wants to hear the chronicle but also hopes to avoid Skinner's glance. She knows he thinks she's fair game for the suggestive attention he pays to her. She finds a secluded spot behind the rigging and listens to his description of the shipping business and the islands in the Caribbean. She learns that hundreds of ships cross these waters every year from May to October, some to the West Indies, others to British North America. Those that are late arriving have to winter over; if it's in the West Indies, soft summer breezes, fruit falling out of the trees and palm trees laden with coconuts make the stay a pleasure. But those who get stuck in British North America are as likely as not to perish in the dreadful winter months. She'd heard about the ice and snow from the men who met with her father to discuss shipping routes and cargo. She'd listened to tales of the savagery of the Indians and the ferocity of the beasts that roamed the forests. Her father had told her about the French Acadians—traitors, he said, who plotted against England and were a constant threat to the good British settlers who struggled to make shelters and find enough food to stay alive. The West Indies, in contrast, sounds like paradise.

"There's where you'll shape your future, boys," Captain Skinner is saying. "For women, of course, it's a different story." Charlotte leans closer. "Concubines are commonplace on Jamaica." Murmurs of assent all round. "Marriage—well, marriage is hardly heard of—and there's some here aboard who'll be glad of that, gentlemen, I tell you."

General laughter. Charlotte's face reddens. There could be no mistaking it: he is speaking to her.

"There's little monogamy there," says Captain Skinner, warming rapidly to his topic. "Every man may have several wives and several children with each one. Their real families are back in England—where they belong!" Laughter. "A man may buy himself a whore for what he pays to fill his pipe!"

Loud and sustained laughter.

Several men turn to look back to where Charlotte stands. She struggles for her dignity but cannot tolerate such raillery. She turns and strides to the hatch.

"Though a pipe may often give as much pleasure!" Captain Skinner calls after her and the men roar.

The moment her feet touch the passengers' deck, she feels a surge of anger. She pushes past two men lounging in the dim passageway and hurries to the bunk she shares with Pad. He's on his back, staring at the ceiling.

"You've not told me the truth, Pad! You've lied to me."

He sits upright, looks puzzled.

"How do you mean?"

"You've deceived me and taken me for a fool."

"I've done *no* such thing. What do you mean, Charlotte?"

Old Hutchins, who bunks across from them, looks over with mild curiosity, but drops his eyes when Charlotte gives him a look.

"You've told me you were taking me to a paradise, where we'd live and be free. But as far as the captain says, it seems to be a paradise only for men. Women there are nothing more than goods to be bought and sold in the market, like the poor Africans."

"It's not so, Charlotte."

"Is it not? The captain's been there a few times more often than you have, Pad Willisams!"

"We won't be anybody's slaves, Charlotte, I know that much."

"You mean *you* won't!"

"No, I won't. The slaves are Africans. The native blacks they call the coloureds. We're regarded altogether different."

"That's not what I'm talking about."

"What is it then?"

Charlotte takes a long breath.

"Pad," she says, "will we be living with the English and the other whites? Tell me the truth."

"I . . . I don't know, Charlotte. Not with perfect certainty. But I do know we'll have nothing to fear from slave masters."

"Who told you that?"

"Friends."

"Friends who?"

"Friends I have—I *had*—in service."

"And what did they know?"

"They *knew.*"

"Pad, did they know that Jamaica is a godless place where women are concubines? That marriage has no meaning?"

"The captain must be a liar, Charlotte."

"A white woman has nothing to fear," a raspy voice says. Charlotte turns to see Hutchins propped on one elbow. "They respect a white person, never mind man or woman."

"What do you know?" Charlotte demands.

"Lived there fourteen years," Hutchins says. He fades back onto his mattress, as though he'd spoken his last words.

Charlotte makes a short sound, not quite a laugh.

"Did you? And did you have a wife there too?"

"Three," Hutchins says without opening his eyes. Charlotte rolls hers. "But none of 'em was white," the old man adds.

Charlotte looks back to see Pad's reaction, but his eyes are closed, shutting her out.

ON THE MORNING of July 7, she comes on deck to find the sails full and the spirits of every person on board lifted. She can't find young Tommy. Her affection for the boy has grown so much, she worries about him constantly. The kittens are having their way all over the ship with the captain's grudging approval. Lucifer is back on the prowl, hardly noticing the brood she'd birthed on board. The stalls are bare, the animals consumed. But Tommy is nowhere to be found. She knows his ailment is getting worse. He seems to be even smaller and his cough sounds like glass breaking in his lungs. When she finds him at last, he is lying on a heap of straw at the bottom of the ladder down to the storage hold, shaking with fever and talking gibberish. "Tommy, it's me, Charlotte." The boy moans, slurring words rapidly one into the other. She can't make out his meaning, but it seems he is being chased. As hard as he runs with his words, his lungs cannot catch up. His breathing is ragged, noisy, his chest caving in with every heaving breath. She's certain now that he is contagious, that touching him could bring about her own demise, but the pathetic sight of this blameless child overwhelms her. She gathers his puny frame into her arms, wraps her skirts and shawl around him and strokes his brow while whispering soothing thoughts in his ear. "You'll stay in the islands with me. I'll need a good boy like you to help me. You'll see, Tommy, this voyage will end and there will be a new beginning."

She stays there for hours, trying to will him to live. He sleeps a little, stirs as if in another nightmare and slips into suspended consciousness again. Then he wakens and begins to cough, to choke, she fears. She can feel his ribs against her arms as the cough tears through his emaciated body. The light around the ladder to the stalls turns to dusk, then dark. Pad finds her where she cradles Tommy; he brings them biscuits spread with molasses and strong tea. He warns her of the danger to herself, and suggests she leave the boy where he lies. The kittens, and Lucifer too, have found the heap of woman and boy and taken their places around them, burrowing into the warm, damp folds of Charlotte's skirts. She wets Tommy's lips with the tea, tries to dribble some liquid into his mouth. Pad returns with his own great coat. "I'll tuck it under him. It might give some warmth to Tommy and protect you as well." Charlotte knows Tommy needs more than a coat, more than her own ministration. "He needs decent food, a doctor." Pad just shrugs—there is no one onboard except the incompetent Parsons.

The ship sails into the night. A brisk wind means they'll change hands on deck and take advantage of the blow. The only sound is the snapping of the sails, the voices of the men above her head. Charlotte naps, wakening when Tommy's coughing wrenches through both of them. Then suddenly he sits up, looks straight at her and in his peculiar way of speaking says, "Yer fair of face, Miss Charlotte. Yer eyes take the colour of the sea. Yer scent is fragrant, like the cattle."

"Like the cattle!" she replies with mock horror, delighted to be teasing him. She thinks it must be a turning point, that the boy has gained his senses. But as quickly as he'd risen, he collapses again like a wicker basket suddenly disassembled. Then his eyes close and he becomes so still she finally realizes he has stopped breathing.

"You poor small boy," she croons to the little body in her arms. "You never managed to find the shore." She's never seen anyone die before, much less held a lifeless body. She rocks the bundle in her arms and tries to reckon what will happen next.

A LOUD CLAMOUR of bells and the captain's voice shouting words she can't hear. Charlotte leaves Tommy's body with Watkins, who had appeared with first light, and hurries onto the deck.

"Get below!" he commands her. "Get below this instant!"

She retreats in confusion. Several men jump through the hatch to the lower deck. Others push her toward it, then pass her down what seems like a moving platform of hands.

"Hasten now!" calls a sailor at the bottom of the ladder and points her toward her bunk.

"What's happening?" Charlotte demands.

"Pirates," the sailor shouts as he runs toward the stern. Charlotte feels the frisson of fear. Had they come so far and suffered such discomforts to die now? She hurries to her lover.

"Pad! There's pirates!"

He jumps to his feet, grabbing Charlotte and pushing her behind him.

"You best get yourself down in the hold, mistress." Hutchins lies on his filthy mattress, his face betraying no alarm. "You'll be prize booty for 'em, that's sure. They'd kill us all to have you. Not that I'd fight 'em. I'm too old for that. Get down in the hold, I say."

Charlotte turns to Pad. "There's hardly strength enough left on this ship to take on boys, much less bandits."

Pad takes her hand and keeps her close while the other passengers huddle in silence. But she detests this, waiting like cattle in the hold for slaughter. She lets go of Pad's hand and crosses through to the aft passageway. There is no one there and she wonders where she might best hide. Ten yards along, she sees light overhead. The second aft hatch is open. She hears distant voices and can't resist the mad impulse to see for herself and climbs the ladder just far enough to peek above the level of the deck. A hundred yards to port is another ship, a large single-masted sloop on a parallel course. It is the first evidence of humanity beyond this ship they have encountered since they had left Bristol, and it has come to devour them.

She looks up and is surprised to see that the *Anton* carries only light sail, although the breeze is strong.

"Surely we must try," she thinks. She looks along the deck to where Skinner and two officers stand at the rail. They face the approaching sloop and are waving their arms. The sloop draws close, its enormous mainsail billowing. Charlotte feels her throat constrict with anxiety so palpable she can hardly draw breath.

Men stand along the rail of the sloop with drawn blades and muskets. What chance has she to hide from these pitiless bandits? They have only to put a few of the *Anton*'s men to torture or the sword and her presence will soon be revealed. A voice rises above the sound of the rushing water.

"Heave to! Heave to now!"

It is spoken by a tall man who stands a head above the other pirates.

"Heave to! We're boarding. Lay down your weapons and you'll every one have mercy from us! Heave to!"

Captain Skinner waves again and calls out.

"Help! Help! We need water! Help!"

"Heave to, skipper!" calls the pirate captain. His hair is black and unbound, as Charlotte had always imagined a pirate's hair would be. It is clear that fear had unmanned Skinner entirely. Her mind races. What can she do? What can she say?

"Help us!" calls Skinner.

"What'd ya say?" calls the pirate.

"Help! Hasten! The pox has struck and we're desperate for water. Take what you will but give us water, we beg of you! Help!"

Charlotte sees four of the *Anton*'s crew appear from beneath the quarter deck. They bear a plank bound with a body wrapped for burial. Charlotte is torn between fear and grief. Another body follows the first. They are tipped overboard with awful slowness and when they are gone, one of the sailors who had carried them slumps to the deck and lies motionless. The others back away from him and turn to the rail.

"Water!" they call out. "Water!"

"What have you aboard?" calls the pirate leader.

"Good cotton!" Skinner replies. "You may have it all, what we have not wrapped the dead with."

For some time the two ships sail on in parallel, not fifteen yards of sea between them, as the pirates talk among themselves. Another of the *Anton*'s crew crumples to his knees; the others give him wide berth.

"How many have you lost?" the pirate calls.

At that moment two sailors appear with yet another bound body. The pirates gather at their rail again.

"What's in that there?" calls their captain.

"A lad who has just died," says Skinner.

The pirate ship veers a little off, then closes again.

"Let's see 'im, then!" calls the pirate.

Skinner looks pointedly at his men, and with great care the two sailors expose Tommy's face to the sun.

"We're short o' water ourselves!" shouts the pirate captain. "Steer straight on! You're not far now!"

The pirate sloop heels to starboard and veers across the wind. Within ten minutes, she is well off.

It is an old trick, as Charlotte later learned, but done well, it always stood a chance. No sailor wanted smallpox aboard. Coming on deck, Charlotte looks at Skinner's leather face and feels an unexpected admiration for him. He makes his living on a dangerous sea and he has the gumption to see danger through. They owe their lives to him, and to the special instrument of their salvation, Tommy Yates.

At noon they stand at the rail as Skinner mumbles from the Book of Prayer. They bind a ballast stone to the boy for weight, his frail corpse not heavy enough to sink. They tip the plank forward and he is gone. Charlotte rushes to the side and looks. The scarf she had put around his thin neck trails behind as he plunges into the deep.

THEY SAIL ON under a strong wind. Danger, Charlotte thinks, is a matter of perspective. The captain's audacity gulled the pirates, but his failure to make a timely landfall or reckon the proper provisions has primed them for death of another sort. The water is nearly gone and their false pleas to the pirates echo in all their ears. Charlotte uses some of the last of the cloudy liquid rationed to her and Pad to make two cups of tea. She crushes a few biscuits under a piece of planking and mixes the crumbs with dregs of molasses she has scraped from the side of the barrel.

"Here's to our good health," she proposes to Pad, who grins back at the strong-willed woman he loves. It had been nine miserable weeks. "If pirates came to us from land, land cannot be distant now," she says.

That evening a young sailor named Jake approaches her. She had found his leering most distasteful when they had first come aboard, but she feels obliged to hear him out.

"I see ye can read words. Can ye tell me the meaning of this?"

He thrusts a bit of paper into her hand. She reads: "Yorkshire Plantation, Jamaica, The West Indies. Courtesy, Master John Frye."

"What does that mean to you?" she asks.

"I'll not be worked to death by some friend to the damned captain who brings men to load ships at the docks. I know Master Frye and I mean to find himself when we reaches the land."

THE NEXT AFTERNOON, Charlotte and Pad lie listlessly on their bunk, bored, testy and tired of the interminable voyage.

"Land ho!"

It sounds distant and for a moment she wonders if this is indeed the call. Then again.

"Land off port bow!"

Charlotte looks along the passage. No one moves. Has every passenger been struck dumb by the news? She and Pad climb from their bunks. Others still sit like statues, though some are smiling. Perhaps the notion of salvation is percolating into their souls, thinks Charlotte, but she for one is going on deck. Abruptly they rise together, clamber to the ladder and crawl up its greasy rungs.

Green masses of land bumping up out of the sea make islands of every shape. Most have rugged mountains that fall into forests the colour of emeralds. Others are hilly with flat plains dotted with palm trees. The islands are surrounded by exquisite turquoise water and edged with white sandy beaches. They can see military forts and battlements on the hills and columns of smoke swirling skyward, a sign of civilized life here in the New World. The softest breeze she's ever felt blows in Charlotte's face.

While the captain negotiates the tricky channel toward the harbour in Jamaica, Charlotte stands at the rail chattering like a child about the wise decision they'd made. For Pad, it is a relief beyond measure. He'd used all the bravado he could muster in telling Charlotte of this place, which in truth he knew almost nothing about. But it was the only place he could think of where he and Charlotte could have a life together. From their vantage point, the island looks indeed like the Garden of Eden. As they get closer they can see the town of Kingston and beyond to great mansions perched on the surrounding hillsides. The plantations she'd heard about spill out of these estates and roll out to what looks like a bustling centre of commerce. Imposing buildings with commanding columns, presumably government houses, are decked in flags and smaller ones, perhaps trading establishments, fill in the rest of what appears to be the main thoroughfare. Between that orderly looking town centre and the dock is another reality. Crowded shanties lean against one another like broken clay pots. Every alleyway produces another angle of huts teeming with mothers and babies, hawkers selling their wares, a scene so colourful—brown skin, vibrant orange, red, green and blue clothing, trays of pink and purple fruit—the scene is like a mural that hangs in the great hall at the governor's mansion in Sussex, back home. The port in front of them is layered with row upon row of warehouses. Soon, she thinks, they'll quit this horrible ship and begin their lives anew.

The arrival at the dock is similar to their departure from England, save the temperature. There are dock masters shouting orders and a collection of vagabonds looking for wayward parcels that may fall into their hands. Charlotte is amused by the activity and not in the least concerned about the safe-keeping of the trunk she packed clandestinely so many weeks ago. All she can focus on now is the solid land that will soon be under her feet, the glorious bath in hot water in which she can scrub the grime from her body and the fresh clothes carefully folded in the trunk that will replace the grimy ones she wears.

THE SHIP is secured, the gangplank is lowered and without a backward glance Charlotte steps her way to the land she has imagined during the long weeks at sea. The passengers on board are rounded up for a tally in the passengers' shed. Jake sends a pleading look to Charlotte as if to say, "Find me Master Frye and get me away from these men." She can't help him. In fact, her legs are wobbling on the terra firma so much she can hardly help herself. They move to the cargo shed and wait for their belongings, trusting the Captain Skinner to fulfill his final duty. Even though personal possessions are to be off-loaded before the cargo, they wait for hours. The sun that had been so welcome when they first got off the ship is unbearably hot. The shredded roof of the shed where they wait provides no relief. The sweat now mixing with the soiled bodice and skirts she wears is making her garments stink. She can hardly wait to cast them off.

Pad strikes up a conversation with the overseer in the shed.

"Is the Willisams family known to you?"

The overseer, a bearded man of fifty, looks at him without

expression. "There are many such families here," he says. "Which do you seek?"

Pad hadn't considered the possibility of a choice.

"Hire a coach to take you to the governor's office at the centre of the town," the overseer finally volunteers. "Ask for Camilla Willisams. She's acquainted with most persons here."

The road to the governor's office passes no shanties. Charlotte cranes her neck at majestic palms, coconuts gathered overhead like string bags of giant marbles. Crimson bougainvillea bracts burst out of the bushes along the trail and mix their sweet scent with the sea air. As the distance between the couple and the *Anton* increases, so do their spirits.

The governor's office is about to close when they arrive and ask to speak with Camilla Willisams. The woman at the front desk, whose skin is the colour of milky coffee and who projects a bland, detached air, says flatly, "Yes." Presuming she is Camilla, Pad steps forward.

"Good day, madam. My wife and I have just arrived from England on the *Anton*."

"Sa ki non'w?" Camilla says. Pad looks perplexed.

"I think she is asking for our names," Charlotte says.

"Willisams, ma'am. You and I share the same family name."

"Ki sa ou vlé?" she asks, in a stern tone of voice.

Captain Skinner had said most people here spoke English as well as Creole, a mixture of English, French and Portuguese, but the woman in front of them doesn't seem to be speaking any language they can understand. Charlotte wonders if it is possible that she wants nothing to do with them? After several more failed exchanges, it becomes clear that the Willisams name is not the ticket to welcome they had hoped for. Camilla finally condescends to use English, and dispatches them to a village at the edge of town where she says they can find shelter with others who are unsettled.

The waiting coachman, who seems more inclined to English, suggests that the nearby village really is their best hope for accommodation. With no one to advise them otherwise, Pad and Charlotte agree.

Fields stretch out on either side of the track. The sun is dropping out of the sky and into the sea with that alarming rapidity they had observed as they'd sailed into tropical waters. It is an orange ball of flame that lights the clutches of families walking arm in arm through the fields toward home and burnishes the smoke that curls from their small houses.

"We're likely going to a way station," Charlotte says. "Some place where arriving passengers stay until they can make proper arrangements." The land around them becomes brown bog, almost undefined in the fading light.

"Ow!" Charlotte swats at her neck. A moment later Pad, too, begins swatting. The air is suddenly full of flying insects that bite at every exposed bit of flesh.

"Mosquitoes," says the driver. "Better you should cover yourselves."

Charlotte pulls her soiled shawl from her bag and Pad lifts the collar of his shirt.

"Whoever heard of mosquitoes this big?" Charlotte wants to know.

It is pitch dark when they pull into the village, a crush of thatched shanties, fires burning in pits in front of the huts. The driver stops at what appears to be the only proper dwelling and disembarks. A European man with a drooping moustache and oversized belly stands on the doorstep and the two speak briefly. Charlotte can see the man looking over the driver's shoulder at her.

The driver unloads the trunk and accepts his payment in silence, then is gone.

"Welcome to Jamaica." The man stifles a yawn. "Hurry in now, before the mossies carry you away."

Pad drags the trunk inside and the door closes behind them. Straw mats are strewn about the floor of the main room, and are separated by curtains of cotton that hang from pegs on the beams above them, just like the dreary curtains that hung between bunks on the ship. It seems a dozen others have found their way to this house, though Charlotte recognizes none from the ship. A fire burns in the centre of the room, some smoke escaping through a hole in the roof while the rest fills the room.

"I'm Lutz," says the man. "What is it I might do for you?"

"Sir," says Pad, "my wife and I have just disembarked from the *Anton,* out of England."

"England? You don't say. Fancy that then." Lutz gives them a broad smile that reveals two prominently absent teeth.

"We need fresh water, baths, food," Charlotte interrupts.

"Food." Lutz rubs the stubble on his chin. "Yes. We have food. And water. But baths"—he lets out a rolling chuckle—"We don't see too many baths here on the plantation."

"Would you be so kind, sir, as to tell us where we are?" asks Pad.

Lutz frowns. "In what sense do you mean, sir?"

"We're entirely new to the island, sir."

"Them's sent you told you, did they not? The Raleigh Plantation is famous enough," Lutz says. "I'm its manager and this village serves its needs. You'll find we ain't got much here, but I can offer you shelter."

"Thank you, sir," says Pad, and he indeed feels a gratitude that almost equals his weariness.

"We get a lot come from the ships, seeking work and a life on the island. And we get many that are running from another life, one they choose to leave behind." His eyes convey a knowing twinkle. Charlotte feels a sizzle of indignation.

"You spoke of food, sir," she reminds him.

Lutz produces slices of bread and mugs of tea from a table by the window and suggests they sit on the bench against the wall. When they have eaten he shows them to their straw mats. Charlotte's heart sinks now, as it had sunk a score of times in the course of that day.

"Never fear, love," Pad whispers. "We're only weary. Tomorrow will be a good day."

"What did he mean, 'those who sent us'?" Charlotte wants to know.

"In the morning, love. In the morning."

They drag their trunk near their pallets and collapse exhausted on the straw.

THE SKY IS BARELY LIGHT when Lutz begins shouting to waken the household. There is a lineup for the basin of water on the sideboard, but tea is brewing, fresh bread is baking in an outdoor oven and, mercifully, there are heaping plates of mangoes for the house full of refugees. When the others have eaten and left, Lutz takes Charlotte and Pad outside into the yard. "You can stay here if you want to work," he says. "I need a man to help the overseer of the plantation. There is a cottage nearby. You can earn your keep with work." He says he also needs a person to do the accounts and inquires whether either of them can read. A huffy Charlotte tells him, "Of course I can read." For that, he says he is willing to pay five shillings a month. Both faces must register their dismay, for Lutz tells them flatly, "Your options are not better than this. If you don't want to stay here, you must go back to town on the cart this morning."

With diminishing enthusiasm for the idyllic life they'd envisioned in these islands, they decide to stay at least until they can get their bearings. The pair move into the dingy one-room cottage at the edge of a field of sugar cane. Charlotte opens the trunk that contains their only possessions to find linens for their straw palette. It's while they are settling into the cottage that Pad first complains of the swell left by the mosquitoes the night before. "They must like your taste," Charlotte teases, relieved that her own bites are small and few. There isn't even time to fully unpack the trunk before Lutz returns and directs Pad to the office of the overseer and tells Charlotte to come to his house to work on the account books.

The next few days are a blur of work, sleep and beating off the pests that crawl over everything in the cottage. There is no possibility to make another plan, much less unpack their belongings. Charlotte pulls a clean frock from the trunk each day and washes the one she's worn, spreading it to dry on a bush behind the cottage. As for the clothes she sailed away in, she tossed them on the fire the very first night, creating a smudge that she hoped would at least keep the mosquitoes away.

EACH NIGHT BEFORE DUSK, though the air is stifling, they stoke the fire to ward off the mosquitoes. Mattie Higgs who stays in the hut next door has told them a smoky fire works best. Each morning, they go to their respective jobs. Lutz informs them that the harvest in the far field must be done by week's end. Agents will collect the cane for export and the ship will depart directly. There is no time to rest.

ON THEIR FIFTH DAY, another morning where rain streams down ceaselessly, Pad complains that his joints are aching.

"It's the working, I should think," says Charlotte. "We have laid like lumps on that ship these months."

Pad's joints continue to torment him and two days later, he develops a fever. Charlotte presses cold cloths to his head at night. One of the women who lives with Lutz—a concubine, Charlotte assumes—advises her to pack mud on the swollen bites.

Charlotte's worry grows to a gnawing fear. Rain continues to fall.

"No surprise, that," one of the other women explains. "It's the rainy season, my girl. It's gonna rain and rain these five months."

The deluge that had soaked the plantation that first day had seemed a welcome relief from the oppressive heat and a good wash for a dirty world. But now every single morning, the rain pelts down on the cottage for an hour or so and turns the fields into swamps and the tropical air into clouds of steam.

Pad grows worse by the hour. That night he groans in his sleep and then he vomits into the vessel beside the bed. On the ninth morning, his eyes roll in his head and he begins to shake violently. Charlotte runs to the main house.

"Mr. Lutz! Mr. Lutz!" she calls. "Please come! Pad is sick! You must help me!"

Lutz sends for a woman who, he assures Charlotte, is known for her cures, a local witch who gathers her medicines in the woods. While they wait for the woman to arrive, he looks at Charlotte with an undertaker's face.

"We got yellow fever here," he says.

"What is that, sir?"

"Bad."

"Where do you have it?"

"On this island."

"It's a big island with many people."

"Indeed, Mrs. Willisams. And many dying." He fills his pipe, regarding her as he does so. "Many widows, alone and grieving, are grateful for the support of a proper man."

THE MEDICINE WOMAN is remarkably old, wrinkly, toothless and not as high as Charlotte's shoulder. Her name is Mrs. Sue. When she arrives at the cottage, she ties a kerchief over her face and indicates that Charlotte should do the same. Pad's fever is raging. Charlotte spends her time running back and forth between the office where she is supposed to be working and the cottage where her man lies close to death.

She asks the woman if Pad's sickness is contagious. "It's the yellow," Mrs. Sue tells her. "Mosquito."

Charlotte lies beside Pad and tries to sooth his delirious mutterings. He'd been her lover for more than a year. She'd turned her back on her own family to run away with him. The voyage had been tough on the pair—instead of being the handsome, affable man who ran the household, he'd been nervous, easily defeated by judgmental glares from the other passengers. But once on shore, she'd assumed his confidence would return and with it, the emotionally powerful bond of their illicit relationship.

Desperate, she lifts her head to his ear and whispers, "Don't leave me, Pad. I'm carrying your child." She watches his face for a response, but there is no sign.

The medicine woman returns with a concoction of juices and tells a frantic Charlotte to wait outside in the soaking rain and the suffocating heat. There's no sound from the cottage. The morning rain lets up, the men in the field cleave the cane, the women tend to their children and Charlotte waits and waits. Then the door to the cottage opens; the old woman pulls the kerchief from her face and says, "I regrets to inform ye miss, your man is dead."

CHAPTER 2

The Atlantic Seaboard

1775

*T*wo of Lutz's men bury Pad Willisams the next morning in a pit at considerable distance from the plantation.

Charlotte picks herself up from the stoop and walks slowly to the house. She can't stay here. Going home is not an option. She's unmarried and by her calculation four months' pregnant. So shocked by the events of the last twenty-four hours, she hasn't even shed a tear and can hardly put thoughts and actions together. She'd suspected in mid-April that the passionate, furtive nights with Pad has resulted in a child but decided not to think about it until they were far away from her father's house. She wonders if Lutz will now see her as a potential new addition to his collection of concubines.

When she gets to the office, he looks up.

"The accounts for the sugar cane must be made ready. Commodore Walker arrived with the high tide in Kingston four days ago. His cargo is off-loaded, except for what he brings to me."

Charlotte says nothing.

"His business with the governor is conducted, and he intends to collect his new shipment from me personally."

She sees through his vanity, his suggestion that the commodore had singled him out as more valuable than other managers.

Charlotte goes to her table and begins to enter the numbers and description of the cargo to be dispatched to the commodore's company. She allows her eyes to flick to Lutz and catches him staring at her. The particulars of the shipment suggest a transaction the size of a prize for Lutz.

THE FIELDS ARE A BUSTLE of workers cutting cane and bundling it with twine, rolling barrels of molasses and rum from the warehouse and lugging sacks of spices to the wagons that will carry the order to the wharf. Bully overseers, whips at the ready, urge them to move faster. In the scant ten days since she has been here, it is clear that there are slaves and indentured servants who work this land. The servants live in this village, but the slaves are kept apart in hovels on the other side of the plantation, marched to the fields in long lineups at dawn and back again at dark. She knows from Pad's reports that they are beaten, tormented and intimidated for the slightest provocation, but when she commented on their treatment to Lutz he'd told her to mind her own business. She hates the place. The grotty shacks the workers live in, the sooty fires they cook at, the hopelessness and the dawn-to-dusk labour are not what she thought a life in the West Indies would entail. Maybe the sprawling mansions she'd seen above the town when they docked would better suit her.

But for the moment, she only needs to enter the numbers of bundles and the date they are placed on the wagon. *July 17,* she writes, but the words that play in front of her eyes are *the day after Pad died*. She's caught in a surge of memories. Pad, so exotic in the household that he controlled. Her pathetic mother relied on him for everything. Her father often took him into his study to discuss the business of the day. Had she stayed away from him, none of this would have happened. Pad may have . . .

"Have you finished?" Lutz interrupts her meditation.

"Soon," she replies.

"You can stay here and work for me," he says.

She decides not to reply.

"Or you can be a wife to a man in the town. You're a comely woman, and will attract a gentleman of position." Charlotte has a flashing thought of another respectable Englishman with concubines and remains silent. The stay in Jamaica has left her feeling powerless and consequently vulnerable, not a condition she is accustomed to. She wants to bolt from this hot, fetid, disease-ridden island and find a place to be anonymous. But where could that be?

LUTZ ANNOUNCES his intention of going to the dock himself. Three other plantation men—all white—have gathered in his office, waiting for instruction.

"There'll be no talk of yellow fever," Lutz growls. "Nor any manner of invitation to bring the man back here."

One of the younger men flips his hand in a nervous gesture.

"Beggin' your pardon, Mr. Lutz, but I for one am happy to go. No need for you to trouble yourself, sir."

Lutz makes an expression of mock horror.

"You'll go, will you, Peterson?"

"Yes, sir."

"You'll go in my stead, will you?"

"Yes, sir. If I can be of help, sir."

Lutz lowers his voice. "Who asked you to do anything but what you're told?"

Peterson shrinks back and Charlotte puts down her quill.

"The Commodore George Walker is as gallant a sea captain and as notorious an English privateer as this ocean has seen in many a lifetime. He's fought the Greek and fought the Turk and fought the Spanish dog—fought pirates off every coast between here and the Mediterranean, which, Peterson, is a sea *far away.*" Lutz's face is reddened with the passion of his admiration. "Commodore Walker sends his ships here for their cargos— molasses and rum—because he himself has much important business elsewhere. But *this* time, Commodore Walker—*the* Commodore Walker—is making the voyage himself. Why is he doing so? On account of *my* crop—*that's* his reason. And I can tell you gentlemen in strictest confidence that Commodore Walker means to take on a portion of the cane and try his hand at the *sugar-refining business.* And I doubt not but that he will do *very well!*"

He pauses to allow the enormity of his words to sink into his subordinates' minds. Charlotte, on the other hand, wonders why a man who could be represented in such a light might make business with Lutz. Walker, a captain of merchant vessels out of London, might be a man not unlike her own father: stern, shrewd, unforgiving.

In fact, she wonders if he could possibly be acquainted with her father. Lutz says Walker operates a trading post in a place called Nepisiguit in British North America. The outpost was financed first by one Hugh Baillie and now by a John Schollbred, both from London. Charlotte is certain she's heard both those names before and wonders if they are financiers who visited her father at their home. Lutz explains, "The trading post is in the middle of nowhere, the vast northeast where winter consumes much of the year—but people say it is well-finished and flourishing on a trade of fur and timber."

The middle of nowhere, Charlotte imagines, an undiscovered place where a woman can shed the past and seek obscurity—perhaps. But what of the cold and wild beasts Captain Skinner had described.

"Tell me more about this Nepisiguit," she asks Lutz, who is willing to oblige.

"It's a tough-minded breed of men who settle in those parts. They fight the climate all the year—to prevent freezing to death in the winter and starving to death when the food runs out. It's not a place I would frequent. But there are opportunities in that northern land. There's money to be made and land to be had. I reckon there are shiploads of dissidents and eccentrics who seek their fortune in that desolate wilderness."

"I want to go with you to the docks to meet your Commodore Walker," Charlotte announces. The scheming Lutz conjures up the scene—an attractive, young British widow by his side like his own bit of bounty when he offers his salutation to the commodore. "You will be welcome," he tells her.

The rest of the day is filled with hurried preparations. The sugar cane is loaded on the wagons, along with the molasses and rum barrels. She understands from the women in the house that it is unusual to ship raw cane. But the details interest her not in the least. The warehouses are readied for the fine lumber Walker promised Lutz he would bring; beauteous pieces of wood Lutz can sell in town for a fine price. "This will be a grand trade," Lutz tells Charlotte.

The trade will be more than lumber and cane, she thinks. Although another voyage by sea is a loathsome concept, the greater concern is making sure she sails away with the commodore.

Back in the cottage at nightfall, Charlotte considers her plan. Should she tell the commodore the truth? That she ran away from her father's home, that she was not married, that she's pregnant? No, that would be folly. He'd leave her behind to wallow in the pitiful condition she'd found herself in. The widow Willisams, bereft after leaving the hearth of her kin to come to the colony with her new husband to serve the King—that would be better. She could tell him the northern clime he comes from is more to her liking, or is there more she can offer? Reading and writing are skills that won the favour of Lutz. Could that be employed again? And her father, how will he factor into this bargain? If he is known to Walker, her plan could be foiled. Charlotte lies down on the bed covered with musty straw and considers her next step. The combination of grief, fatigue and the need for secrecy and cleverness overcome her and the next thing she knows, it's dawn. She decides the course she will take. The trunk that was hardly unpacked is secured for moving when the time is right. The incoming tide will bring her salvation.

SHE SETTLES on the carriage bench beside the repulsive Lutz for the ride to the dock. The distance is shorter than what she recalls from her journey just eleven days ago. The horses move unwillingly in the morning heat. Charlotte wishes she had a parasol to shield her face and shade her body. She lifts her shawl over her head, trying not to disturb the pins and combs she's arranged in her hair. The dock comes into sight, the vagabonds are there as before, masters shouting orders. And out in the channel she sees a ship anchored in the turquoise waters beyond the dock where the wagons wait.

There is a flurry of activity. A small craft has been lowered to the water from the schooner. It rows slowly to the pier, and when it is secured a man dressed in the plumes of a naval officer steps out in the company of other, clearly subordinate men. Even as Lutz's face is contorted with warring expressions of greed and awe, Charlotte's face remains a mask. Behind it, her heart sinks. Commodore George Walker is an old man. What else had she imagined? She'd imagined, as she now realizes, that she might cast a spell and make a young heart beat fast enough to spirit her away from this sweltering stew. The commodore and his party advance toward them, and even at ten yards Charlotte sees the sort of seasoned features that suggest their owner's ample powers of insight into her own shallow scheming.

The introductions are formal. Lutz dances from foot to foot in ill-disguised eagerness. Charlotte is introduced as his assistant. A mercy, she thinks, and better than whore, which I shall probably be if I don't get away from here.

Walker is styled by his aide as Commodore George Walker, Esquire, Late Commander of the Royal Family Privateers, Justice of the Peace for the County of Halifax in the Province of Nova Scotia and proprietor of Nepisiguit. He is a man of moderate height with fine, ruddy features, blue eyes and thick white hair. Charlotte drops a half-curtsy and nods her head. As though she is suddenly transported into the presence of her own family, her shame is intense. Walker shows little concern for her and she tries to melt into invisibility. As the party walks the length of the docks, pausing here and there to make observations and comments on the facilities, the main topic is the cargo and the need to offload and reload without delay.

Charlotte is absorbed in her own lament about the opportunity she sees slipping away. She hadn't been listening to the discourse between the two men so when she hears her name she's jolted back to attention.

"Mrs. Willisams?" It is the aide. "Might the commodore then have the pleasure of your company at dinner?"

She looks at the man with astonishment and sees that Walker and Lutz have walked on ahead.

"Dinner?"

"This evening. At Harper House."

"Of course," she replies. "Please inform the commodore that nothing would give me greater pleasure."

The young man returns to the main party, and Charlotte hurries to join them. They then walk to the carriage that would carry the commodore and Lutz to the commodore's lodgings. The wagon that is to take Charlotte back to the plantation draws up. At this moment, Commodore Walker breaks off and approaches her.

"Mrs. Willisams," he says, "I wish to express my deepest condolences." His voice is surprisingly light and pleasantly tinted with his Scots brogue.

"Thank you, commodore."

"And thank *you* for consenting to join us this evening. I regret that Mr. Lutz will not be able to be there."

"How unfortunate."

Her heart is racing, her mind spinning. The wagon bounces along the rain-rutted path. What was at work in Lutz's porcine brain? Did he imagine she would give herself to him in return for passage? Curious, because he might easily—however regrettably—have anticipated obtaining such favours if she was trapped here.

—

SHORTLY AFTER DARK, she is summoned to the house. She finds Lutz pacing in the main hall, his face transfigured by satisfaction.

"A great business, woman. A great business."

"Why do you not join us, Mr. Lutz?"

"Me? What could I do but interfere? We have done good business here and much more to come. And you, Mrs. Willisams, life will go better for you, I can tell you that."

"In what way, Mr. Lutz?"

"I'll see to it that you have a better house here. Tomorrow, you'll take the Roberts house. That drunk and his whore have no place on this plantation. You'll have his place, you will. And money."

"May I ask what is required of me?"

"Required?" Lutz pulls his head back in exaggerated puzzlement. "Required? Nothing but that you continually assure the commodore of the wisdom of this business and my very great regard for him."

"I see."

"There is the wagon now. Go."

Charlotte stops at the door, her thoughts unformed.

"Thank you, Mr. Lutz," she says.

Lutz comes to the door, holds it open, standing near her.

"Do not, *Mrs. Willisams*,"—he splashes a liberal dose of acid on these words—"do *not* let me hear"—his foul breath washes over her face—"that you have denied the commodore any of the favours a man might ask a woman. That would be a most dreadful mistake."

He shuts the door.

That's it then, Charlotte realizes. I am to service a very old master rather than a merely ugly one.

HARPER HOUSE is the Jamaican country home of the sixth Earl of Ruffield, who now hardly visits the islands and is an old friend and associate of Walker. The pomp and ceremony of the place remind Charlotte of Lord Lafford's house in Sussex, where she had been presented on the occasion of her eighteenth birthday. She stops short when the brown-skinned servants wave her toward the double doors and suppresses the ill thoughts of the truth she conceals and the mixed-race child she carries. Then assuming the grandest pose she can muster, she sweeps into the room where the commodore waits.

For a time after the commodore greets her, they stand together in the drawing room and sip Madeira wine. She had had the wagon ride to determine the tale she should tell, but who knew what the wheedling Lutz had said to Walker. Whatever he saw to be to his advantage, certainly. Better sail as close to the truth as possible, while steering off its sharpest rocks. She could say she now found herself to be wasting dreadfully in these tropical climes and would prefer to . . . ah, the rub. Prefer to what? She could hardly return to England. Indeed, there is real danger Walker might actually be acquainted with her father.

Dinner is announced. They have hardly settled into their chairs when Walker leans across to her.

"Dear Mrs. Willisams, the very kind Mr. Lutz has told me of your loss and I offer again my deepest condolences to you. Now please, you must tell me your circumstances, for I assure you I am your most attentive listener."

She had not expected so vigorous a probe. Before she can conjure up a reply, he continues.

"Mrs. Willisams, this is no place for an Englishwoman on her own. What shall you do?"

And at that moment, and wholly to her own astonishment, Charlotte Taylor begins to weep. From weeping she falls to explaining, and from explaining to telling the truth, or as much of it as she dares. He shows no special response and raises no query. As she speaks, she regains her composure and is able to insert an innocent fiction about letters of introduction stolen at sea. When she is finished, ending with her beloved husband's burial—he who sought to serve his King in the heavy clay of a land he never knew—there is silence.

Finally, Walker speaks.

"I don't know of a ship returning to England this week," he says. "But you may sail with me and then leave for England from my trading post in Nepisiguit."

"Nepisiguit? Where is that?"

"It's in British North America near the Gulf of the St. Lawrence, my dear. It is my small part of His Majesty's colony of Nova Scotia. I have certain knowledge of a ship that will sail from there in early September and I will arrange that it take you home."

She looks at the weathered face that regards her steadily and sees no trace of baseness or deceit. The commodore lifts his claret glass to his lips, sips, then sets it down.

"I confess that I can propose only this circuitous route. But you *cannot* stay here. It is intolerable that you should do so. You are not bred for such a place, as is clear to see, and there are those here who would willingly take advantage of your innocence. I intend to raise anchor as soon as the cargo is stored and the tide is high. That will be early tomorrow morning. If this is agreeable to you, Mrs. Willisams, please do leave all arrangements to me."

And that is the end of the discussion about her departure. Throughout the rest of the meal, the commodore entertains his guest with stories of his first voyages to the West Indies. He tells her how he had sometimes thrived and sometimes not as he traded in those changeable waters. Indeed, the islands had new owners so often, he had felt compelled to inspect the flag in every harbour to know whether he would enjoy the welcome of Britain, France or Spain—countries not always in perfect agreement. At some point, as he pours her port, she is cognizant of the fact that, save the stories of events long past, he had spoken not a word on his own personal account.

"You have not mentioned your family, commodore. How you must miss them, at sea so often."

He looks at her a long moment, but his expression is opaque.

"I am a widower, madam," he says. "And childless."

She is without a reply. How could she express condolence for his loss without appearing condescending in respect to his childless state? He might, perhaps, have preferred to remain childless. As indeed, at this moment, did Charlotte.

At the door he kisses her hand and again Charlotte feels a surge of emotion. Her suspicion and plotting had been undone by a gracious man's simple kindness. Then a servant leads her not to Lutz's plain wagon, which had been dismissed, but to the commodore's own carriage.

As she draws into the village, Lutz is leaning in a chair against the front of his house, a mug in one hand, his pipe in the other and a bottle at his side. A single lantern burns overhead.

"Was the dinner to your liking?" he asks.

"Yes."

Suddenly he's upon her. Grabbing her arm in a viselike grip, steering her into his office, slamming the door behind them. He pushes her into a chair and stands before her as though she's on trial.

Lutz snorts. "And what of our good commodore? Did he meet with success?"

"I understand you have made good business together."

"Hmm. But did he meet with success here, in the petticoats?"

"Mr. Lutz?"

He steps toward her.

"I think he did," he slurs. "Or God help you."

"I've done nothing to displease the commodore. I ask you to leave me alone."

"We have made a bargain," says Lutz, "and now I'll have you!"

"You will not!"

He stands a moment, breathing heavily.

"If you will not give over, I'll beat you—and you should know—I've beat many before you."

Charlotte sees the lust and anger and drink combined in the man's already cankered countenance.

"Mr. Lutz," she says, grasping at a tone and subject that might reach him. "If you were to beat me or take me against my will tonight, word must reach Commodore Walker. It would spell the destruction of the trade you do now with the commodore and all you hope to do. Do not let the drink destroy all you've done."

He stares at her in the carefully balancing manner of a drunk. Finally he says, "You will lay with me when he's gone, woman."

Buying herself what time she can she replies, "I owe much to you, Mr. Lutz."

"Damn you *do* too! You owe me a great deal!"

Muttering threats about what he'll do if she dares to leave this room, he crosses to the anteroom at the back of the office. Charlotte hears the scraping of the chamber pot on the floor as he draws it forth with his foot.

"I shall piss myself if I have no relief," Lutz says. He chuckles and sets the candle down while fumbling with his breeches.

"Let me help you," she says and without stopping for even a fraction of a moment she crosses the floor, grabs the candle and is out the door in a single movement. It is black as pitch inside. Lutz roars and as she bolts down the stairs she hears the chamber pot rumble across the boards and Lutz fall heavily, cursing her.

She extinguishes the candles and runs across the field to Mattie Higgs' hut.

"Mattie! Mattie!" she calls outside the woman's door. "It's Charlotte."

She appears, sleepy-eyed.

"Mattie. Let me share your straw tonight. I fear mine may be infested."

She rises at dawn, finds Mattie is already gone and returns cautiously to her hut and seeing it undisturbed, she makes the final preparation to leave. She selects apparel suitable for travelling and this time, being knowledgeable about sea-faring, carefully packs the items she would need for the voyage in a parcel and ties it with twine. She also gathers a few of Pad's personal effects—a square of cotton he often wound around his neck, the three silver strands he'd bent into a bracelet and the packet of seeds from the garden that he'd tucked in with his belongings, promising that one day he'd plant a garden for her like the one she left behind. There isn't another thing she wants to bring as a reminder of this place. The trunk is ready, so is the parcel. She scribbles the day's thoughts into her diary.

July 18—I will leave Jamaica today with Commodore
Walker. I'm not sure about his intentions. He behaves so

*graciously, almost as though I am his ward. I have a feeling
he knows more than he lets on. It is not possible that he is
acquainted with my father. Surely it is not possible. He
thinks he's assisting me in getting back to England, but
I have no intention of doing that.*

*I ought to go to the wretched plot where Pad is buried.
But getting there will create too much attention. I feel ill at
the prospect of going there anyway. Maybe that's why
Mama always fell ill when she was expected to do something to her disliking. Pad would not want me to be left
here to become a concubine, to struggle without him. I can
hardly wait to leave.*

Then Charlotte walks to the main house, helps herself to a
cup of tea and a slice of the morning's baked bread, takes her
place at the table and begins the day's entries as though nothing
whatsoever has changed. Lutz finally appears at the door, looking the worse for his night. She resists the impulse to look up lest
she betray her anxiety.

He prowls around the premises, bellowing orders, directing
his prurient gaze at Charlotte. The wagons make the short trip to
the dock a dozen times. Charlotte waits, barely able to concentrate on her chore, wondering if this nightmare is really coming
to a close? Lutz has gone to the dock. By now Charlotte is pacing
back and forth to the tea stand, trying to lessen the tension she is
feeling. The tide will soon be high. She fears she's been left
behind.

A WAGON APPROACHES. Charlotte dashes to the door. It is
Lutz, alone, and bearing an envelope. Her heart tumbles into a
pit deep in her breast.

He enters the office silently and lays the letter on her desk. The seal had been broken.

"Now you are exposed," he says.

So it was to be for her—unending punishment and salvation unendingly denied. For a moment she sits numbly. She looks down at the letter. She sees it is addressed to Lutz. She unfolds it and reads the opening lines.

"I know you will be pleased to learn that I am able to convey Mrs. Willisams to her home in England, though I can offer only an indirect route through my trading post in Nova Scotia. In token of my gratitude for your kindness to her, I am sending over a dozen bottles of my best port, originally a gift to me from—"

"You are a damned whore!" calls Lutz, but Charlotte is already out the door, her heart bursting with joy.

MORNING IS ALWAYS the right time for a departure, when the ship and the day set out together and nothing but prospects lie ahead. The sky over Jamaica is clear that morning and a steady breeze blows in the channel that crochets the islands to the sea. The birds hover and call. The air is fresh and sweet with the distillations of the tropics. Charlotte stands near the fo'c'sle. She can see Commodore Walker in busy conversation on the quarterdeck and beyond him and the little *Achilles*'s wake the hills of Jamaica. How beautiful, she thinks, as its landscape diminishes to a glittering emerald. A young man climbing the fo'c'sle stops partway up to greet her with a smile.

"Morning, madam."

"Good morning."

He is perhaps twenty, his blond hair curling out from under his cap, his blue jacket and bright white shirt a match for his eyes.

"Captain would like to know if you're well, madam, or have need of anything." The Scots lilt is most pronounced.

"I'm very well, thank you. Who are you?"

"Able seaman Will MacCulloch, madam."

"Are you already an able seaman, Will?"

"I'm recognized as exceptionally able, madam, and hope soon to be third mate. When Rockwell moves on, as I'm certain he will."

"I *am* impressed."

"Thank you, madam."

"What are we doing now, Will?"

"We're just putting on sail, madam." They look together to the yardarm, where sailors are still unfurling canvas. "From here we'll tack through this channel until we turn north into the Gulf current. It'll take us straight along the coast of America. Though first we must sail east to pass Cuba."

"I've heard of Cuba. Is it not an island?"

"It is, madam. A Caribbean island."

"Will we round it this morning?"

Will laughs. "No, madam. It's a great big island, but it's no ower muckle. We'll sail a day to round it, though we're already near its eastern end. Then we'll need to stay close inshore to catch the wind and that's when we must look out the sharpest for pirates."

"You can't frighten me, Will. I've encountered them already."

"On your voyage over? I hadn't heard."

"Oh yes. Our captain told them we had smallpox aboard and tipped some things like bodies into the sea to convince them."

"It sounds an unlikely trick, if I may say so."

"Well, it worked." Charlotte tries not to picture Tommy's face, exposed to the sun.

"Well, we also have to be on the lookout for fierce storms, which blow here in the summer months," Will says. "If one strikes, we must beat for shore, sure enough. These schooners are wonderful ships, fast indeed. But they'll heel over quick enough in the wrong sea."

The *Achilles* tacks toward the open water. She looks at Will and inserts a note of nonchalance in her voice. "Do you know this place where the commodore lives in this Nepisiguit?"

"It's na a wee cabin, I can tell ye. The captain's built a fine flourishing business there. He does mostly fish and lumber in the fair seasons and shipbuilding in the winter. He lives verra well at Alston Point." He laughs. "We *all* live well when we're there."

Charlotte studies Will's face. "A paradise, then?"

"Well, it's faroff from proper civilized places. The northeast, it's terrible big, madam. A body that lives year-round in those parts might think winter eats up much of the year."

A faroff place, Charlotte repeats to herself. She looks up at the billowing sails—there are six now and the schooner heels a little to starboard as the wind catches her and pushes her toward the open sea. The gulls screech and wheel about the bow with excitement of their own. A place far away from proper civilized places, she thinks. A place where a person could shed a past.

Will knows he's found a listener and he climbs the rest of the way to stand by her.

"An' s'truith, a lot of them that settle in those parts are a strong-minded breed, an' so they must be, if they don't want to freeze to death or starve when the food runs out. It's not a place for lads without the likes of the commodore to set things up for us. But if you don't freeze or starve, to some tastes it's a beautiful place. There's money to be made and land to be had."

"Is there?"

"Oh aye, madam. Shiploads we see, comin' to seek their fortune in that wilderness."

"You set your store by Commodore Walker?"

"Aye, madam. He's an honest man, and a gentleman. I've seen him give us wages from his own pocket when the owners were tardy. And the man can trade with anyone."

Sure enough, ponders Charlotte.

"The English don't set much store by the Indians and the French Acadians. But our commodore has no problem wi 'em. He's the only Justice of the Peace in the whole area, so he settles the quarrels and performs the marriages and baptizes the newborns and buries the dead. British, Indian, Acadian—it makes no difference to him. His services are available to anyone who wants them." He also tells her there are no white women at the trading post, but that she'll be well taken care of during the stopover before she sails for England.

"A proper businessman. A modern man."

"'Deed, I think he's so."

The cabin boy approaches them.

"Mr. MacCulloch, sir, captain says you are to escort the lady to her quarters."

"Thank you, Mr. Harding."

"Must we go now?" Charlotte asks Will.

"It's only to show you, madam. You'll have no restriction aboard this vessel. Unless the captain makes 'em."

It is apparent that Walker outfits his ships according to a policy different from that applied by Captain Skinner and the company who employed him. Will leads Charlotte to her own quarters, a small cabin quite near the stern, comfortable and not without its pleasing touches. As this is a cargo vessel, there is a crew of only a dozen men commanded by four officers.

A sailor sets her bag on the bed and departs.

"I'll go about my duties, then," Will says.

"You have been most kind. My understanding from Commodore Walker is that the voyage should take three weeks, perhaps four if the winds should not be favourable."

"That is my experience, madam."

"We'll have plenty of opportunity to speak then."

"Thank you, madam." And he turns to leave her.

THE GLIMPSE into Walker's life offers her a detail of the man as well as the place. She retires to the welcome privacy she's been allotted to ponder the days ahead and promptly collides with the beam overhead, forgetting the cramped space of a ship, and almost knocks herself senseless. Except for an angry-looking welt on her forehead, she is not injured and seeks relief on the bed secured to the wall. The bed is covered in a huge, hairy animal skin—a forest beast, she supposes. She rolls it back and finds another skin, this coverlet for warmer climes, she assumes, calculating the heat of this day. Beneath the skins, there are sheets—a luxury she hasn't known since she left home. They are coarse, like jute, but are an appreciated covering all the same. They remind her that inside the trunk she packed so scrupulously that last day in England, she had removed the white cotton overlays from her own bed and tucked them in with the items she felt she may need. What will become of her in the land she is sailing toward? And how is she to cope with the unpleasant events that have gone before?

SHE WAKENS to a knock, stands, pats her hair, opens the door. Will again. Clearly her minder.

"I'm sorry if I have interrupted, madam. It's well past midday."

"Is it truly?"

"Captain Walker and the officers would have you join them for the evening meal, madam."

"Will that be the usual arrangement, Will?"

"I believe so, madam. You will dine with the officers. And most fortunate they are, if I may say so."

She looks up with some pleasure, but he is already gone.

THE OFFICERS' MESS, like her cabin, is not without its charms. The walls are well panelled, though not painted, and the brass sconces are of good workmanship. Introductions are accompanied by sherry, with service by the cook and the boy Harding.

When the five sit down for soup, Jack Primm, the first mate, makes mention of the Carolinas with a dismissive sneer. On first impression, Charlotte wonders to what extent the man's name had shaped his character. He seems prim indeed for a senior sailor, his long face pale, his lips most often pursed.

"What is the importance of these Carolinas?" Charlotte asks.

Primm sniffs.

"We pay the price, madam, for our slackness there. How many jackanapes did we permit to raise their voices against His Majesty while we whistled our way along? Now we shall pay."

"Och, Jack." Commodore Walker shakes his head gently. "We should have had to pay sooner or later, no matter."

"The Tea Tax was your great mistake, gentlemen," says Sullivan, the second mate. He is a burly, snub-nosed man with an unruly mop of red hair much the colour of Charlotte's own. "You must mind your manners when you rule."

"Indeed," says Primm. "An Irishman would tell us so."

Rockwell, who is third mate and youngest of the officers, is not to be left out.

"The Tea Tax was very much to the colonists' advantage," he says, looking about the table for support. "It would put the smugglers of tea out of business and the tea itself would be less dear."

"Of course you're right, Mr. Rockwell," says Walker. "But consider, sir, that more was at play than cheap tea. The Tea Act, alas, was another signal of British control. That is how some colonists regarded it at least. *And* they saw it to favour the East India Tea Company."

"Which it most certainly did," says Sullivan. "Capital soup, by the by."

"It is, yes," Charlotte adds.

"You must hear enough about all this in England, Mrs. Willisams," proposes Sullivan. "Surely it's the constant talk."

"I think it is," Charlotte admits. "But I'm ashamed to say we young women are seldom party to such talk."

"And so it should be, my dear," says Commodore Walker. "You have enough to do, learning how to manage our homes and children, without listening to such rubbish."

"You *must* know of the Tea Party," says Primm, "whatever else you may not hear about."

"I think I have."

"Oh, it was plenty exciting," Rockwell bursts in. "The damned colonists started to send back the tea and then in Boston they stopped the unloading and then at night a crowd of them dressed up as Mohawk Indians and threw the lot in the harbour!"

"It was actually a great crime," Walker avers. "Three hundred and forty-two chests of tea—almost ten thousand pounds of profit and taxes."

"Yes," Sullivan chuckles. "And by God the English government is vexed that their mismanagement should cost so much. But it will cost much more."

"I fear you're right in that regard," Walker says and for just that single sentence his normally light voice darkens in a manner Charlotte has not seen before.

The door bangs wide and young Harding carries in a steaming tureen. When opened by the commodore it displays a thick mutton stew supporting a half-dozen massive dumplings.

The others draw long, appreciative breaths. Apart from her first meal with Walker, she had only dreamed of such food in many weeks at sea and in Jamaica.

"You will find, madam, that a sailor's victuals are always ample at the start of any sea journey," Primm instructs her. "Later you may find them somewhat otherwise."

"In the past, we would have taken on new supplies in Carolina." Walker speaks as he ladles the stew. "It's a fine stretch, the Carolina coast. You have the protection of miles of seaward islands, with plenty of harbours inside for great vessels *and* for the like of the *Achilles*."

"The weather's awfully favourable," Rockwell adds. "A great deal better than Nova Scotia. They have little in the way of winter, yet are far enough north to escape the oppressive heat of the West Indies."

"Oh thanks to ye, Rockwell," says Primm. "Your erudition is always of the greatest assistance."

Rockwell turns pink and the others laugh.

"At any rate," Walker says, "the present troubles now cause us to give those shores a wide berth. If this breeze holds, we'll be nigh past the Carolinas with our supplies but half-consumed.

The lesson of the sea, however, is to count on less food and more foul weather."

"I think we gentlemen might do better than to try to frighten our guest," Sullivan interjects and looks convincingly solemn. "This can hardly be what she expects of us."

"Do we offend, madam?" Primm inquires.

"Not at all, sir," Charlotte looks around the table. "Not at all."

"Nonetheless"—Walker lifts his glass—"I think it is in order that we pause to salute the person who has brought the rare gift of beauty to the *Achilles*. Mrs. Willisams, you are a brave woman and an inspiration to your sex. Gentlemen, I give you Mrs. Charlotte Willisams."

"Mrs. Willisams, Mrs. Willisams," intone the others as Charlotte looks to her lap.

Walker refills her glass.

"I had occasion to sail to the Carolinas thirty-five years ago with my ship at the time, the *William*. My mission was to defend the settlements from Spanish privateers. It wasn't rum and molasses in the hold then. We had thirty men, twenty guns, thirty-six small arms and thirty-six cutlasses."

It is not difficult for Charlotte to see she provides Walker with a fresh reason for the telling of his tale. And quite apart from the wish to see the conversation veer from the subject of herself, she finds delight in his stories. She could easily set this white-haired salt in the role of the young man he was not that many years before: dapper, determined, undoubtedly courageous.

"The province of North Carolina paid me ten thousand pounds for the relief of those shores," he says. "*And* they offered me a large grant of land in thanks." He stops and takes a pensive sip of wine. "Which I refused." He takes another sip. "Perhaps wisely in view of the explosion soon to come."

"There are plenty who will flock to the King's banner and many who want it rent asunder," chimes Rockwell.

"Indeed," says Walker. "As we may see at this very table, there is no uniformity of opinion, even among officers of Her Majesty's merchant navy."

ALONE IN HER CABIN, her lightness of spirit evaporates somewhat and the hard truth of her own condition settles upon her once more. Pad, who would have preserved her honour in marriage, is dead. What would happen if the commodore should learn that she is pregnant? And what if he did not? Will she need his help? She takes out her diary and sits wondering how she can compress the events of the day when there is a knock on her door.

"Who is it."

"It's Will, madam," comes a soft but urgent voice.

She opens the door.

"Will. Come in. What is the matter?"

He steps in and closes the door.

"I have come to see that you have all you need."

"Thank you, Will. I am well provided for."

She sees he holds a bottle in one hand.

"Have you been drinking, Will?"

"I am wedded to the rum, madam. Will you join me in a small glass before you retire?"

"No thank you. I'm not certain that is proper, Will."

"Och. I only propose a glass, then I'll be gone."

She can't help but smile back at him and nod.

He sets a glass on her writing desk and fills it to the brim.

"Careful, Will. It is strong drink, I think."

"There's none stronger, madam."

"Will you have a chair? I have only one, but I can sit on my bed."

He sits.

"What manner of beast is this?" she pokes at the great black fur that covers the bunk.

"That would be black bear, madam, but ever so dead."

"I'm not sorry. Do they have these at Nepisiguit?"

"They do. I've seen 'em myself, foraging for the berries and such. They can turn against a man, if the mood takes them. And then they won't just kill him in a moment, but eat him too."

"God preserve us. Tell me more about Alston Point."

"It's a bonnie bit o' land that juts out into the Baie de Chaleur—that's what the old Frenchman Cartier called it—the Bay of Warmth. What a dickens would make him call it so I don't know. It's only warm by comparison with the North Atlantic. But that's where the commodore's built his summer camp. Five large stores an' all sorts o' outhouses and such. He even has himself a battery to defend the place."

"But who would dare attack him?"

"Aweel, madam, ye ken the French. Ye canna trust them. An' now there's them from the colonies who hate the English, though they were Englishmen themselves a few years before. They'll be makin' mischief, be sure. But to say, the commodore has his winter house farther along the harbour."

He pours himself another glass.

"He commands the only trading post in the great northeast, all the lands around the bay and the great forests that grow to the south and the west. Lumber, moose hides, bearskins and furs of all kinds. Whale fat as well—fell guid troke. That's Scots, madam, for excellent business. Tusks of the walrus an' the fish. All them waters swarmin' with cod, herring, mackerel and salmon—so many they are, the fishing boats make two or three runs a day into the water. Then, in the winter months, the commodore sets his men to shipbuilding."

Charlotte feels sleepy, and knows that no matter how talking with Will chases her ghosts and fears away, it is time for him to leave her. Standing, she says, "Will, I confess I must retire. I am tired."

"I shall leave you to your dreams."

He draws himself up and opens the cabin door. "Sleep well, madam."

WHEN DAWN BREAKS two days later, she knows they have left the tropics behind. The water is transformed from turquoise to navy blue, white caps trim the small waves and the salt air, though still warm, is fresh. For days thereafter, the *Achilles* is carried north in the current. By day, Charlotte watches the ceaseless labour of the sailors—the mending, tarring, braiding, patching, climbing, sawing, nailing—and tries not to take an unseemly interest. Yet she wishes she could be part of the crew if only to have something to do. She is instead expected to stroll the deck, rest in her quarters and be available for dinner conversation with the officers.

She regularly retires to her cabin and takes up her copy of *Clarissa*.

> . . . *But here is Miss Harlowe, virtuous, noble, wise, pious, unhappily ensnared by the vows and oaths of a vile rake, whom she believes to be a man of honour: and being ill used by her friends for his sake is in a manner forced to throw herself upon his protection; who, in order to obtain her confidence, never scruples the deepest and most solemn protestation of honour.*

So it was for Clarissa. But I have escaped all vile rakes, Charlotte thinks. And am I not, in fact, the one who never scruples the deepest protestations of honour?

There is a knock and when she opens the door, it is Will, who had not spoken to her since his late-night visit.

"The captain would have you join him for dinner, madam."

"I dine with the officers each evening, Will. Is this one to be different?"

"The captain asks if you could join him in his quarters for dinner."

"Ah. Very well. Thank you, Will. Tell Captain Walker I would be most honoured."

"I will, madam. Dinner will be at eight."

SHE ATTEMPTS to lift her hair with pins and combs, but her success is limited. Here for a second time she would be the private guest of the commodore. She thinks again of his grave, weathered countenance, the brilliant shock of white hair, the perfect poise with which he takes command of his vessel. And wonders again of his intentions.

At eight, Harding comes to escort her on the short walk to the captain's cabin, it being a deck up.

Walker's private quarters are a frank delight, with every appointment possible in so small a place. The furniture is of quality and deeply polished. There is a good Turkish carpet on the floor and several charming paintings in the rustic style. A small fire glows in the grate, not unwelcome now, as they are wafted ever farther up the coast toward the North Atlantic Ocean.

"What a splendid sight you are for these eyes, Mrs. Willisams."

"If you would call me Charlotte, commodore . . ."

"If you will call me George."

"Thank you, George. Your kindness has deeply touched me."

They settle comfortably in chairs before the fire. Walker attends to the filling of their glasses with his old Madeira while Charlotte seeks better knowledge of her saviour. His fame as a British privateer was widespread, as she now knows. He was particularly remembered for valour in his engagement against the Spanish battleship *Glorioso*.

"But the wilds of Nova Scotia? However did you come to be there?"

"Ah, my dear. You've seen a little hardship already in your young life, but much more may lurk for any of us. Twenty-five years ago, in London, there was a group of exceptionally greedy and politically influential owners of a squadron of four ships. The ships together were known as the *Royal Family* and I was in command of those vessels. These owners were most injudicious—and that is the best I can say—in their handling of others' monies. When it became clear that the company was in a state of calamitous ruin, someone had to be blamed, someone had to be made bankrupt. I was that person. Someone also had to be imprisoned for debt that wasn't his. I was that person too. Five long years later, the House of Lords heard my case and cleared me of all charges."

"You were betrayed."

"Betrayal, my dear, is a common recourse when the loss of money is encountered. Upon my release, I sailed immediately for Nova Scotia. The King's administrators are not always as wise as they might be or as we might like. No one in the colonial office in Halifax had any interest in the northern shores of Nova Scotia when I arrived in 1764. The fishery, of course—everyone knew it to be a trade of very great proportions. But the French settlers—have you heard of them, the Acadians?"

"I have."

"They were transported by their thousands to cause us less trouble. A most unpleasant, most regrettable business. They had been firmly anchored in their Arcadia, as they called it, for a century and a half and one way and another, many came back, or other Frenchmen came in their place. His Majesty's government saw the French peril as very real."

"And was it?"

Walker stares into the fire in silence. "A bad business indeed," he finally says. After a moment, he looks up.

"Look, your glass is empty. This must not happen."

He pours, then sits back and stares into the grate.

"It was most difficult to persuade English settlers to move into an area so distant from the populated southern regions. But as a younger man I had once been charged with the task of charting the coastal waters of my native Scotland. I established fishing posts there and settled hundreds of families. I saw a valuable prize for the taking in this New Scotland, largely despised, like the old. That is when I established the fishing station and trading post at Alston Point. It was 1768."

"It seems almost more than one man could do."

"If you live long enough, my dear Charlotte, and must work for a living, it is surprising what comes about."

There is a knock on the door and Harding enters holding a tray almost too wide for the door.

"Come in, my good man, come in and set it down here. That's it. Very good. How is everyone tonight?"

"They are all well, sir."

"Very good. Have Mr. Hampton send you up with a flask of my best claret."

"I have it ready, sir."

"Good. Fetch it then."

Walker lifts the covers.

"I'm a Scot by birth, Charlotte, but I love my roast beef as any Englishman."

"Oh, George. It looks splendid!"

"Here. Thank you, lad. You may go, and see you get some sleep."

"Thank you, sir."

Walker fills Charlotte's glass with claret.

"Your health."

"And yours, commodore."

They eat a while in silence.

Hoping to avoid the conversation about her so-called circumstances she guesses she's here to have, Charlotte asks him about Nepisiguit.

"I'll get to that detail in due course, but now I want to talk about you."

She sits very straight in the chair he has provided and waits for him to take the lead in the discussion. She knows he's a man who doesn't dawdle with words and she's quite certain now that he knows more about her than she has considered.

"Are you by chance the daughter of Charles Howe Taylor?"

Her cheeks flush. She drops her head and in a barely audible voice says, "Sir, I am his daughter." Charlotte doesn't know how to continue the conversation and sits staring into her skirts until finally conjuring up the courage to ask him how he had discovered the truth.

"Lutz told me more than your widowhood. He said he was suspicious about your circumstances from the moment you turned up at his plantation. He saw you as a woman of some means and, how can I put this—your man as one of fewer means."

Walker takes care to describe the predictable background of couples who flee their homes for the New World. He doesn't want to back her into a corner or force a lie, so continues gently, "Invariably they are running away from something. In your case, Lutz wondered if it was a forbidden marriage or, perhaps, no marriage at all."

But how did he tie this presumption to her proper name, she inquired. "Lutz told me that the plaque on your trunk is inscribed with the name Charlotte Howe Taylor. Now I have seen it for myself. In truth, your person—your flame-coloured hair, your height, give your identity away. You are the image of your father."

Now clearly anxious but in some ways relieved, Charlotte has questions of her own. How does he know her father and what will he do with her when this voyage is over?

The commodore assures her that his intentions are honourable. "You couldn't be left with that reprobate Lutz. He would have used you unpleasantly. I am hoping that I can still convince you to return to your father's home on the ship sailing from Nepisiguit next month." Charlotte is trembling. Her father would shun a pregnant daughter. Can she tell the commodore the truth? Instead she asks, "How has my father come to be your acquaintance?"

He tells her they were in business together in the merchant marines. In describing the business arrangements, he also submits his concerns about the lagging economy the men worked in. "England is suffering in financials. Trade isn't as profitable as it was. And the threat of war with the colonies takes ships and men from the trading business." She asks about Misters Baillie and Schollbred and whether they would have been visitors at her father's home. "Yes, they are known to the general as well, business associates they are. They may have frequented your home but that I doubt, as they conduct their affairs in grand offices in London."

He changes the subject, saying, "Tell me of your life in Sussex."

Charlotte persists as there are details she needs to get on the table.

"George, as you now know, I left my family in haste, without my father's approval. What I can tell you about the life I left behind is that I have an inheritance, a sizable sum from my maternal grandmother. As a woman alone, I need to secure my lawful right to that income."

There, the matter is on the table at last. Then as though considering her surprising commentary, the commodore shares a tale of his own.

"Well then, now that we are sharing more intimate details, let me sound you out on a matter. I have received recently a letter from a very dear friend in Edinburgh. He is a man of sixty-five and never married, but enjoys the fruits of a long life and a busy one. He is vigorous in every respect but wearies somewhat of matters of trade."

"Unlike yourself."

"We are both alike and unalike. But as I say, he is in Edinburgh. Now my friend writes me not a fortnight before I sailed to Jamaica to tell me of a somewhat extraordinary turn of events. It seems his lifelong patron—I cannot tell you the man's name because he was a person of high note in that city—his patron made certain investments in certain coal ventures in Yorkshire by which he was to lose his entire fortune and, as a consequence, he suffered a most terrible shock about a year ago and was carried off within days."

"He died of grief for his fortune?"

"He did, his good wife having died some years before for quite different reasons."

"Pray, what became of the coal mines?"

"It would seem there were none, not in the particular parcel of Yorkshire claimed by the principles in this case. But here is my concern. My friend's patron had a daughter, an attractive woman whose prospects were damaged beyond repair by her father's misfortune. Of course my friend was most solicitous of her well being and offered his assistance in every way possible. But—here it is—he was quite unprepared for her confession that she loved him with all her heart and desired only to be his wife."

"She sought the security of his fortune."

Walker carefully shovels a scoop of coals onto the tiny grate.

"This he naturally considered. But to test her in this regard, he offered to make her a dowry that would restore some measure of respectability to her position. Still she has professed her love, saying that she saw in him measures of honour and courage that surpassed those of any younger man."

"And which he possesses?"

"In my judgment, this is a true estimation. And so it is, my friend writes me. Can it be imagined, he writes, that a woman so young, so properly bred and of such beauty as to draw the admiration of any who encounter her, could form a true attachment to a man in the winter of his years?"

He sits suddenly forward. "Now look. You've emptied your glass and you've left potatoes here, swimming in gravy. I cannot have it."

They eat the last of their meal in silence. In fact, she is unsure exactly how she should answer, or how her answer could be of help to Commodore Walker's friend.

"George, I can claim no special wisdom in these matters," she finally offers.

"Who among us can, my dear?"

"But I have a sense."

"Yes. Yes, I'm sure you have."

"Your friend is a man whose life has brought many satisfactions and rewards. Naturally there may be others who would like to share in these, but few could hope for success except a woman, especially a young woman—and this is exactly who makes a claim."

"But even if she were to have other reasons, my dear, you must address whether, in your opinion, such a person could conceive of a true and lasting love for so old a man."

"She might form many bonds of strong regard, George, some seeming very much like love. But I do not believe such bonds would be the love your friend seeks. That love is the love that arises between men and women of more equal age."

Walker nods with slow assent.

"His hopes are dashed then," he says.

"You did not speak of hopes, George, but said only that your friend's feelings were tender ones. And I see no reason why they should be trampled underfoot by a young woman's vagaries."

"Absolutely well said! In fact, I must confess these are my own sentiments precisely and I shall write to him as soon as we are in port and give him these very words, if I may have your permission to repeat them."

"Of course you have. But now I must press you in turn. You have told me of these troublesome times in Nepisiguit, and that American privateers are wreaking havoc on outposts such as yours."

"That is hardly surprising."

"And that they are assisted by the Indians and the Acadians, with whom you trade."

"Alas, this is so."

"But why would you trade with men who join in arms against ourselves and our King?"

"The answer is perfectly simple, though the question reveals intelligence I would often be glad to discover in my own people. The answer is that we canna judge others by category but by their individual actions. The ancestors of the Acadians I know learned to be good hunters and good fishermen from the ancestors of the Indians I know. If we in turn learn from them and reward their teaching according to our ability, we have nothing to fear from them."

"But surely the tales I was told of Indian massacres are not entirely fabrications?"

"The Indian nations are many and widespread. Some tales are true, others are not. I speak only of the Indians I know, the Indians of Nepisiguit, the Micmac. They are my friends."

They speak on and the fire dims in the grate. It is dark by the time the commodore comes to the end of his story. He suggests the cabin air should be amply cooled now that the sun is well gone and that the gentle seas ought to bring a fine sleep this night. Outside on the deck when he walks her to her cabin, he reverts to a formal tone and says, "I bid you good evening, Mrs. Willisams." Charlotte thanks him for his hospitality and adds, "My name remains Charlotte Taylor."

"Thank you for your company," are his final words.

Charlotte undresses and lies on her bunk in the dark. It is measurably cooler now and she has recourse to the lighter blanket of pelts. The bear, she has decided, makes an admirable rug. Her sole concern as sleep claims her is that the commodore had made no mention of her inheritance, although she is certain he has not forgotten it.

The lamp is long extinguished when Charlotte is jolted from her sleep with a menacing crack of thunder and the realization that she is suddenly very cold. She retrieves the hairy black bearskin from the floor to protect herself from the frigid air but the thunder—cracking like a gunshot now rather than rumbling like a cart of stones being unloaded—is announcing a storm that will likely mean she has to go below. She no sooner considers the option when Will comes to her quarters in great distress telling her to get below. "Take cover. It's a nor'easter. Tie yerself down to the pole in the hold and stay there until I come to fetch ye." What is this nor'easter, she wonders, but quickly grabs the bearskin and finds her way to the ladder. On the way she can see that the wind is lashing the deck and the sea is rising and falling like a mountainous landscape. It's an awesome sight, unlike any storm she'd seen before. At this stage it seems to be even wilder than the one she survived in the mid-Atlantic.

For three days the nor'easter blows. The men in the crew take turns staying below to dry out a little, eat and rest before returning to the upper deck. The rain pounds down on the ship, threatening to drown them where they hide. Charlotte wonders at times which direction they are taking. She fears the gale-force wind will blow them over into the pounding sea. When Will comes below, he tells her the wind is not the problem. It's a rogue wave they're frightened by. "It could swamp this schooner and we'd all be sent to the deep." Charlotte begins to calculate the likelihood of a rogue wave and realizes that the longer they are stayed in this storm, the more likely it is that the one would find them. It's a long way to come to drown before reaching the shore, she thinks.

But there's more to do than worry. She tries to keep the tea ready, to scrape mould from the last pieces of cheese so that she can put them with slabs of equally mouldy bread and have some sustenance ready for crew members when they come below. There is still a good supply of water and the food will last for many days yet, but the bread and cheese are all she can reach from the place she is tied to and she dares not release herself as the ship tosses violently in the brine. No one has slept during the days and nights of being dashed about in the storm. On the third day, Will takes a fall from the ladder and when he struggles to his feet his arm is dangling by his side, broken. There's nothing to do but lay it—straight she hopes—onto a board and wrap it with ties of cloth she finds by the stores. Will manages to smile at her throughout her ministrations, even as sweat beads on his pale brow.

They are, all of them, nearly exhausted when at last the rain begins to lesson and the wind dies down. "'Tis over," Will tells her, "blown itself out." It is safe to return to her quarters and she's relieved to get out of the hold. Back on deck she finds the commodore looking little the worse for wear and asks him whether the storm has pushed them ahead or cost them time. He points his finger to the northwest and says, "In that distance we will soon see land. We've been alongside Nova Scotia throughout this storm. Miscou Island is ahead. We need to sail around the north coast of Miscou and then you'll see a sight you won't soon forget."

THE FOLLOWING MORNING, the dark green coast of northern Nova Scotia lies high on the horizon and she can make out the island they are approaching. The commodore invites her to join him for breakfast and speaks his mind immediately. "You are a curious woman. I have noted your interest in where this ship will sail and the history of the people in these parts. It sounds to me as though you may plan to stay in Nova Scotia once we land. Is that a possibility?" She has thought about this conversation a dozen times and is still uncertain about the position to take. Now almost five months' pregnant, her secret is becoming harder to conceal.

"I wish to stay on this side of the ocean," she tells him.

"There are no other European women at the post," he replies.

She says she already knows that—Will had told her. He states his case again.

"It is most unusual for a woman to be alone."

Silence from Charlotte.

"There are men to marry, men who can take care of you," Walker proposes.

She wonders if this is an oblique reference to the story he'd told her about the aged suitor and the young woman. Is her future in the New World predicated on marriage to the commodore?

Then he says unequivocally, "Charlotte, I am convinced that a hasty return to England is in your best interest."

Before she can say another word, he dismisses her with a curt, "I have duties to attend to."

She is on her way back to her cabin when the coast comes into clear view. "Land, bloody land—thanks be to God," Charlotte cries. Soon they steer around the high cliffs of Miscou still being swept by a stiff Atlantic wind and suddenly sail into the calm of the Baie de Chaleur. Charlotte catches her breath at the sight of a land that captures her soul. A beautiful wilderness lies before her. Forests of fir trees drop off into fields of glistening seagrass that wave over long, sandy beaches. The water around her is teeming with fish. Will is at her side and tells her the huge marine mammals with the horizontal flukes on their tails are called whales. They move like undersea mountains, riding up to the surface and slipping out of sight again. The smaller ones with tusks are walrus, he says. The cod are so plentiful, she thinks, she could scoop them from the water with her hands. She can hardly believe the long journey from England to the West Indies and now to this place called Nepisiguit is over. Standing in awe at the ship's rail and remembering defiantly what has gone before, she vows, "I will make my own way." As the incoming tide sweeps the vessel to Alston Point and the home of Commodore Walker, Charlotte is determined to tame this wild and enchanting land and make it her own.

CHAPTER 3

The Baie

1775

*W*ioche stands on the Second Rock, alone except for Atilq. He had come here at first light to watch the movement of men at the shore of the bay. It's his habit. His father had taught him this among other things: you learn most about men when you watch them unseen, since every man does alone what he will not do if watched.

Wioche pulls his wolfskin around his shoulders, the on-shore wind being brisk this late August morning. He takes a piece of dried whale meat from his pouch and chews it slowly, looking at the empty horizon. He looks down at Atilq, who tilts his nose out across the bay to demonstrate that he would not be seen to beg. Wioche reaches again into his pouch and tosses a piece to Atilq.

"Where is your ableegumoocj-k today?" he asks the dog, and Atilq raises his ears because he knows the word *rabbit*.

The wind brings a sound from the direction of the English outpost—footsteps. He follows the sound with his eyes and sees a woman stepping through the brush from the commodore's lodge toward the beach. There were no women among the English, but all the People knew the commodore's ship had been in the bay since yesterday. Evidently, though an old man, he had brought a woman with him. Wioche watches from the Second Rock. The woman in the long dress stands half a head taller than the men he knows at the lodge and has hair the colour of raspberries. No one among the Salmon People stands taller than Wioche and no *woman* of any people. He squints his eyes against the rising sun, watching her stealthily find her way to the shore.

THE SUN has already made its way fully over the horizon and is bathing the water as well as the sands with its rays. Morning gilds the sky. She takes a step forward and stops in her tracks. A giant bird with blue-and-grey feathers, a long angular neck and long, spindly legs is standing like a solitary custodian gazing out over the water. She stands as still as the winged creature, taking in the sight. The bird is grand but vulnerable, so lonely in its repose. She feels the solitude—her own as well—and thinks, This isolation here—it will be my saving grace as well as my struggle. She knows the life beyond this compound must be different to the comparative luxury Walker enjoys. She knows, too, that her own future has been reduced to survival. But above all, Charlotte sees the opportunity here. The genteel covering that she has worn for twenty years has begun to peel away. The lessons of the West Indies ripped off the first layer, exposing her vulnerability. But the mantle of this general's daughter was rent piece by piece as the reality of food, water, shelter, pirates, rebelling colonies, wild beasts and nature's ferocity exposed the life of a settler in the New World. While she stands here in the dawning, she knows there is still a level of naïveté that could defeat her, but she also knows she has pioneer in her bones.

"Why ye be to the beach at this early hour?" Will calls out. The bird she's been watching lifts off the sand suddenly and soundlessly, its massive wingspan spreading to a width that astonishes her, its neck coiling as it takes flight. Charlotte watches the bird circle toward the sea and asks Will, "What is that magnificent creature?" He tells her it is a great blue heron. "There are many in these parts. They stand for eternity at the shore." She wants to know when the tides change. "It was a low tide at about three o'clock this morning," he explains. "Did ye not hearken the squawking of the birds?" So that was the sound that had wakened her in the night. "The gulls fight for clams on the flats of the low tide," he says. She asks what the flats are. "That ye'll see later," Will promises. "But for now, ye must come to the house. The commodore asks for ye at the breakfast."

WIOCHE KNOWS the men will be coming to trade soon and lets his thoughts stray to the molasses the white men bring, the strange sweetness that rivals honey and syrup, the fierce mother of rum, the devil potion that possesses its drinkers. He whistles softly to Atilq and together they move off the rock to a canopy of young trees, a vantage point closer to where the trade will take place.

IT'S MID-MORNING when Charlotte sees the Indians approaching. Eight maybe ten, walking down the long path that leads from the forest on the hillside to Alston Point. They are carrying something—furs perhaps, piled on a tarpaulin that's slung over two poles. She's anxious to be present when the commodore goes out to greet them, but a residual fear still lingers so she waits and spies on them from a distance. One speaks to the commodore in English. They want to trade the goods they carry for the molasses and rum he brought on the schooner. There's a lot of talking, must be the way they make the trade, she thinks. At last, the exchange is made. She has lost her chance to speak to an Indian and sulks about it when the commodore returns to the house. He tells her that he has to go to the camp to meet with their leader, Chief Francis Julian, later in the afternoon and that she can go with him if she likes.

He has no special instructions for her while they walk the short distance to the camp except to say the Indians are known as the People of the Salmon and are respected for their medicinal remedies. The camp is situated at the top of a hill that overlooks the harbour on one side and the bay on the other. Walker explains, "It's a fine location for a camp, high enough to be dry but close enough to the water below to have easy access to the canoes and a fresh-water lagoon that empties into the harbour immediately below the camp."

Closer now, she can see that the camp is surrounded by trees—spruce, poplar and an abundance of birch. The black-water murky lagoon separating them from the hill they need to climb to the camp necessitates a tricky crossing over a collection of logs. Near the top of the hill she gets her first glimpse inside the camp and calculates a dozen tents in a clearing and one long, low log house set apart from the rest. There are a few cabins, shacks really, nearer the woods. An enormous fire pit in the middle of the camp is where all the action is—animal skins are fastened to frames by the fire—to dry, she supposes—women are cleaning fish and dogs are hungrily lapping up the refuse the women toss to the ground. All at once the visitors are noticed.

People come from all directions—little ones, old men,

young girls and their mothers and grandmothers and the yapping dogs gather by the fire looking toward them.

Walker tells her the man coming toward them is Chief Francis Julian. The hearty greeting the two men exchange makes it obvious that they have known each other for some time. Charlotte is transfixed. The frightening tales she has heard of savages—scalping, raiding, stealing, pillaging—are suspended when Chief Julian tells her she is welcome at the camp.

WIOCHE IS NOT AMONG the people who gather around the fire. He's carefully concealed, watching the English commodore and this strange woman by his side. He rubs Atilq's head to sooth his own anger when he hears the English words. He knows Chief Julian speaks the commodore's language because it's good for trade with the English, who rarely learned the language of any other. But it rankles—this deferring to the foreign men. As the chief's appointed traveller, his job is not to trade the pelt of the beaver or the hide of a moose. He trades information for the chief from camp to camp in the Mi'kmaq region, information that increasingly concerns the white man standing in this camp. Wioche had long known the language of the French as the French had been the powerful strangers in the time of his father and his grandfather and his great-grandfather. The Salmon People spoke in their own language to the French, whose little brothers *les Acadiens* had lived in these woods and fished these waters so long. Wioche reluctantly learned to speak the English white man's language as well.

MARIE STANDS by the fire with Josef, who is three, and Marc, who is four, and watches the English arriving in the camp. Chief Julian comes forward to give greetings. He knew well enough how to be a friend to strangers and draw advantage from them. The old commodore was no exception, though he is less a stranger than most English.

Marie does not wish to offend the woman who appears to belong to the commodore, and she is careful not to allow her inspection to become a stare. But it was impossible not to marvel at so strange a shape. The woman is an odd creature. How had she grown so tall? And though the skins of the English were often pale—paler even than that of her Acadian husband, André—they were never in Marie's experience as pale as this, and the hair colour was—it was unnatural.

Yet for all that, the woman behaves just as women among the People were expected to behave. In the presence of Chief Julian, she speaks not a word, though her voice had echoed up the gully as she'd approached. Now the commodore and the chief walk aside to speak alone, and the red-haired woman stands among a crowd of strangers. Marie stoops to stoke the fire for tea and drops her berries and leaves in the kettle propped on stones in its midst. She probes the sand with a stick to check if her bannock is ready.

A *bois brule*—married to a white man—she prides herself on baking better bannock than her sisters. Not that *les Acadiens* had eaten the bannock, of course. The Scots—a kind of English— had passed that good food to the People many years before. Indeed, her own grandmother had baked bannock. But it was a white man's food nonetheless, and André Landry was a white man and that made her bannock better. She straightens up to call at Josef, who was about to plunge himself straight into the fire.

"Get back!" she says. "Or you will burn up like the devil!"

She speaks in Mi'kmaq. The children understand French well, but it had come to her with difficulty and more so because André spoke the language of the People. Since they had hid *les*

Acadiens from the British soldiers for twenty years, many of the People who did not speak French before now spoke it well. This was the wisdom of Chief Julian, who had seen that the French would return some day in numbers. Already there were signs that this was so. There were no English here in the land of the People, only some Scots and French from across the water and a few of the old *Acadiens* returned. And the commodore, of course, and his men. But they were not ordinary English.

The red-haired woman waits awkwardly and Marie glances at her belly. Was this the way with such long English women, that their bellies stood out a little beneath their dresses? Or could she be with child, the commodore's child perhaps? Who would know about this? Marie wondered.

"Here," she says to the woman, her voice low, as it always was when she spoke French. "Here is food." She begins to poke at the ashes with a burnt stick.

The English woman draws close. "Do you speak French?" she asks in that language but also softly.

"A little, from my husband," says Marie. "And you? Do you speak French too?"

"Yes, a little."

"Josef!" she calls. "Come back or I will tie you!"

"Are these your children?" the red-haired woman asks.

"Yes. And my husband is *un Acadien.*"

"How beautiful they are! You married a man who was not one of your own."

Marie smiles shyly. "I married the man I loved."

"Yes," says the white woman. "Yes."

Marie uses two sticks to pluck the bannock from the coals and shakes the sand from the flattened bread. She gives a piece to each of her children, and a piece to the woman.

They chew a minute in silence while Marie wrestles with the propriety of her thoughts.

"May I touch your hair?" she finally whispers.

"Of course."

"It's real?" asks Marie.

"Yes, of course it is." She leans forward to let Marie touch her hair and asks, "What's your name?"

"Marie Landry. What is yours?"

"Charlotte," she answers, her eyes as blue as the sky. "Charlotte Taylor."

FRANCIS JULIAN is in his fifty-third year and his hair is long, almost to his waist, and the black is shot through with grey. His skin is the colour of buckwheat honey, but this is a matter of no note, since this was the colour of the skin of all the Salmon People. His nose is high and arched, and his dark eyes are veiled by their upper lids. This, too, is unexceptional. In summer, he wears a wolfskin draped over his otherwise bare shoulders and his trousers are baggy and woollen, courtesy of the white traders his people had come to know. His moccasins are made of deerskin, soft and carefully beaded. These, too, are as they should be. Francis Julian is in every way unexceptional except in respect to his mind, which is uncommonly clear.

At thirty he had seen the extension of English power when even the proud French generals could not assess its true nature. The learning of English had been the greatest challenge of his life. "I have killed the mother bear," he would often say, "but I did not fear then as I feared the shifting face of the language of the English."

His prescience has had its reward, and the Salmon People knew greater prosperity than they had known in the memory of the oldest man among them. And had there been no other Englishman, his friendship with George Walker would still have bettered the lives of every one of the People.

Except for the rum. Francis Julian knew the English goods for what they were—easements of life's burdens. The rum, too, had come disguised as a blessing. But it had stolen the souls of his best. What could he do now about the rum and the men who brought it? This was a friendship to preserve. After he and the commodore had spoken at length, they part again as friends. What had the upstart Americans who were rebelling in the colonies to offer that was better than this?

The English start back down the path and the commodore sees Wioche, alone on the ridge above them. Charlotte walks beside Walker as the entourage descends from the camp.

They pick their way down the path without speaking until Charlotte sees the lone figure on the outcropping above and to their right.

"Who is that?" she asks.

Even from fifty yards, he is a striking figure, taller and more muscular than the other men of the Salmon. His sleek black hair flutters in the breeze as he turns to watch them pass below him. He makes no gesture, but Charlotte feels the force of his gaze fall directly upon her.

Walker looks up briefly.

"Wioche, the chief's favoured man, he's called the traveller," he says. "Something of a dark horse."

"I'm most intrigued, commodore, with this encampment and these people," Charlotte begins. "Can you tell me how they live there? Do they live all together in that great hut, or in the little cottages and tents? Does every Indian have many wives, as I have heard?"

Walker stops in his tracks. "Charlotte, I beg you. Allow me to give some consideration to the news I have just heard."

He starts down again. Scolded, she falls silent, but keeps pace with him, her newly adopted boots making her sure-footed on the rough forest trail. After the experiences of the ship, she could not conceive of any cause for less than complete candour between them.

Finally he stops and turns to her. "Charlotte, the outpost may come under attack by American rebels. That is the simple fact. That is the news."

"What will you do, if I may ask?"

"What I *must* do, is to depart for Quebec. I'll consult there with others in His Majesty's service about this matter. I can only say, Charlotte, that I repent mightily that I may have put you in danger. And I thank God for your imminent departure."

BACK AT ALSTON POINT, a canoe had arrived from Restigouche across the bay bearing news. Walker is huddled with his men in the main house and Charlotte is not intended to be party to any of it. She walks out to the water and surveys her new surroundings.

Alston Point is almost entirely a dune of sand. It juts into a channel to create a large harbour off the Baie de Chaleur. Its stands of white pine carpet the earth beneath them with softly scented needles, and the sands by the water are dotted with shards of white clam and indigo oyster shells like quarter moons. Charlotte is drawn to the peculiar nature of the tides in the place, tides so extreme they leave swaths of the bay uncovered in their retreat, as is now the case. The gulls are landing in their hundreds, prancing and pecking furiously into holes on the sandy, rippled flats and snatching up creatures, a savage spectacle. As she walks, she considers the dizzying flow of events. She had entertained the idea of remaining with Walker here for some time, long enough at least to consider her plight more carefully and arrive at a course of action not wholly determined by others. But if he is to leave for Quebec by canoe—and she knew he could not be persuaded to allow her to accompany him on such an adventure—how could she remain here without his patronage and protection?

Back in her own chamber, she loosens the stays of her dress and feels a considerable relief. Her pregnancy has remained her secret, but—she calculates the time—it is late-August and the quickening has begun, wondrous and foreboding at once. Her midriff has thickened and her breasts are swelling. Soon she would have to let the stays out.

There are fourteen men gathered in the dining room that evening, and a palpable air of excitement pervades the room. When Charlotte enters, the entire group—ship's officers, trading-post roustabouts and leathery canoeists just off the water—rise in courtesy.

"I shall never again be one woman among so many men," Charlotte says as she takes her chair.

"Or half-men," a grizzled fellow mutters from the table's end to polite guffaws.

It is a comfortable dining room, with some respectable English furniture and even several French pieces. When Charlotte points these out, Walker smiles cryptically. To the victor has gone the spoils, apparently. These were living cheek by jowl with an assortment of animal-skin carpets, aboriginal pottery and religious symbols such as heavy silver crosses.

On this occasion, the first course consists of clawed monsters called lobster, boiled and served broken in pieces on platters. They strike Charlotte as a most unnatural food, but she is coming to terms with extracting the white meat from the bony shell as well as the thick grainy bread, a taste, too, that she is bent on acquiring. The men are drinking rum as always, but this libation is not extended to the woman among them. The commodore's sense of what is appropriate seems at least in part to be determined by the company he keeps.

When the plates are cleared, a haunch of venison is brought, and good gravy. After serving it, Walker clears his throat auspiciously.

"Charlotte," he announces in a tone that seems curiously formal, "I have excellent news. I've been most anxious for your safety, as have we all—and all the more because of our imminent departure—in view of these various alarms. But now these men, just arrived from Quebec, tell me that we may expect the arrival here at Alston Point of the *Hanley*, bound for Bristol. It may appear within the fortnight but will stop only to drop letters. We shall attempt to make every arrangement possible before my departure, but I have asked Mr. Primm to remain here as your protector and guardian."

Charlotte nods without speaking.

"Needless to say," Walker concludes, "I am most relieved."

Later that night, she finds him alone in the small room he calls his study, where his books have a place on sturdy shelves and his papers a place on a capacious desk.

"George," she says without preamble. "You must know how grateful I am for your concern. But I wonder if I might not await another ship."

"Another?"

"You have provided me with an opportunity that few such women as I can look for, that is, to see the New World in the company of enlightened men. I beg you not to abbreviate this exceptional circumstance."

Walker looks at her.

"Charlotte, I'm flattered indeed. And were the season not now so far advanced, I might consider your request. But we cannot be certain of another ship. The crossing will become increasingly dangerous with each passing week. And were you to fail to find any ship, I cannot contemplate your staying in this place through the winter."

"Will you remain here yourself, George?"

"Of course. But these winters, Charlotte. Nothing in your experience would allow you to imagine their fierceness. They are a test even for the strongest man."

"What of the Indian women we have seen?"

"They are a remarkable people, Charlotte, but they are not the likes of you."

"And the Acadians? Have there not been Acadian women here these two hundred years?"

He looks at her without expression, then smiles.

"You must allow me to assure you, dear Charlotte, that your request is impossible. But here is something I can offer."

He takes a sealed letter from his drawer and hands it to her.

"This is for your father's eyes. I think when you see his response, you will appreciate my wisdom. If you've been rash, you were rash for love and that speaks well of you and lies very much behind you. The general will read here the sort of daughter he has, and I tell you, he will be proud and forgiving."

"My father," Charlotte says, her voice without expression.

"You will make a proper marriage, Charlotte, to one of those good young men of good family that Sussex teems with. You and your husband will be happy, live in a fair house and raise fine children. Could any woman want more?"

He stands, places a gentle hand upon her shoulder.

"The past is done, Charlotte, and no longer to be feared."

THE NEXT MORNING, after a breakfast of fried potato and salt pork, the commodore spreads a large, hand-drawn chart across the main table and several men sit with him.

"Charlotte?" She stands nearby, not wishing to be seen as too curious. "Charlotte, do come and see where we are going."

He draws a finger from the small house that marks their place at Alston Point on the shore of the Baie de Chaleur along the breadth of the bay to its western shore where it meets the Restigouche River.

"Thence, we shall travel through the eastern hills of Quebec to the St. Lawrence River."

"Why, sir, will you not travel by sea when you have a ship of your own?"

"We save a week by avoiding the Gaspé Peninsula. We will follow the Restigouche and make a series of portages. Once on the big river, and with the blessing of a favourable wind, we will paddle in haste to the ramparts of Quebec."

ON THE NIGHT BEFORE Walker's departure, Charlotte paces in her chamber, burdened by her deceitfulness to the man who is her benefactor. Her anguish is interrupted when a bluish light flashes across her room. It's so peculiar she wonders if it is an omen. It appears again, then vanishes. Wondering what it could be, she exits her chamber to investigate and finds Walker outside surveying the night sky. It is a sight to behold. The heavens are awash with great waves of blue luminance that spiral and dive in galloping columns like a game of chase. "The northern lights," he says, "the Indians call them megwatesg. They come at this time of the year when the weather is starting to change. Chief Julian says they are the lights of the Great Spirit."

"What are they really, George?"

"I know not, Charlotte. Some charged vapours of the air, some curious lightning in these more northern regions."

"They are not spirits then?"

"We leave the spirits to the Indians, Charlotte. Our reason does not allow them. God Almighty is enough of a spirit for Christian men."

They stand together, mesmerized by the astral vision above them—the safeguard and the salvaged—under the surreal firmament of the Baie de Chaleur.

He turns to her and she can see his face by the mixed lights of the sky and the lantern in the window. "Provided you have no objection, I have decided also to leave Will MacCulloch here to watch out for you. I can see he is very fond of you and feel assured he will see to your needs."

"I'm most grateful to you, George."

The next morning, the convoy of six canoes paddles away.

FOR THREE DAYS after the commodore's departure, Charlotte keeps to herself. She twice saw Salmon women on the flats, and Salmon canoes paddling out of the bay and back from time to time. But she contents herself with mending the plain dress she favours most and reading from Walker's library. There she discovers to her delight a book entitled *The Fortunes and Misfortunes of the Famous Moll Flanders* and found a heroine who, battered as she might be by circumstances, offers more inspiration than the wilting Clarissa.

In the evenings she eats with Will and the ever-watchful Jack Primm and others of Walker's employ. With the exception of easy banter with Will, there is a rather thin courtesy at the table and talk among the men of rebellion and trade.

On the fourth evening, Primm turns to her directly.

"Mrs. Willisams, excuse me, Miss Taylor," he says pointedly, "I have every reason to think that the *Hanley* shall put in soon to this harbour. The wind has been favourable for some days now and she is well captained."

"This is the ship bound for Bristol, Mr. Primm?"

"It is. I would advise you to see that you are packed and ready."

"I will see to it, Mr. Primm."

After dinner, she walks out to the shore and watches the long lines of birds flying into flocks like pointed arrows. Walker had said they were a kind of goose, though she could hardly match these distant travellers in the sky with the honking geese and ganders of Sussex barnyards. The evening sky casts a pink glow over the fluttering seagrass, the distant forests of pine look like black columns of sentries shadowing Alston Point and the sandy beach washed by the water from the bay seems to blink in the last of the light. For a moment, she feels the peace of eventide.

MARIE LANDRY carries her basket out onto the flats and wraps her blanket robe about her tightly. Already the season is turning and the air is both cool and wet. She has enough mussels for the meal, but she wants the fat clams too. They're hiding in their bubbling holes, but she knows how to winkle them out of their lairs. The gulls soar and dive, but she pays them no heed.

There, at the edge of the flats, is the red-headed English woman, alone. She walks with her head down, her English dress shrouded in a man's long coat, but with no air of despondency. Rather, she seems absorbed by the things, living and not living, left exposed on the sand. Marie walks to her and Charlotte looks up and smiles.

"Do you gather"—for a moment she cannot recall the French word for *mussel*—"food?" Marie asks.

"Mussels," says Charlotte. "I find them rather good. I never ate them at home."

"In England?"

"Yes, I never ate them in England. We never see them there. Not in Sussex, anyway."

Marie shows her own collection.

"Oh, what an excellent lot! I see you gather your food from the sea here, as we do in England too, though not so much. We *do* eat—I can't recall the French for them, but we call them oysters."

"Oy-eesters?"

"They have dark shells with thick sharp edges and you eat them alive."

"Oh yes, we have them here. *Huitres.*"

They stand for a moment looking across the bay.

"Such a wild, empty land," says Charlotte.

Marie points toward the seaward island Charlotte had rounded on the *Achilles* and traces her finger down the outline of the coast.

"My husband's parents have moved there, to Caraquet, south from that island of Miscou. That was five months ago. Now we stay with my parents."

"Does your husband like to stay with your people?"

"Oh yes. He is an excellent fisherman and hunter."

"But he is comfortable with *your* people?"

"André is one of us. He speaks our language very well. We have taught him and he has taught us. That's how it has always been with *les Acadiens.*"

They stand again in silence, each resting from the effort of speaking in a language not their own.

"Where is your husband?" Marie asks suddenly.

"He has died."

"Oh."

They walk on. Marie whistles to the sandpipers skittering along the shore. The two women stop, and Marie bluntly says, "You are pregnant."

"I am." Charlotte tries to walk on, but she cannot withhold her own wretchedness. She feels a hot tear course down her cheek.

"What shall you do?" asks Marie.

"I don't know, I truly don't know," says Charlotte.

Marie bends to collect the cream-coloured clams, which withdraw their fleshy necks into their shells as soon as she has plucked them from the sand.

"The commodore is sending me back to England."

"Back to your home?"

"Yes—where I *cannot* go. My father will not have me with this child."

The Indian woman puts a small dark hand on Charlotte's.

That tender gesture undoes her.

"I cannot explain!" Charlotte says, trying to swallow the rising emotion that's constricting her throat when she cries, "What shall I do? Who can help me?"

Marie looks at her dumbfounded and says, "You cannot go home with your baby?"

"No! And *he* will not let me stay in his outpost here!"

"Where will you go?" she asks.

"I don't know!" All her poise and dignity leave her. Tears pour from her eyes and she reaches out blindly to take Marie's hands and says, "I need someone who can help me."

"Stay with the People," Marie Landry says in her slow, careful French. "We will keep you safe."

FOR TWO DAYS it rains, a slow, misted drizzle that matches the weather to Charlotte's mood. When at last it stops, the sky turns a pale watery blue and Charlotte leaves the lodge for an afternoon stroll. She has adopted a miscellany of apparel that suits these excursions and protects her from the weather. She favours the boots and had cut a dress to make a simpler skirt, which she wears with a shawl she had stitched so that it would hang loosely over her now-let-out bodice. She had been somewhat inhibited from venturing away from the water on account of bears, but understood from her conversation with Jenkins, one of the outpost men, that bears had other business on their minds in this season. Apparently the beasts slept in dens all winter, buried in snow. She suspects that this is in several respects what the human beasts may also do.

She sets off with no firm idea of her direction, but it is unlikely to have been an accident that she finds herself on the path that leads up in the direction of the Indian camp. And in the woods just off that path, she hears the voices of women: Marie and another woman are stooped over gathering leaves from a bush. They look up at her approach and Charlotte's heart lifts at the sight of Marie's broad smile.

"Hello."

"Hello, Marie. What are you doing?"

Marie shows her a wide basket with a number of smaller baskets inside.

"Upsoolemanokseel," she said.

Charlotte holds the tiny red berries in her hand. They look like chokecherries to her.

"What do you do with these?"

"Tea," said Marie. "Very good tea, but you may eat them also."

"Without cooking them?"

"Yes. A little."

She nibbles a berry. It is bitter almost beyond description.

"I think I would prefer the tea."

Marie laughs. "This is Anne," she says.

The other woman is taller than Marie and although she wears clothes much like Marie's, her features are not that of an Indian. Her French is fluent, better than Charlotte's, with a curious country accent.

"There are still *les Acadiens* among us," Marie explains as they put berries in their baskets. "Both her parents are French."

The three walk together to the edge of a clearing where a grove of white birch stands in the watery sunlight. Marie takes a cloth from her basket and carefully unwraps it to reveal an iron-bladed knife. She begins to cut pieces that look like mushrooms, the shape of half-plates, off the white bark from the living tree. Elsewhere on its trunk, Charlotte can see the evidence of earlier cutting.

"Is this, too, for tea?"

"No." Marie cuts with determination, stretching up to harvest fresh pieces from higher on the trunk. "This we boil and mix the juice with bear grease and rub it on sores. It's good medicine for sores."

"And see here," says Anne. She opens the sack she carries and shows a half-peck of soft brown cylinders the size of a man's finger.

"Cattails," says Charlotte.

"These are for the throat when it is sore."

"A cold."

"Yes. But you boil them for a long time to make a drink. Wioche says some hunters must carry just a piece in the mouth to keep off devils and cold."

"Wioche?" She recognizes the name.

"Wioche has learned the medicines of the elders," Marie says. She packs some leaves to cover the basket of berries. "He knows much about these things, more than any man now among us."

"Some of us think he knows too much," Anne says, and both women laugh.

"Oh," Marie exclaims and snatches up fistfuls of leaves from a plant in the clearing, pronouncing a word that Charlotte could not hope to repeat. "These we burn and put the ash in corn. Very good."

"Really?" Charlotte marvels. "Ashes in corn? We don't do that in Sussex either."

Marie turns to Anne and speaks in their own language. Then to Charlotte.

"Later, we'll go on the high rocks and collect the—what, Anne?—the blueberry leaves."

"Ah," Charlotte smiles. "For tea. I know."

"Oh yes," says Anne. "Tea for the old ones, whose old bones ache. There is good in those leaves."

"Is there? Good in tea?" Charlotte laughed. "Though, if I'm honest, I will confess to liking China tea, which is what my family drinks in England."

"Here we make good tea from roots of the spruce and sarsaparilla and pine needles and juniper needles too."

"Goodness! So many teas?"

"Oh yes." Anne smiles, pleased to pass on her knowledge. "There are leaves for the hearts of the old people too."

"And you can chew the gum of the spruce tree," Marie adds.

Anne makes a face. "Yes, but it's better for patching the canoes."

They laugh together.

THEY HAD COME to the lagoon and the two women begin to cross the path of logs without looking back. Charlotte follows.

In the camp, Marie takes Charlotte's hand gently in hers and leads her away from Anne, who is speaking with an older woman.

"Look! Come!" she says.

They pass through the cluster of cone-shaped tents—wigwams—to a group of small shantylike constructions at the edge of the woods. Children play outside two of these. Fires burn near the entrances. One shanty is closed, quiet.

"They have been the houses of *les Acadiens* who hid among us," Marie says, her voice soft, conspiratorial. "Now some have found new homes."

Charlotte regards the little structure in front of her, which seems almost to have sprung up from the floor of the forest. It is built of logs stacked up one atop the other and tied together with spindly tree roots. Birch bark covers the outside. The roof is thatched with boughs.

Marie makes a soft noise, and Charlotte turns to follow her gaze. A tall—very tall—Indian man is walking toward them.

"Wioche," Marie whispers, but Charlotte knows that already.

He approaches unsmiling and speaks to Marie in the Indian language. She answers and opens her basket, takes out several leaves on twigs and he examines them, pronouncing judgment with grave authority. Marie asks a question and he answers, nodding in the affirmative. Marie smiles, turns to Charlotte.

"Charlotte," she says.

Wioche bows.

"Wioche," Marie says.

The three of them stand a little awkwardly.

"Marie shows you the plants," he says—in English.

"I'm most struck by her knowledge," Charlotte replies.

"Food and medicine are the first matters," he says.

"Certainly, such matters are indispensable," says Charlotte.

They stand again unspeaking.

"It is good to see you among us," says Wioche.

He bows again, turns and walks away. Marie looks at Charlotte.

"He's unaccustomed to speaking with English women," she says.

"No matter," says Charlotte. "I rarely have the opportunity to speak to Indian men. So we are even."

Marie suggests they go inside the cabin. It's one windowless room, sunlight filtering through the holes in the roof. The earthen floor is smooth. Sealskin lines the walls. A neglected chimney that looks as though it might collapse at any moment stands nonetheless, evidence of long-extinguished fires at its base. There is a cot, built on four tree stumps that someone has covered with furs. She suspects that someone is Marie.

AT THE TABLE that evening, Will MacCulloch busies himself with his meat as Primm turns to Charlotte on the matter of her walk.

"And apart from this danger of animals, which cannot be

discounted, especially for one such as yourself, who must go unprotected with a musket or even a pistol, there is the matter of the Indians. I must warn you that these relations are most delicate and that minor incidents may have lasting consequences for all of us."

"I don't doubt it, Mr. Primm, and shall bear your words in mind at all times."

Primm looks at the others.

"I ask more of you, madam, than that you should bear my words in mind. I ask you not to venture up the hill to the Indian camp."

"I understand. How far may I go in that direction?"

Will catches her eye, winks and looks quickly back at this meal.

Primm shoots another glance around the table in a silent demand for support.

"I do not say that you shall go thus and thus far in any direction, madam. I am concerned only for your safety and the safety of the outpost as a whole. That safety, as you know, has been entrusted to me."

"I shall do everything in my power, Mr. Primm, to help you uphold your obligations, which I see are burdensome."

"They are not burdensome, Miss Taylor, but merely to be properly discharged."

"I feel you do very well."

Primm pinches his lips shut.

"Thank you," he finally says.

Will dares then to glance at Charlotte, she smiles at him.

"How is your arm, Will?" she asks.

"'Tis far better, madam, than 'twas. I shall soon be myself."

—

AFTER THE MEAL, Primm takes Will aside in Walker's own study.

"MacCulloch," he says, his voice low. "I am most concerned that this woman may cause us some problem."

"How do you mean, sir?"

"She is of an undisciplined constitution and this is known to Commodore Walker, who has charged me with the responsibility of assuring that she is safe and more particularly that she boards the *Hanley* as planned."

"Yes, sir."

"It would not do for this to miscarry, MacCulloch."

"Certainly not, sir. A grave miscarriage."

"For that reason, I am charging you in turn with the special duty of surveying Miss Taylor at all times when she is beyond these walls, and reporting her whereabouts to me."

"I understand, sir."

"You have strayed before, MacCulloch, and the commodore's eye is on you."

"I ken it well, sir."

"Here is a place where you may especially regain his favour,"

"Indeed, sir, and I shall endeavour to do so."

"See now that the firewood is brought in, MacCulloch."

"I will, sir."

IT IS EVIDENT THAT, if she is not to be aboard the *Hanley* and bound for Bristol, she will have to make the move to the Salmon encampment. There is no doubt that it will take a clandestine effort to see that done. She cannot simply haul her trunk up the hill, even if she were able to do so. Indeed, it must not be seen to be missing. She would require some measure of assistance and some of deception. She thinks of Will, but that would be unconscionable.

THE NEXT MORNING, when the men are out of the house, Charlotte opens her trunk and removes its contents. She carefully folds these into large squares of cloth that she cut from rolls in the storeroom and ties each bundle with twine.

Throughout that day, as the opportunity presents itself, she carries these out of the house and deposits them in the woods not far from the climbing path.

As the afternoon darkens and the men are gathering for their evening meal, a party of Salmon fishermen approaches the shore and several come up to the house, laughing and talking noisily. Jack Primm goes out to meet them and returns with two large salmon strung on a line.

"Excellent fish," he says. "Wonderful size. See these are cleaned, Mr. MacCulloch."

THE NEXT AFTERNOON, Charlotte lies in her bed in the commodore's house and reads a chapter from the life of Moll Flanders. Then she drops the book on her rounding belly and drifts into sleep.

Will MacCulloch is keeping watch. He sees the ship, goes straight to Charlotte's chamber and knocks.

"Who is it?"

"Hey, you wi the reid heid!"

"Will!"

"Och, madam. It's not me that wants you. It's Mr. Primm. The ship has come!"

She throws the door open.

"Are you certain, Will?"

"It's a big ship, madam, and must be the *Hanley*."

"Help me, Will."

"I shall, madam. What will you do?"

"I must run to the Indian camp."

"What do you need then?"

"To run, Will."

"Ye don't need me to run, madam."

"That's so, Will. That's so."

She snatches at the fur coat the commodore had given her and her few clothes.

"Who will see me, Will?"

"No one for the moment. But place your pillows under the covers, so you appear to be here or they shall skin me for helping ye."

"Shall you be punished for my deeds?"

"Not at all, madam. Hasten, now!"

"Here. Quick! Is the fire alight?"

"I know not. Quickly!"

She goes to the grate and drops the letter to her father on the coals.

"Madam, the grate is cold and your paper will be found! I shall burn it for you! Hurry now! I can see Primm's wee boat in the bay!"

She runs to the back door and opens it.

"Will!"

"Madam?"

"What a fine man you are!" she whispers.

"An' ye shall be a proper Englishwoman if ye don't get away now."

She dashes from the house and up the path toward the encampment. She passes the place where she had hidden her possessions—they were no longer there. Her path is chosen now so she forges ahead, crosses the lagoon on the log path, enters the clearing and stops in her tracks. The fire burns low and the People of the Salmon are gathered together in the centre. They turn their heads as one and look at her. On the ground beside the fire where they have gathered are her possessions, still in their bundles. She sees Marie and realizes her eyes are filled with tears. She could do nothing but walk forward.

PRIMM COMES THROUGH the door with the two sailors. Will is stoking the fire.

"MacCulloch! Fetch the lady!"

"Yes, sir. Is the ship here?"

"It is and no time to be lost! They will come with their boat to bring our letters and be gone straight!"

In a moment, Will is back with the news. The men run to the bedchamber and there was the shape of a woman, but no woman.

"You've let her escape, MacCulloch!"

"No, sir. She did na gae oot from here, sir."

"She did—while you napped in front of the fire, no doubt. By God, MacCulloch, you shall rue the day you knew Jack Primm!"

He looks around him in the greatest agitation.

"Now, every man! Search the grounds, for she cannot have gone far but is in likelihood crouching in the woods. MacCulloch, join the search! I'll deal with you later!"

THE OLD MAN regards her with sad eyes.

"Charlotte Taylor. Greetings. I am Francis Julian, chief of my people."

He seems taller now than when he had stood beside George

Walker on the trading day but displays no air of importance. Not knowing what better to do, Charlotte curtsies deeply.

"You are here by invitation of Marie Landry, wife of André Landry. This is no fault of yours. Nor of hers. But we know you to be in the care of George Walker, who is a friend of the Salmon People. And we know it is George Walker's wish that you return to your father aboard the ship that is now anchored in the bay. So we may not welcome you into our camp, but must wish you a good voyage."

Her knees tremble, but she is determined to show no weakness.

"Chief Julian," she says, "I have no welcome in the house of my father and ask you to give me refuge here."

Julian shifts his weight uneasily.

"Charlotte Taylor, I cannot know the matters of your family. But you are in the care of George Walker and he would see you safely returned to your home. This wish we must honour. Go with the Great Spirit."

"Chief Francis Julian."

All eyes turn to Wioche, who walks forward and stands in front of the chief.

"Speak, Wioche," the chief says.

"We know that you have led us well in these years. If the Salmon haven't suffered in these struggles between the French and the English in our land, it's because of those things you have done and said. Is this so?"

With this question he turns to the People and the men around him nod.

"But we must not be too eager, Francis Julian, to please the English. This woman, as Marie Landry tells us, is with child and seeks to live among us. Does she not flee her English father as our little brothers *les Acadiens* fled the English? Did we not give them shelter here, though their own French people had deserted them? Why would we deny it to a woman alone? This is not the tradition of the Salmon. We deny it, Francis Julian, because you as a man of honour must deny it, though your heart says otherwise. Is this so?"

Again he looks at those around him and all feel compelled to nod.

"Therefore, Francis Julian, here is my request. If you will walk out of our camp for an afternoon hunt of the deer, and if this woman Charlotte Taylor should come to seek shelter when you are gone, I, Wioche, as the son of Amoq't, will grant her welcome. I have made no promise to the Englishman. On your return, you as a man of honour will not revoke the welcome I have given."

There is everywhere a murmur of consent.

"Wioche, son of Amoq't, I hear you. You speak well, as did your father and you are as subtle as he. But this subtlety is best applied to the messages you carry to the people in other camps. You cannot revoke my promise or supplant my place as chief. The father commands the daughter, and in his place, the father's friend brings her home."

"Ah, if I may interrupt ye, chief, an' meaning no offence whatsoever."

Silence. Eyes turn. A fair-haired boy in the well-worn suit of a sailor, one arm in a sling, walks slowly from the edge of the group, where he had stood unseen.

"Ah, chief, I'm William MacCulloch and in the service of George Walker and His Majesty's merchant marine. Nou, chief, I wish, if I might, to say a word on behalf of the English and a few others, if you'll let me do so."

He looks around, but no one speaks.

"Nou I may leuk an Englishmaun to ye, chief, but I'm not. I'm a Scot and so too is George Walker. I wanna tell ye what ye seem not to ken—that this woman Charlotte Taylor is in actual fact Charlotte Willisams, married and nou a widow. And, chief, in the customs of her country, a married woman is no longer at the disposal of her faither but is a free body, as free as ye, chief. That's not all I hae to say. The other is on account of Commodore George Walker, who is a fine man, a Scot and as guid a captain as any of us will ever ken. But he is a *maun,* chief, an' I'm here to tell ye—and don't ask me how I ken this, chief, 'cause I will never tell ye—I'm here to tell ye that the captain—auld as he is—wanted this bonnie wife for himself, but she told him nay. She seeks a younger maun for a husband and a faither to her bairn. The captain is a maun of honour, chief, and would do no wrong on account o' the devil. But ye might understand that he did not seek to see this woman ivery day in this place he calls his hame. Much better she should be in England, with a faither who does not own her and does not want her. Do ye stairt tae see the thrust of me argument here, chief? I hope ye do."

With that he turns and walks away. Charlotte watches him go, stunned by the lie he told for her and not for a moment did she imagine that she would never see him again.

Chief Julian stands silent and studies her closely.

"I am the chief of the Salmon," he says at last, "and I have heard all that has been said. Today I will go into the hills and hunt the deer as I did as a young man. Tomorrow I will return. While I am gone, Wioche, son of Amoq't, will act for me as he has in the past."

With that the assembly rises and the People return to their tasks.

—

JACK PRIMM SITS at the long table, his rum bottle his only companion. Bob Simpson looks in at the door.

"Can I fetch you anything, sir."

"You cannot. Is she gone?"

"We're still looking for her, sir."

"Not the wretched woman! The *Hanley!* Is she gone?"

"She was gone before dark, sir, when her boat brought letters for the commodore."

"I am damned then."

"Are we to resume the search in the morning, sir?"

"What matters now?"

"She may be in danger, sir, in them woods."

"Let her die there. Bring me for now MacCulloch and I shall tell him his punishment. There's some satisfaction."

He fills his mug with rum again.

"He don't seem about, sir,"

The HMS *Hanley*, bound for Bristol, catches a good evening breeze from the west and sweeps toward the wide Gulf of St. Lawrence.

"We thought to carry a woman," says Captain John Robbins.

"Aye, sir, but sudden illness confines her now and she must wait a later ship. But this letter, sir, I am entrusted to carry to her dear father in Sussex, who is himself sickly. It may be their last communication, sir."

"Alas, a melancholy burden."

"It is, sir, but I am honoured to carry it."

"And who pays your fare?"

"I shall pay my own fare, sir, if you will but employ me. I am an able seaman, sir, and can do the work of two men as is attested by these papers, sir."

"And your arm?"

"It is almost healed, sir, and I shall soon not favour it."

"Your name?"

"Will MacCulloch, sir, at your service."

"A Scot."

"Awhiles a Scot, sir, an' whiles mony anither!"

CHAPTER 4

The Baie

1775–76

*T*here is much to learn. There is no written language, only storytelling and drawings she is unfamiliar with. The legends of the Mi'kmaq are full of superstition and mythology, relying on the past to fathom the future. She's enchanted with the analogies and the use of hieroglyphics.

She had already discovered a veritable pharmacy in the woods with Marie but wonders how she'll keep all the medicinal remedies straight. Eat this, don't touch that. Boil one, scrape the other. How will she ever remember? And by now she knows about Gluskap, the legendary alter ego of everyone in the camp. The stories about the shenanigans of Gluskap are about monsters and wisdom, magic and moral laws.

The people, including the few Acadian families that remain in the camp, eat communally around a great fire. Charlotte quickly learns that food is either roasted over the coals or poached by putting it in bowls of water heated with red-hot rocks. Sometimes steaming is the method of choice when, for example, lobster, cod or bass are put on top of the coals and water is sprinkled over them until they are cooked. Meat such as moose and deer are usually roasted but also poached in the deep bowls, the rocks being replaced when they cool, about every ten minutes with a new supply from the fire.

The women cook with an assortment of ancient utensils carved from trees and bones and European iron pots and knives gained through trade—or theft, according to some of the gossip she's heard. The children are much adored and do whatever they like, slipping from one woman's lap to another with the ease of fish moving through water, playing about the fire and, depending on their age, helping themselves to food from the spits or swallowing portions that have already been chewed by their parents. The men sit separately.

Charlotte stays with Marie, trying to mimic her behaviour, learn her methods. The chores are very much divided—the men hunt the animals, the women go into the bush to skin and butcher them for food, clothing, utensils and materials to patch the camp together. They only kill what they need; nothing is wasted, except perhaps the rum that the women tell Charlotte is arriving in an ever-increasing supply and is often blamed for everything from ill-will to a poor kill.

Before the meal is begun, Marie makes it clear that Charlotte should watch carefully, that she must learn the ways of the camp. The chief approaches the fire and tosses a handful of herbs onto the coals. The aroma they create is sweet and savoury. Charlotte understands it's sweetgrass from the bay and sage from the woods, together they apparently create the scent of the earth.

Chief Julian looks her way and says, "We burn sage to take away evil and bad thinking and sweetgrass to invite the good."

He's carrying a long feather that he waves in all directions so the smoke wafts onto the food and the people sitting in the circle.

"It's the feather of the eagle," Marie whispers. "Our legend says it is the message of life and hope from the Great Spirit. When you hold it, everyone will respect you, no one will interrupt you."

Chief Julian begins to chant, to call out to the north wind, east wind, south and west wind. He prays to Mother Earth for the children, the eagle and the women and men. Charlotte feels the power of the ancient ritual and lets the smoke waft around her while realizing what a very long way she is from her own traditions.

One evening after the meal while everyone in the camp is still gathered in the circle, she asks the chief how it is that the Acadians came to live with the Mi'kmaq. Chief Julian rises—as though a ceremony is about to begin, she thinks—walks over to Marie's husband, André, and hands him the eagle feather. It is the signal that André has been invited to tell the story.

The night is cool; she wraps herself in a mooseskin hide offered by Wioche and moves closer to the fire as André begins. "Les Acadiens sont arrivés ici il y a cent quarante ans." It is an extraordinary tale of small victories over the harsh climate, crushing defeats at the hands of the British, abandonment by their own government in France and ultimately betrayal and expulsion. It is also a story of resilience, and endurance, of abiding music and masterful storytelling. Charlotte has spent a lot of time with Marie and André by now. She'd met his parents when they visited from Caraquet and joined the extended family when they went berry picking or walked along the flats looking for clams. Her impression so far is that the Acadians are a people so comfortable in their own skin, one could be forgiven for thinking they had triumphed here on the north shore rather than being turned into fugitives.

André continues. In 1755 when a war was stirring between Britain and France, the unimaginable happened. The Acadians, who had refused to take sides in the warring, committed a crime in the eyes of the victorious British and needed to be punished. Long suspected of being in collusion with the Indians, who were a thorn in the British side, the new masters decided to rid the land of the people whose roots were planted deeper than anyone else's save the Indians in the soil of Nova Scotia. Families were shattered during the hurried expulsion, children being deported on one ship, parents on another, fathers were banished to one colony, mothers and children to another. The upheaval was catastrophic; many died en route. The Great Expulsion saw almost every one of them—more than eight thousand—banished, sent back to France, dispersed to other colonies as far away as South Carolina and Louisiana or pursued relentlessly until they died on the run of exposure, hunger or were slaughtered like hunted animals. Their land was confiscated, their footprints nearly wiped away.

André's family and a few others managed to stay by hiding in the Indian camps, ultimately raising their families there and preserving what was left of l'Acadie. Although there were families who found their way home earlier, most did not return until now, when a modified government in Nova Scotia decided the Acadians were no longer a threat to British rule. It is twenty long years after the expulsion.

There is a hush over the camp when André comes to the end of his story. More tea is served as the embers die and a flagon of rum is passed around while the Mi'kmaq, the Acadians and the Englishwoman among them watch the coals glow, each caught in their own considerations.

LATER THAT NIGHT, Charlotte finds her diary and writes:

They have been here for five or six generations and seem to be a breed apart, these men and women of L'Acadie. They can finish one another's sentences when they tell their stories of wild beasts in the forests and the wonders of the deep. Their stature is not great, most are quite short. But they're like people I've never known before. As rough as the brine, as harmonious as the tide and as crafty as the fox, they are shaped by this land they have adopted. They steer their boats by the stars and measure the season by the thickness of an animal's fur. They have a quirky way of talking to one another—self-deprecating double entendres in a cadence as musical as the fiddles they play. They can trick the animals into their soup pots and trick themselves into believing their lives are blessed. As for their relationship with the Micmac, in many ways one has become the other—in language, in clothing, in the food they eat and the ways they live. The best of each being borrowed as one's own.

IT'S OCTOBER when Commodore Walker returns. Charlotte had thought there would be a warning, some time to prepare for the explanation he would demand. There wasn't. She is working with the other women, drying fish to store for winter when suddenly he is standing before her.

"May I ask what it is you think you are doing?" he demands.

When she stands to respond, he is flabbergasted at her obviously pregnant shape. "You are with child," he utters.

"Too true," she replies.

It's a crisp autumn afternoon; the leaves have turned to gold and scarlet, signalling the season had changed as well as Charlotte's location during the commodore's long absence.

"I thought your return would be announced to me," Charlotte says, unable to find a more polished way to speak to the man who had been her benefactor.

"It was unexpected, by me as much as by yourself. I was very delayed in Quebec and endured a long and arduous return voyage." Staring at her pregnant belly, he adds, "But I see that expectations of all sorts are matters of moment."

She cannot help lowering her eyes.

For a moment he doesn't seem to have any clear notion of what else to say. He clears his throat. "I do hope you are well."

"I appear to be in perfect health."

They stand awkwardly in the clearing, near the wigwam of Francis Julian, where the main fire blazes in the clearing. The chief himself and the two members of Walker's staff idle at a discreet distance. Wioche has made himself scarce.

"I cannot express the shock and—yes, displeasure— I experienced in hearing of your conduct at the time of the *Hanley*'s departure," Walker says. "But now I see you, I . . . I cannot retain those feelings."

"I'm glad of that."

"You are wilful, Charlotte, but you are courageous. A man would be a great dolt not to acknowledge it. I should have respected your request to remain. I wanted only to discharge my duty as I saw it toward your father."

"I know that to be true. You've been like a father to me, kinder than my own."

"I . . . I have believed myself to be your friend."

"You are, George."

"I have spoken to Chief Julian, and we are both of the opinion that you would find accommodation at my house a welcome change. Charlotte, you are under no obligation to please me in any way on account of your father. And there won't be another ship bound for England until the spring."

"I need to give birth here, George, where there are women around me."

"I understand that, but you have not come yet to term. I think you could return to your people safely for a week or two."

"My people?"

"English people, I mean. We are at the winter lodge now. It's less than a mile west of this camp. Come enjoy some of the comforts the old life offers."

FRANCIS JULIAN WATCHES the reunion with some relief. The harbouring of the Englishwoman is not without its complications, her growing friendship with the son of Amoq't among them. Julian will do what he can to assure her permanent installation in Walker's camp, but for the moment he offers his guests the opportunity to share his meal.

When everyone is finished eating and the pipes are lit, Chief Julian's granddaughter Miq whispers to Grik'las, her maternal grandfather. Julian nods toward the old man, and as his wife extinguishes two of the three lamps that hang in the wigwam, he leans toward Walker. "Grik'las will tell us the story of Gluskap and winter," he says in English. "It is a story for Miq, our little one."

Grik'las, a remarkably weathered and toothless man, begins by meeting the eyes of every person in the room in turn. When he is satisfied that he has the attention he deserves, he launches into his narration in what sounds to English ears like a tuneless song.

Julian waits for the old man to pause and then interprets for his guests.

"Winter was a giant who lived in a large house in the north. Winter's very breath withered the trees and they could make no leaves or fruit. He covered the corn, the rivers and the animals in frost. This brought famine and death to the People." He looks down intently as he again listens to Grik'las. "Gluskap saw this was not good. He went to the house of Winter to ask him to stop. But when he entered the house, Winter breathed on him and froze him. Luckily, Tatler the loon was nearby. He flew into Winter's house and wrapped his wings around Gluskap until he thawed.

"'You must go to Summer, the queen of the south,' said Tatler, 'and tell her of your plight.'

"So Gluskap ran to the sea and sang for Spout, the whale, who came and carried Gluskap on his back. The clams peeped a warning along the way whenever Spout got too close to the shore, until finally, they reached a land covered in flowers. Gluskap jumped off Spout's back and swam to the beach, where he saw a rainbow because there is always a rainbow in that land. He followed the rainbow and, at its end, in a house made of the vines of grapes and all the grasses of the world wound together, he met the queen called Summer."

The chief pauses in his translation to wait for the old man to catch his breath and carry on.

"Now Summer fell in love with Gluskap," Julian interprets, "and said she would follow him anywhere.

"'Come with me to the north,' said Gluskap.

"Spout carried them back to the north and they saw only ice and snow. When they reached the house of Winter, the giant was waiting. He blew on the couple and Gluskap felt his blood run cold. But Summer smiled and Gluskap felt warm again. Each time Winter blew, Summer smiled. Finally, Winter melted to the floor under the force of her smile. Summer now went with Gluskap across the north and awakened everything the giant had frozen. Buds burst open in the trees and grass and corn sprang to life and water ran in the rivers.

"When they returned to the house of Winter, Queen Summer said to the giant, 'You have been too greedy. Henceforth, you are banished from Gluskap's country for six months of the year. You may return only if you agree that you will be less harsh.'

"Winter rose from his floor, glad he was not completely melted.

"'And I will rule the land six months of every year,' declared the queen."

Grik'las finishes speaking and looks around with an expression that conveys both his own satisfaction and a request for approval. Miq smiles up at him.

"And so she has always returned," Julian concludes.

"Never precisely the same tale twice," Walker says in a muffled voice to Charlotte.

CHARLOTTE ADDS two large sticks of wood to the roaring fire and dips a finger in the kettle. It is already hot. She lifts it from its hook and adds the steaming water to that which already half fills the great tub beside the fire. Here truly is a luxury almost equal to that of her father's home. She crosses to the door and assures herself again that the latch is secure, then lifts her gown over her head and steps carefully into the tub. This is her second bath in a week.

She sits down slowly, amazed by the round bulk of her abdomen, warmed and supported by the water. She allows her eyes to close and her thoughts to slow. In the distance, she can hear the crack of hammers as Walker's shipbuilding enterprise proceeds apace, the business of making money neverending. The baby shifts, jabbing her in her groin; she is carrying low now. She shouldn't remain much longer in this house of grunting, sweating men. She tries to think of Pad, whose soul and flesh she had once found so thrilling, but her thoughts would not remain with him, though she makes every effort to persuade them.

She puts her hair up before she joins the commodore and his men for dinner, a rite that strikes her as odd now that she has passed so much time among the Mi'kmaq. To show off her long white throat was something her mother had always encouraged her to do, but in this place and climate it seems a foolish invitation to cold breezes or worse. She contemplates letting her hair down again, but then convention stays her hand. For these few days she would play the proper Englishwoman, and perhaps distract some of the men's eyes from her condition.

Unlike the summer quarters at Alston Point, the winter house has few windows, a larger hearth and almost nothing to adorn its dark wooden walls. After they had finished a haunch of venison, platters of cod and chunks of bannock, Walker offers a round of port.

Walker, sure of the loyalty of his men, is complaining openly about his financial backers. "I must fend off sharp practices at every turn. They alter the accounts in their own favour. They refuse my requests to seek more generous grants of land, without which we can hardly hope to increase business."

"Indeed. Honest men must wonder why we make such exertions for their benefit," joins Primm, who had been uncharacteristically muted in her presence this whole last week. "They pay our efforts no heed at all."

"And I cannot rely upon His Majesty's officers in Halifax," Walker continues. "I have asked for governing authority here in the north but am quite ignored."

The others nod in silence, but Charlotte speaks up.

"Sir, do they not recognize your achievements here on the Baie de Chaleur?"

Walker looks at her.

"My achievements? They hardly recognize the Baie de Chaleur *itself*. It might as well be in the South Seas for all they care. They might then take a *greater* interest."

"If I may say so, sir, your description of their actions only adds to my impression."

"What impression is that?" Primm ventures to ask.

The other men shoot careful glances at one another. They know the woman well enough.

"My impression of the conduct of our countrymen since they have come to this land. It seems not to have been conduct becoming to Englishmen."

"It's a rude world, Charlotte," Walker replies. "Who would you compare us with?"

"I would compare us with the Acadians."

"What!" Jack Frome cries. "Madam, you take a low view of us altogether!"

"I would compare us unfavourably, sir."

"Madam, if you were a man, I would take offence."

"Now, Jack." Walker smiles at Charlotte. "My dear Charlotte, do you really imagine we conduct ourselves less well than the Acadians?"

"Is it not a fact, George, that the Acadians have lived amidst these Indians for a hundred years or more and never fought with them, or once impinged on their territory without a fair arrangement? Is that not a stark contrast with our own bellicosity, our many hedgings and agreements?"

"The problem with the world, Charlotte, is its complexity. You speak of Scots. Even as we sit here by our fires, Scots lords enclose the lands of their countrymen and throw women and children onto the highways without means or livelihood. The French plot and meddle to retain their power in Europe and threaten us with war—or practise it—at every opportunity. I would not be surprised to see them within our lifetimes make another bid to conquer all of Europe, even England."

"Which they shall not do!" declares Jack Frome.

"Here here!" comes the ragged round of agreement.

"I would not have the blood of these Acadians on my hands for all the world," Charlotte says with passion. "We might have lived in peace with them."

Primm speaks up. "In the past and elsewhere, madam, when one nation defeats another, those disloyal to the victors are put to the sword. You see how we English compare."

"We allowed them to die on ships, instead."

"Charlotte." Walker leans forward with no trace of impatience in his expression. "His Majesty's government has permitted the Acadians to return. Grant us that."

"To find their farmlands occupied by British settlers."

"There *is* a right of conquest, Charlotte."

"Spoken like a privateer, sir."

The table falls silent.

"Pass your glasses, gentlemen," says Walker. He fills each with deliberation. "Charlotte, in the Salmon camp here you have met an Acadian named Landry."

"André Landry. I am acquainted with him and better with his wife, Marie."

"His family lived in a place called Caraquet, just south of Ile Miscou. During the expulsion, they took refuge among the Mi'kmaq. Alexis Landry, uncle of this André, was a leader among these Acadians and apparently made clandestine visits to Caraquet to discover the condition of his old property. The land was in fact unoccupied, the gardens overgrown but otherwise unharmed.

"When I arrived at Alston Point to start this fishery, the governor in Halifax appointed me magistrate for all of Nepisiguit. Alexis was among the Acadians and Mi'kmaq who traded at the outpost. He resolved to plead directly with me for the return of his property. Other Acadians tried to persuade him of the folly of such an action, believing I would punish him for his effrontery. He approached me nonetheless and I granted him official permission to settle on his own land. No British policy forbade it. Alexis immediately set to working the land and rebuilding a house. His relatives meanwhile cowered in the woods, fearing events could turn against them again, or hoping for the overthrow of our regime. Eventually a move was deemed safe and most of the Landry family repaired to Caraquet. A few, such as André, decided to remain with the Indians. Perhaps they preferred it there."

Charlotte doesn't have the heart to point out that such clemency had been conditional on the decency of one man. "With your permission, George, I shall retire."

SHE PUTS THE DIARY DOWN, gets into bed and is soon fast asleep.

The knocking is persistent. "Charlotte? I would speak with you, Charlotte." It is Walker's voice.

She slides from the bed and stands in momentary confusion. She had been dreaming of her father, the general, of some past day when things had been right between father and daughter, and the shelter of his parental concern still stretched over her. It had been peaceful there.

Her room still glows from the fire in the grate, but she lights a candle before unlatching the door.

"May I come in?" A dishevelled George Walker stands at her door. His jacket is askew, his white hair tumbling onto his forehead.

She steps back so he can enter.

"Your fire is low," he says. He bends slowly, carefully places three pieces of wood on the coals. She thinks him perhaps unsteady.

"Do sit, George."

"I hope I have not disturbed you."

The silence stretches as Walker stares at her. "Are you quite well George?" she finally asks, hoping for both their sakes he isn't going to embarrass himself.

"Charlotte, your child soon comes to term."

"In five or six weeks I think."

"And the Indian women will attend you?"

"They are kind, George."

"I know they are kind, Charlotte, but . . . then you shall have a child."

"I shall."

"And no husband. And, Charlotte, you can't be planning to remain forever with these Indians."

She sits on the edge of her bed and rests her hands on top of her belly. "No. No, we cannot."

"And you have had some breach with your father and will not on that account return to England."

"You're right about that too."

Silence. "Where is the letter I gave you for him?"

"I threw it in the grate on the day the *Hanley* arrived."

"It is destroyed then?"

"Well, in fact, the grate was cold. Will took it and said he'd burn it for me later."

"So it is in Will's hands—on its way to England."

Charlotte gasps. "That never occurred to me. What exactly had you written to my father, George? It's my inheritance I need and now you can understand why. The letter you wrote, can it support my position about gaining my inheritance?"

"My God, woman, you confound me with your presumptions. I am certain Mr. MacCulloch has schemes for this letter that will not serve you or me. I am just as certain that neither of us has heard the end of it."

He meets her eyes now, a suitor with a case to state. "I have the means to support you and the child. I can offer you a life here, if this is what you choose, but we could also live in England, or in Scotland. I have a house in Edinburgh, a fine house." She looks at him, sorry for him, wanting to give him the respect of serious consideration.

"George, I think you've had a little too much to drink tonight. Is it not better that we should speak of this tomorrow?"

"No!" He stands suddenly, swaying. "By God, Charlotte, must you persist in folly?"

Charlotte stands. "We shall speak tomorrow, George." And the commodore bows to her once and leaves the room.

In the morning, before he is awake, Charlotte slips into her boots and treks back to the Indian encampment, where no one pretended to know her mind better than she did herself.

HER LIFE IS CONSUMED thereafter with preparing for the coming winter. It is already so cold at night, she keeps a fire going and sleeps under bearskins, staying as close to the embers as she dares. The birds are flocking up—flying in V formations and landing in the marshes in great migratory herds, preparing to leave for warmer climes. It is a sign she'll forever associate with the laying down of food for winter.

Her back aches, her feet swell, the child in her womb is moving constantly now. She has already marked November on the earthen patch she uses to keep track of the months; she is heavy with child and calculates a mid-December birthing. The women in the camp seem to take special pride in their mental and physical toughness in labour. She knows almost nothing about delivering a baby and wonders daily if she has the courage for the birthing.

A SOFT MORNING LIGHT fills her hut. Charlotte holds her hands out above the bearskins and studies them, roughened by labour and raw weather, the painful blisters on her palms now calloused. Calluses, she had learned, are what a body needs. Her whole spirit is becoming just a little calloused, as she feels it must if she is to survive.

She had added wood to the fire at dawn and crawled back beneath both her furs. She is in no hurry to rise but is content to lie in the cot marvelling at the child stirring in her belly. The wind outside the hut is rising. By her best calculation, it is the first day of December. The last arrows of geese had vanished over the southern horizon some weeks earlier. The women had finished filling their pits with onions and roots and had hung to dry ropes of wild grapes, sarsaparilla, spruce roots and balsam buds. By day Charlotte had smoked and salted meat and fish with Marie.

"How can we ever prepare enough to last us through the

winter?" she had asked as they had rubbed salt into the split bodies of a half-dozen enormous codfish.

"We don't have to preserve all we need. The men will hunt moose and deer, and will fish through holes in the ice too."

"There are fish below the ice?"

Marie smiled. "Where else would the fish go? The water is their home."

"So you are sure we shall have enough to eat."

"Yes." Marie stopped work to meet Charlotte's eyes. "But sometimes the hunt is bad and sometimes the fish punish us and they refuse to bite. So we need to do all we can now."

"Of course."

"But the hunt is good here and we can stay in our village all winter." Her face was lit in the broad, easy smile that is her most striking feature. "I don't like to move."

Charlotte sucked her finger where the salt had invaded a cut. "Sometimes a body must move from an old home to a new," she said. "It may not be altogether a terrible thing."

Marie smiled again. "Charlotte, you left your home for love. But to move because you must eat is not the same thing." She resumed salting the cod.

THE FIRE IS CRACKLING well now, though she notices a chink in her chimney where the glow of the fire shows through. She would have to ask Marie for advice on how to repair it, or perhaps Wioche. Her breath blossoms above her in the still-cold air. She had returned to her hut from Marie's wigwam—when was that? Was it a week before—the moon, she remembered, had been a thin crescent in the west. She had returned to find a mountain of spruce boughs piled against the outside walls to buffer them against the wind. Moss had been stuffed into the cracks in the walls and roof. A moose hide had been stretched over the floor and the walls inside lined with more boughs.

It had been Wioche's work, Marie confirmed it.

"That is how he speaks to you," Marie had said.

Charlotte's comfort is that, if she becomes too cold, or too alone or too alarmed by the sounds in the forest that stand like a dark wall only yards from the back of the hut, she can join Marie's family in their wigwam. There, twelve souls—Marie and André, their children, Marie's sister with her husband and children—twelve warm bodies—are a refuge she could scarcely have imagined not long before but had sought with gratitude on three occasions so far.

At last she can put off the day no longer. Rising, she wraps more layers of shawl around her and then shrugs into the fur coat the commodore had given her. She opens the door and goes out into the grey morning.

The rivers that flow into the Baie de Chaleur are frozen now, though the tide on the bay still rises and falls each day. Towers of ice stand stranded on the flats and dwarf the Salmon men who venture out in search of fish. It begins to snow, gently at first, dusting the trees and leaving patterns of white on the pine-needle paths. She lets the snow fall on her face, feels the lightness of the flakes and marvels at their shapes. Marie is carrying wood to her wigwam.

"Hello, Charlotte!" she calls. "Are you well?"

"Oh yes. I wished very much to call upon you, Marie, but your house was quiet."

"Josef had a fever last night, and he is still sleeping. Don't worry, the fever has broken—he'll be okay by tomorrow."

"Well, Marie, I've decided these winters of yours are not so impossibly bad. It's not as cold as I thought it would be."

Marie regards her without the usual smile. Even as they stand together, there is a rustle in the treetops overhead. Both women look up. The pines on the ridge to the east make a sound between whispering and whistling that carries toward them.

"Three days," says Wioche, who appears as he usually does— out of nowhere. "A storm for three days," he says. "From the northeast."

Charlotte remembers the wind that had almost blown the *Achilles* to its destruction. Behind Wioche stands the frail thing that is her house, branches piled around it but little of the snow the Mi'kmaq said would protect her from the winter winds.

"Charlotte," Marie says. "Gather as much of your wood inside as you can and quickly, before the snow makes it wet. See that your other wood is covered by skins well secured with stones. And come to our wigwam when you have need."

She hurries away, but Wioche lingers. "The hawks have stopped flying," he says. "Rabbits and squirrels will soon disappear into their holes. We'll do the same."

"I've seen storms before," Charlotte insists.

"This will be the first storm of winter."

"I shall manage," she says. She drops her eyes as she passes him on the way back to her cabin.

By midday, the cloud cover is so low it seems to skim the tall trees. The snow is falling faster now. She's fascinated that something as white as snow can produce so dark a day. Every now and then she opens the door of her hut to watch the swirling snow, now falling like blankets tumbling to earth and being whipped into drifts by the wind. She can make out the shadowy figures moving from one wigwam to another.

The heat from her fire is warming the room and although puffs of cold wind still penetrate the walls, Charlotte is comfortable enough that she settles down with her diary. She notices after a few paragraphs, that her entry is almost all about Wioche—the way he turns up when something is wrong, his attentive explanations about food, shelter and the traditions of the Mi'kmaq, the walks she and Marie take with him—and writes, *I must pay less attention to this man, lest I offend his family.*

As the hours pass and the snow mounts against her front wall, a glance outside confirms that she can't even see the camp. She feels trapped inside. Late in the afternoon, the wind takes on a sinister howl. Smoke blows down her chimney in gusts and snow sizzles in the fire itself. She stokes it higher. By evening, the woodpile is already diminishing and she curses herself, thinking, You have hardly enough for one night, never mind three days.

She wants to go to Marie's house, but Marie had been the one to warn her never to venture outside in a snowstorm at night, even a few feet from your door, because you might never find your way back. She untwists the cords that hold the door tight and allows it to open a few inches. Instantly, snow sweeps into the room, and the door is forced open wider. She holds on to its frail frame for a moment, mesmerized by the storm. A roiling world of white lit a lurid orange by the light of her lamp and fire pushes its way into the hut. Charlotte pushes back, but the force against her increases. She struggles hard, slowly edging the door closed against the wall of snow, then twists the cords to hold it shut.

THE WALLS GRIND and groan around her. She is unbearably cold. Bending to the dwindling fire, she feeds kindling to the embers until they catch, then piles on more wood. Now, by the light of the flames, she can see snow has drifted into the corners. The hut shakes around her with each new gust, and more snow finds its way into her shelter.

Only the hearth itself is dry. I really must go to Marie, she thinks. A particularly vicious blast of wind tears into the roof above the door. The thatching makes no sound as it is sucked up into the night. The opening between the logs is six inches wide at that point and a yard in length. The blizzard bellows into the room.

"Help me!" she shouts, but can barely hear the sound of her own voice. She stares at the break, her eyes stinging in the smoky darkness. The bearskins. She snatches one from the cot and stands on tiptoes to push it into the gaping hole. The funnel of wind abates and the snow settles in the room, until the next gust sends the pelt and more snow crashing on top of her. The fire is hissing. She scrambles from under the bearskin and stumbles to the hearth before the snow puts the fire out. Drifting snow is everywhere. She piles wood on the blaze, it burns fiercely. Smoke quickly collects along the underside of the roof and fights past the snow to escape through the gaping opening. More thatching soars into the night as the wind gets fresh purchase on the gash.

She heaves the last piece of wood on the fire and sits down on the cot exhausted. Wonderful heat radiates from the old stones and warms her where she sits. She lets her eyes close a moment. I am warm, Charlotte thinks and stares dully at the fire. Like beads of rubies, each with its own sun inside, little flames rise up the length of the chimney. It's beautiful, she imagines. The fire will melt the snow. She looks at the brilliant flickers where the chimney pierces the roof and watches their progress along the underside of the thatching around the chimney. Then as if waking from a stupor, she screams, "My God, the house is on fire! *The fire cannot stop the snow, and the snow cannot stop the fire. I cannot fly this place. I cannot stay!*" The chimney now glows its whole length, a bright crimson tracery visible through every seam and crack. The flames fight to escape from their nest and make their way under the blanket of snow. Frantic, Charlotte grabs the basket from the wall, scoops snow from the floor and throws it at the flames that ring the chimney at the roof. The snow falls back in her face. She refills the basket, and once again throws snow at the flames. The flames crackle fiercely in the thatching. "I have to get out of here," she cries. But the roofing has collapsed in front of the doorway, blocking her escape.

Wioche takes off his left snowshoe and uses it to dig through the drift against the front wall of the hut. When he is halfway down, he kicks at the door.

He drives his foot at the door again and again and when the ropes break he and the storm both tumble in. Charlotte Taylor lies on the floor before him, her hands over her eyes.

"I am sorry," she says.

SHE AWAKES TO CALM, the comforting arch of the wigwam poles overhead, and intense sunlight slanting through openings in the birch bark making patterns on her furs. For quite a long time she lies there, listening to sounds outside. She hears the cawing of crows first, then the laughter of children, then the voices of women as they go about their work, muffled it seems in a great softness.

Marie appears in the doorway carrying a steaming bowl. Charlotte smells squash soup and sits up so eagerly Marie smiles.

Charlotte takes the extended bowl, with thanks, and props it on the ledge of her belly.

She ladles the soup into her mouth voraciously; never had anything tasted so delicious.

"You've been asleep for most of two days," Marie says. "Through the rest of the storm. No wonder you are hungry."

Charlotte lowers the bowl. "I'm sorry, Marie," she says.

"Why are you sorry?"

"For everything. For the destruction of the house you gave me."

"Your house is still there," Marie says. "But I believe you should not stay in it."

"It didn't burn?"

"The men put out the fire."

"Wioche?"

"He got you out and carried you here—this is his wigwam. Don't worry," Marie says, seeing Charlotte's face. "He is staying with another family."

The door opens and Wioche steps in. A child cries in the distance. Marie rises from her place beside Charlotte and hurries past him.

"It sounds like Josef has fallen off the woodpile again," she says.

Charlotte struggles to rise.

"Stay seated, please," Wioche says. "Now is a time for rest. You have enough labour ahead." He speaks slowly, with care, the same way as he speaks his own language.

She doesn't know how to express how sorry she is for the trouble she has caused, or how grateful she is to him for saving her life.

He sees her shame and obligation, and speaks first. "You fought to preserve your own life, Charlotte Taylor. It is we who thank you for that fight and we were the ones who placed you in such peril."

"No, that's not true."

"We thought of you not as one of the English, which we knew you to be, but as one of the Acadians, who have lived among us for more than one hundred years. This was a great mistake, a great discourtesy. I am the one who is sorry."

Charlotte can think of nothing to say in the face of such generosity, and again Wioche saves her. Taking the bowl from her hands, he asks if she thinks she could eat some more. She nods and by the time he returns with another helping of soup, lazy steam curling from its rim, she has composed herself enough to thank him gravely.

THE MI'KMAQ have no tradition of coddling an expectant mother, so Marie is pleased to see Charlotte shake off the aftereffects of the blizzard and join in again with the chores of the day.

The next afternoon, which is milder and sunny, Wioche and three companions return from the woods with a large doe. A little later, he approaches her as she is adding an armload of wood to the main fire, holding two sets of webbed wooden nets.

"Snowshoes?" she asks.

"Yes. Come and learn this."

"Won't I just sink with my belly so large?"

"These are excellent snowshoes," Wioche says. There is a lightness about his expression she is happy to see. "You won't sink."

"I have work to do," she protests again, though none too vigorously.

"Here, I will help you strap them on." And he squats to show her how it is done.

Experimentally she takes one step and then another. One had only to lift one's feet a little higher and keep them a little farther apart. As she follows him into the deep snow and slant-ing light of the woods, she feels a surge of exhilaration.

He is a few strides ahead, his dog at his heel. "You cannot travel in winter without them," he calls. "But with them, you go wherever you want."

"I want to go down there!" She is pointing down the slope toward the shore of the partially frozen bay. With her hair bundled under shawls and her shape unrecognizable under many layers, she isn't worried about the men from Walker's post.

"Come," Wioche says and turns in that direction. Charlotte trails after him, carefully setting her shoes in the firm impres-sions he makes.

They cross the snow-drifted beach and he leads her to a sand dune that has been whipped into a natural shelter above the high tideline on the bay. Snuggled against the sand and watching the slushy water form ice crystals below them, they toss lumps of snow into the water, challenging each other for who can throw the farthest. Wioche seems boyish in his enthusiasm.

Charlotte leans over to take off her snowshoes and sits up again, puffing from the exertion. The dog sits too. Wioche pats him, then draws a handful of hazelnuts from his pouch, already broken from their shells. He pours them into Charlotte's hand.

"I do love hazelnuts," she says, smiling at him.

His dog is looking at him beseechingly. "Atilq," Wioche says. "You don't like hazelnuts."

To Charlotte he says, "You learn the way of the People quickly." Then he draws a circle in the sand and marks two long, straight lines through the left side of it. They are facing north. He says, "Do you know what that means?"

"I confess I have no idea," she replies.

Wioche explains, "It says, meet you at west side of lake in two days."

Charlotte draws her own circle and says, "This says meet me at the north end of the camp tomorrow. Right?"

For a time they sit without speaking, looking out on a distant stretch of shore.

"I think, you do not much care for us English," she says suddenly.

He turns to her. She can't read his expression, but the boyishness is gone.

"No?"

"I don't think you do, no."

"Why do you say this?"

"From what I hear *you* say, to others in the camp. And I remember your speech, when you so gallantly attempted to persuade Chief Julian that I should not be returned to Commodore Walker's care."

"I don't wish to speak against your people. Not to you, a guest in our village."

"Well, I shall do it for you if you like. But please, I would be grateful if you would speak your mind. I need to understand these things. Your distaste for the English is not because we're a white people—this I know. You seem to think kindly enough of our French cousins."

"I know little of the French, only of the Acadians."

"But they are French."

He looked at her as though she was missing an important distinction.

"The *children* of the French," he spells it out. "The forgotten children."

"Is that the reason you favour them?"

He puts a hazelnut in his mouth and chews it slowly, staring away to the shore.

"When they came—long, long ago—they were so few and we were so many. Our ancestors took pity on them and taught them what could be taught. They listened, but they would not come into the woods with us or cut the trees or hunt the deer. We thought them fools, but good fools." He spits out a piece of bitter skin and scuffs it thoughtfully into the snow with his foot. "It was we who were the fools. The day came when others arrived who were not content to live along the shore."

"The English?"

He makes a low sound in his throat and the smallest nod of his head.

"They lived, those Acadians, as best they could, and they died. We died too, and more of us died than them. They lived here, only here, on these lands by the sea. They made their little fields in the marshes. They made their small boats. They learned from us and we learned from them. They planted gardens and apple orchards. They watered the land. They fished the waters. Each father had more sons than his father before him. Each mother had more daughters. But never did they do us harm. The People and the Acadians made no treaties. They fought no wars. We let them live and they brought us iron and wheat and rum and cloth."

"The English destroyed this?"

"No. The English were far away. Sometimes, when wars went well for them, they said they owned this land. The French fathers were far away too—when wars went well for *them*, they said *they* owned it. But neither showed care for the Acadians. The Acadians paid no heed. They were no man's friend or enemy. That was their way.

"But that is not *our* way. We help our friends and fight our enemies. The English in the south were our enemies. We fought them and we killed them. My father, Amoq't, killed many in Chebucto and Canso. I, too, have killed."

He sees that he has shocked her. "That is the face of war, Charlotte. The English kill, the French kill and the People kill too, each as he feels he must."

He looks at her and sees anger and something else in her eyes. For a long moment, he does not look away.

They walk home together as night falls. George Walker is waiting for her. He wants reassurance that Charlotte has coped with the storm and that she is aware that winter will not let up for months to come. Back at her hut, he asks what preparations she has made for the baby and, finding scant evidence of any, begins to wonder if she is denying the facts she must confront. He suggests she come to his lodge for a few days. She accepts, reluctant to leave but feeling the need to preserve her friendship with Walker. She packs a sack of clothes and together they snowshoe back to the winter post.

While they take tea and hot biscuits dripping with molasses, he fills her in on the increasingly bold moves of the privateers.

"The river to the south, the Miramichi, is crawling with these disloyal brutes. They destroy everything they come upon and many say they do it with the help of the Indians. Have you heard such accounts at the camp?"

She has but is hesitant about tattling to the commodore. So she decides to dodge his question by suggesting she is so busy trying to keep her own life in order she has no time to decipher the accounts of others. For now she tells him, all she wants is a hot bath.

The time at Walker's is restful as she feels his protective

custody and enjoys it to a point, but she wants to get back to the camp.

The little hut that had almost taken her life is waiting for her. In her absence, Marie, André, and Wioche had organized a work party that spent an entire day thatching, chinking, stacking branches, piling snow and hauling firewood. The interior has become an embarrassment of furs: bear, seal, rabbit, otter, beaver, fox.

"I have more of these than the richest woman in London," Charlotte declares. André has made a cradle and filled it with woollen and cotton coverlets that Marie stitched together from English blankets. Charlotte meanwhile busies herself during the daylight hours arranging and rearranging the few goods she has—by the fire, away from the fire, against her old trunk that Walker had delivered, by the walls. As the stocks of bannock and fish accumulate, she counts them a dozen times a day. She catches Marie staring at her knowingly from time to time.

It's past mid-December when she wakes before dawn and feels it in her back: not a pain, in fact, but a twinge, returning from time to time. It is not the ache of lifting firewood or hauling poles.

Today, she thinks.

Dawn is cold and windless. All morning she collects kindling. By noon she can feel a palpable tightening that lasts a few seconds. She continues to work. Marie comes out of her wigwam and walks across to the hut.

She stands looking at Charlotte a moment. "I'm going to cut wood on the hill."

"Don't," Charlotte says.

———

BY LATE AFTERNOON, Charlotte lies on her cot. Anne tends the fire. Marie makes tea and calls out the door to her children. Her mother, Militaw, comes by from time to time. Flat, smooth rocks are heating in the fire, firewood is piled as high as the roof. All is ready, but Marie can feel the trembling of the Englishwoman, who has never even seen a birth. Still, Marie thinks, there is heart there, and even fear weakens when the heart is strong.

These women have all been here before me, Charlotte thinks. She is frightened, but beyond the fear, she feels an anticipation so consuming, she shakes continuously. Then, as the sun sinks through the trees, the rush of warm water between her legs announces the inevitability of labour. The Indian women call out excitedly.

Afternoon turns to evening, becomes night. By then she cannot breathe hard enough to relieve the pain, can hardly catch her breath.

"Perhaps something is amiss," she whispers when she looks up to see Marie's brown eyes near her own. Marie smiles.

When an especially severe pain has passed, Anne crouches on the floor.

"Like this," she says. "Like this."

The women lift Charlotte in their arms and help her crouch by the bed. For a while the pain seems less.

By midnight, she is struggling not to scream. If I could only rip this baby from my body, she thinks, and be done with it. Marie recognizes the signs and makes a lowing whistle like an owl at the door. Her mother, Militaw, comes with the bark of a dogwood tree, ground into a fine powder, lights it and urges Charlotte to inhale the smoke hoping its narcotic effect will take the edge off her pain. But she only coughs and moans, clinging so tightly to Marie's hand, her fingernails draw blood. They boil water, add wild sarsaparilla; she swallows a little of the liquid, then stiffens again with pain. Both women know the baby will soon be born, and Charlotte needs to be able to push the child out. Marie goes back to the door and makes another whistling sound—the short, sharp call of the whippoorwill. A moment later, Wioche, his face furrowed, hands her a flagon.

"Soon," she says and shuts the door. When the rum courses down Charlotte's throat, it dulls the stabbing pain. A few powerful contractions later, when she hears Marie saying, "Poussez, poussez," she pushes with all her might, again, one more time. Her near delirium takes her thoughts to the dog Atilq and the webbing of snowshoes imprinting the snow, to Wioche and hazelnuts. And at that moment, her baby comes squalling into the world.

"Elizabeth," says Charlotte when they set the baby on her breast.

WIOCHE ENTERS THE CABIN silently and stands by the door witnessing the tender bond of mother and child. He has a gift for the baby. A bunting bag he made from rabbit fur and lined with the delicate skin of a deer that he had rubbed with bird's liver until it was as soft as fat. Marie shows her how to tie the bag to her body and keep the baby close.

The women in the camp bring food, make tea and tend to Charlotte and little Elizabeth. Commodore Walker turns up with more blankets, food supplies and a miniature sleigh his men have crafted so she can pull the baby through the snow. He'd been curious to know what this baby would look like but had seen several children in the West Indies who had been born to mixed-race parents so isn't at all surprised by the light brown skin and the dark eyes of this newborn. Satisfied that baby and mother are healthy, he encourages Charlotte to come to the lodge for a visit and bids them goodbye.

The rhythms of life rock gently for mother and child during the days that follow. For Charlotte, it is a time to nest, to discover motherhood, to be astonished by the ties that bound her to this baby.

She hadn't given a thought to Christmas when Marie tells her the wondrous eve is this night and that she should come with Elizabeth to the ceremony that will be held outside, around the fire. Charlotte tucks Elizabeth into her bunting bag and wraps a blanket around the two of them before they venture out into the frigid air.

The firmament is a mass of blinking stars; the moon dusty with frost when the camp gathers to kindle the flame and light the darkness of Mother Earth. Like most customs here, there is a mix of Mi'kmaq and Acadian, Old World and New, the Indian creation story, the Catholic nativity. A great fire roars into the sky as Chief Julian holds up the eagle feather and gives prayers of thanks. Then they begin to chant.

> Nujjinen wa'so'q epin, jiptug teluisin
> Megite'tmeg, wa'soq ntlita'nen jiptug
> Ignmuieg ula nemu'leg ule'tesnen . . .

Charlotte ferrets out the English meaning from Wioche. It is the Lord's Prayer. To hear it chanted in this humble camp of birch bark and bearskins, of people drawing nigh, is a moment so divine, it touches her soul. She draws her baby close and feels the glory of the night. Then to her own surprise, she asks Chief Julian for the eagle feather, signalling that she wants to speak. In a voice as clear as the night air, she sings a carol, the one she sang with her family every year on Christmas Eve.

> Adeste fideles, laeti triumphantes
> Venite, venite in Bethlehem
> Natum videte regem angelorum
> Venite, adoremus, venite, adoramus,
> Venite, adoramus, dominum!

There in the wilderness, by the light of the fire and surrounded by the spirituality of two peoples she has come to know, Charlotte covers the final distance between England and the New World.

THE DAY THE NEW YEAR begins dawns clear and crisp. With the trees bare, Charlotte can stand in the main clearing and make out the movement of the men at Walker's post and ice fisherman in their shelters on the harbour. She knows that Francis Julian has invited the commodore to a feast that night.

The cooking fires are already burning when she emerges from her hut that afternoon to prepare a bed of coals for the slow roasting of haunches of the fine moose Nab'tuq and his party had killed the day before. Marie and four companions had gone out to butcher it and carry it back. The fire rocks are heating in another pit and four iron kettles that will boil cod are secured in their places. Snow blankets the customary litter of the camp, but the women have cleared it from the meeting place and stamped flat what remained. They had covered the ground thickly with boughs, then covered the boughs with skins and blankets.

Charlotte had been no more familiar with the methods and means of cooking in her own country than with those of the

People. Food, she reminded herself, was a part of life that young women of good families associated only with their parents' dining tables, not with the kitchen. But that very long year of 1775 had transformed her. Now she observes everything the women do, on occasion making notes in her diary while they chuckle at her kindly for having to write down what every woman knows.

As the sun slips into the tracery of tree branches to the southwest, the People gather. As it sinks into the black profile of the horizon, a line of torches appear, announcing the arrival of George Walker and his party—six men in all. The people take their places in a wide circle, men and women separately. The forest is wrapped in darkness. The fires blaze up. Chief Julian approaches the central fire and throws in a handful of herbs. A sweet aroma fills the bright clearing. Now even the sky above darkens to indigo.

The chief chants to the four winds and Mother Earth for the eagle and the People.

Julian takes his place. This is a signal. At last long knives carve the steaming meat. The bannock emerges from the hot sand. A babble of laughter and talk erupts as all the People begin to eat at once.

When the sky is black and the stars blaze coldly and the meat has been carried away and the fires are loaded with fresh wood, a lone drummer begins a careful double beat, like a human heart.

Francis Julian stands. He speaks in the language of the People and then, in turn, in English.

"George Walker has lived as our neighbour some seven years," he says.

Around the circle, a hundred eyes turn to the commodore.

"He has proved a friend to many. His enterprise has been an

advantage to all. He has come to me now to ask if we repay him by concealing our thoughts and our actions. This is too big a question for one man to answer. Tonight, I call on all the People. Speak your hearts. We have no debt to George Walker except the debt of friendship. Let us repay it now."

This is greeted by scattered murmurs of assent. Walker stands and looks around the circle.

"The People and I are old allies and associates in trade." He speaks in a slow and deliberate English, pausing between sentences as Julian translates for his people. "We wish to remain so. I look to Chief Francis Julian as a trusted friend. I am pleased to be asked to address you.

"You may know me to have been this autumn in Quebec. There I met with representatives of His Majesty's government. I have also been in communication with our officials in the port of Halifax.

"The People are now well acquainted with events to the south. The American colonies are moved to agitate for independence from Mother England. A Virginia landowner named Washington is at the head of their army. This Washington is even now gathering that army against His Majesty's forces.

"These events might not have been my direct concern or the concern of the People. We are not able to fathom the rights and grievances of all the parties. We wish only to trade in peace. But you will know that the rebellious colonies have not been content to dispute with British forces on their own soil, but are determined to carry the matter north. In August a man named Smith entered the Saint John River in a sloop with a band of rebels and burnt Fort Frederick and the barracks there. He took four men prisoner and captured a brig of 120 tons. Montreal is fallen and a thousand colonial troops are camped outside the walls of Quebec. My own party was only by great indirection able to enter and leave that city.

"We know now that native elements are lending aid to these rebels and that some braves of the Mi'kmaq and Abenaki have again taken up arms against British forces. I have received intelligence that confirms rumours that earlier reached Chief Julian's ears: these same elements intend to attack private British holdings in Nova Scotia. My outpost must expect to be among those attacked."

For a moment it looks as though he intends to say more, but instead he suddenly sits down. Francis Julian takes his place.

"In the days of war between the British and the French, the People fought on the side of their friends, the French. Many of our Nation travelled south to take that fight to the British in the American colonies. Now that war has past. The French king no longer rules these lands. The British live among us and it is the British we must count as friends. The People do not attack friends.

"If any here tonight have knowledge to share, they may speak openly and with honour."

He sits down. The pipes are lit and passed. A hush falls over the circle, with only a few low voices, a few furtive glances.

Wioche stands slowly. When he speaks, he uses the language of the People, but his tone is so edged it chills Charlotte. When he is finished, he does not resume his place.

Francis Julian responds. "Wioche, son of Amoq't, to whatever actions you have taken, do not add discourtesy to our guests. Commodore Walker speaks English, as you do. Address him that he may understand you."

For a long moment, Wioche looks first at Julian, then at Walker. Then he speaks.

"No man of the People is surprised to learn that we must now make account to the only Englishmen in three days' distance. This is their way."

He looks slowly around, and Charlotte feels his eyes briefly touch upon her.

"You say, Francis Julian, that we fought the British in the colonies to the south, but there is more. We fought them wherever we could. They were our enemies. Now you say that war has passed and that we must be their friends. But the war between the French and the English is an ancient one and not yet ended. You would have our People rush from side to side according to the fortunes of those nations. Better we keep our own counsel."

He stops. After a time, Chief Julian answers.

"Wioche, do you counsel that we should be enemies to none? If so, then we are of one mind."

Wioche stands some time without speaking, then says, "The People need make no account to old friends or old enemies. We have earned the respect of both."

"Wioche, son of Amoq't, do you have knowledge of attacks on this or any other British settlement?"

Wioche is silent.

"Or are your proud words a cover for your knowledge?"

Wioche regards the older man without expression.

"Francis Julian, you are a good and honourable man. May your governing of the People be wise and your friendships reward you and not bring you bitterness and regret."

With these words, he turns from the fire and walks to his wigwam. Three other men follow him. The rest of the People look from Julian to Walker, their eyes wide.

"Wars make many wounds," Julian says. "Some unseen."

George Walker stands, his men follow suit.

"Chief Francis Julian," he says. "We extend our thanks to you. Your feast was grand and your actions above reproach. I bid you good night."

He bows to the chief, nods to Charlotte and leaves. His men light their torches at the fire and walk into the forest behind him, following the path to the winter lodge. The sky is alight with stars and the sparks from the fire rush brightly upward as though to join them. The stars stand still, cold, and white, and the sparks die out among them.

NO ONE SPEAKS of the scene at the feast, but in the following days there is no sign of Wioche. Then early one morning he turns up at Charlotte's hut.

"You'll be safe in the care of the People," he says.

Charlotte laughs. "You sound as though you are saying goodbye." She is curled up on her cot, shrouded in the bearskins.

"I'll return," he says.

"Then you *are* leaving." She hears the alarm in her own voice. "Why go in such cold as this?"

He steps forward, strokes the baby's cheek once, twice, with a single finger. Charlotte looks up from Elizabeth.

Wioche regards her. With an almost unnatural slowness, he extends his hand and with the same finger he had used to stroke Elizabeth, he touches Charlotte's cheek.

Then he turns and leaves. A cold wind blows in from the door as he pulls it shut behind him.

IN THE FINAL DAYS of January, at the onset of the season called Abugunajit, the snow-blinder, Charlotte's hands and feet become permanently cold, as though their top layer of skin has somehow separated itself from the rest of her. Deep cracks open in her fingers and sometimes bleed. Her face feels weather-beaten, though she has no mirror to see it by. The hems of her skirts often hang hard and frozen from beneath the robes of fur. But the baby thrives.

Francis Julian visits her twice. She asks him about Wioche, but he makes no reply. She sees the chief often in solemn conversation outside his wigwam with other elders.

On the day she believes to be February 20, when she had counted three more snowstorms like the great blizzard in December, she awakes in her cold hut and knows she cannot continue as she is. She goes that morning to Marie to ask if she can share a space in their wigwam. Marie lays a hand on Charlotte's face.

"Oo'se," she says. Welcome.

The men go daily to fish through the ice, but, as Marie had foretold, the fish were offended and had decided to punish the People. A day of chopping ice and sitting by the hole often produces only a few smelts. Antoine Denny kills a thin moose two miles to the north and half the camp goes out to butcher it while hungry wolves watch at a distance.

On several occasions Charlotte indulges her urge to ask the women about Wioche and, when she sees them glance at one another, wishes she had not. But no one knew his whereabouts. She sometimes stands on the high knoll and looks down toward the outpost and imagines the men inside, smoking their pipes, drinking their port, eating their roasted venison. She even allows herself to imagine George Walker's tall grey house in Edinburgh, the chandelier that might be suspended over a table of polished mahogany, the servants who might hover around it during dinner. Once, she thought of her old home in Sussex.

The grass in the great meadow would be green in February and the first daffodils would soon appear.

SOMETIME IN MARCH, Gluskap's queen awakens in the south and remembers her promise. She is still in no hurry, but little snow falls and one day it even rains briefly. That same week, Wioche returns. She ducks out of the Landry wigwam to see him standing by his own place in conversation with the chief.

That night the other women speak in whispers. He had been on the Milamichi, as they call the river to the south. No, on the Restigouche, they say. No, he had travelled to Gaspé. They say, thinks Charlotte, but they don't know.

The next morning, he approaches her at the big fire.

"Are you well?" he asks.

"Yes. And you?"

"I am very well." Perhaps for the first time since their afternoon in the sand shelter on the shore, she sees his broad smile.

"Today they begin the syrup," he says.

"What is that?"

"The syrup from the maples."

She makes a puzzled smile.

"Hasn't Marie told you?"

"Of syrup?"

"It was her surprise, perhaps. Come with me."

She is anxious that he should see her skill with the snowshoes. She ties Elizabeth into her bunting and they set off.

"I'm as quick as you!" she cries.

"No!" he calls. "Much quicker!"

They pass swiftly along trails already well worn through the remains of winter drifts. The trees, the ones whose leaves turned scarlet as though signalling their final splendour before dying in the fall, are now running with something called sap. The gnarled old trunks stand silently giving forth an opaque viscous offering to the survivors of winter. They find Marie and the others collecting the sticky drippings into a vessel and setting it over the coals of a fire. It steams and bubbles and after a long while turns into a pale amber liquid as thick as treacle. "Taste," says Wioche, offering her a stick he has swirled through the syrup. She blows on it so she won't burn her mouth and declares after the first taste, "It's like candy."

The maple syrup is also sustenance for the overwintered camp. Every tree in the maple bush is fitted with a funnel and vessel to catch the dripping sap. They boil the bounty and pour it over everything, meat, bannock, dried mouldy berries and even plop it into their tea. The sugar brings energy, so does the change of season.

WIOCHE CUTS WOOD and stacks it by her house. He repairs the roof again and stops the places at the base of the walls where meltwater would enter as the season progressed. But at night, as she lies in her bearskins, the snores of the Landrys around her, she hears angry voices from across the camp and knows Wioche's is among them.

On a soft evening in early April, with the sky still bright in the west, he speaks to her.

"I have fixed your house and cut your wood and a fire is set in your hearth. You can come home now."

As they cross the ground together, they pass old Militaw, who smiles to see them.

THEY EAT A LITTLE while the baby sleeps in the furs on the cot.

"I must leave here again, Charlotte."

"When?"

"In the morning."

"How long will you be gone?"

"I do not know."

Without another word, he leaves her.

THERE'S AN AIR of anticipation for the coming spring during the last cold days and freezing nights of winter. One day in April, the river ice that has been creaking and groaning as it grinds and bucks in the rising and falling temperatures begins to buckle, the broken pieces colliding in sucking and cracking explosions. Now loosened from the binding shores, the chunks move, slowly at first and then suddenly in a roaring whoosh, they are flushed out of the rivers to the bay.

The blessed season of rebirth begins. The land is bursting with buds; the sea brings an easy harvest. Birds are laying their eggs. Lobsters trapped on the flats are scooped up during the low tide. And the rivers are once again byways for travellers. The commodore and his men move from their winter lodge back to Alston Point in a convoy of dories, canoes and a new sailing ship they had constructed through the winter.

It's early in June when Commodore Walker invites Charlotte to dinner to meet his shipping colleague, a man who has come by canoe from the Miramichi.

She fusses as best as she can with her frock and her hair and wraps Elizabeth into her bunting bag for the walk to the lodge at Alston Point. Clad in a blanket shawl and knee-high mooseskin boots, she sets out on the familiar path with some apprehension.

She's still dusting the dirt from her boots when Walker strolls out to greet her. As she turns her head to bid him good afternoon, she realizes his guest is beside him. Before she can collect her thoughts, the commodore says, "I wish to introduce you to a trusted colleague and a most eminent gentleman, Captain John Blake, one of the finest masters in His Majesty's merchant marine and a veteran of life in this New World." Turning to the handsome-looking man beside him, he continues, "May I introduce Miss Charlotte Taylor, a charming woman, recently from England and her wee bairn, Elizabeth Willisams."

Blake steps forward. He is a tall man with a strong nose and chin. His expression is determined, his bearing erect. "Madam," he says, "your fame has gone before you." She extends her free hand and he bows to kiss it.

CHAPTER 5

The Nepisiguit

1776

*C*harlotte's head is spinning from the bewildering speed of events when she stands at the fire in the centre of the camp and asks Chief Julian for the eagle feather.

She'd seen John Blake often, sailing the newly built ship around the bay to test its seaworthiness and at dinner with Walker and his men at Alston Point. Last night he'd suggested they walk together on the beach after supper. It was a mild night, the moon was nearly full and the water's edge shimmered beneath it. Her feet sank into the wet sand while they walked in silence, Elizabeth asleep in the bunting bag on her back.

Blake spoke first. His voice held something that made her turn her head to him.

"I must go to the river inside the week," he said.

"Oh yes? To your home on the Miramichi?"

"You may, if you choose, come with me as my wife."

He had not looked at her as he said this, staring instead at the incoming tide. The bluntness of the proposal left her speechless. They walked on.

"You will not then?" Blake finally asked.

"I am most deeply affected, sir, that you should make such a proposal. I confess I am not prepared for it."

"It is unfortunately the case, Miss Taylor, that here in this new land we have seldom the luxury of long meditation. I have heard you speak to George Walker of settling here and heard you inquire about land. In truth, Charlotte, a woman alone cannot survive here long without a man. This is to simply state the truth. Nor will your faith in these Indians reward you at length."

"They have been my friends."

"They have been friends to many, as have we. But this land shall see great change soon enough, and the Indian will not benefit much."

"I am sorry to hear you say so."

Blake stopped and turned to her. "Nevertheless, I cannot debate this matter with you. I am a man with prospects and I am an English person like yourself. I have proposed marriage to you because I want to have a wife and because I believe you might make a fair one. I say on my own part only that I would make a faithful husband."

"I don't doubt it, John."

"I have no patience with London fripperies, or any fripperies. I do not deny myself to be a hard man, but it is a hard land and I am suited to it."

"It *is* a hard land, John, but full of promise, is it not?"

"Charlotte, will you marry me or no? If no, I am most sorry to have encumbered you with my poor plain speeches."

"Would you really have me as you wife, John Blake? And Elizabeth as your daughter? You hardly know us."

"I would."

Charlotte did not know quite where her answer came from, but she found herself saying, "Then I shall be your wife."

They had walked on again in silence.

SHE FINGERS the eagle feather nervously while she tells the men and women who'd sheltered her these many months that she is to be married to John Blake. They are not in the least surprised as an unmarried white woman is a rarity—even when that woman is Charlotte Taylor. She has an ache in her throat when she begins her goodbye.

"I hope the smoke from the sweetgrass will give me the courage and goodness I have felt in this camp. Your stories of the beginnings—the creation, the land, the ways of the people both Mi'kmaq and Acadian, will be carried forever in my heart. It is my hope that we will meet again. Thank you from my mijuajijuit, Elizabeth, and from me, your nedap."

There is much nodding in approval. Tea is passed around the circle. Now it is Marie's turn to ask for the eagle feather. She tells Charlotte she has un petit cadeau for her soeur and gives her a pair of moccasins stitched across the toe and foot in minute puckers. They are violet in colour, the skins dyed with the juice of blueberries, the sides ornamented with the exquisite quillwork of the People.

"I made them from moose calf," Marie tells her.

Then Wioche stands, takes the eagle feather from Marie and hands Charlotte a blanket with a slit in the middle, made from the long soft hairs of the young moose. When Charlotte slips it over Elizabeth's head, it falls in folds around her and envelops her with the warmth of a people.

Later that night Charlotte writes in her diary:

I will leave this camp soon, but I hope its lessons will stay with me forever. Here, there is a season and a meaning to everything. They hunt when the moon is full. Pick berries when they slip easily from their branches after a summer storm. Peel the birch bark from the trees in the early morning damp of the day. And oil the skins of the moose when the hot sun is overhead. They find their way by the constellations and know the seasons by the moon. Heavy banks of snow mean the wigwams will have less wind and be warmer. The higher the hornets build their nest, the sooner winter will come. They can mimic the owl, the loon, the wire-winged crackle, the mink, the deer and the moose. Each sound is employed to attract a meal, to issue a warning, to respond to an omen. They listen to the messages that come from the animals as well as the heavens. I am the richer for my time in this place.

It's a fine morning, cool and clear when she rises at dawn on her wedding day. The trunk that has become a table of sorts is empty now, her clothes packed for the voyage to the Miramichi. She decides to leave the well-travelled chest with Marie, as there's no room for it in the canoe. But the cradle and the sleigh must come. John Blake had grumbled about that the day before when he loaded Charlotte's worldly goods into the canoe. "I can as well build these once we're at the river." But Charlotte had insisted, so he'd strapped the cumbersome contraptions onto the canoe and paddled away to Alston Point.

When Elizabeth is fed, Charlotte dresses the baby in the soft animal skins that are her only wardrobe and walks out of the hut that has been her home for nearly ten months. André steps toward her and presses a packet into her hand, "Pomme de terre pour planter," he says. She tucks his gift into her pocket and turns away from the camp. Wioche and Marie walk with her, all three with much to say and a short time to share their thoughts.

It's Wioche who bids the final farewell. "You give Gluskap a fine story to tell. May it be continued on the Milamichi."

Charlotte wonders if she will ever see them again. She wishes the ache in her chest would go away. She wonders as well what the morrow will bring. With baby Elizabeth strapped to her back and a braid of sweetgrass dangling from the bunting bag, Charlotte walks into the lodge to be married, for better or for worse.

THEY ARE MARRIED on the twelfth day of June 1776 by George Walker in his capacity as Justice of the Peace for the County of Halifax, settlement of Alston Point, Nepisiguit, His Majesty's colony of Nova Scotia. They stand in the main hall of Walker's house and face the wooden cross that hangs on the east wall. In the absence of a soaring nave, a rose window, an altar and a chalice, this cross is God's sole emblem during the prayer services Walker occasionally conducts. Charlotte had dared to suggest that they might conduct the ceremony in the clearing overlooking the bay, but the men would have none of it. She would have liked, too, to have Marie and Anne at her side, but in light of her betrothed's sensibilities, this drew only frowns. No matter: she had made her choice and now must follow it.

Jack Primm is present, and Dan Crocker and Bob Simpson and half a dozen others of Walker's men.

"I require and charge ye both—" George Walker speaks the words with care, his Scots burr rippling the cadences of the Book of Common Prayer, which he holds somewhat awkwardly at arm's length. "As ye will answer at the dreadful day of judgment when the secrets of all hearts shall be disclosed, that if either of ye know any impediment, why ye may not be lawfully joined together in matrimony, ye do now confess it. For be ye well assured, that so many as are coupled together otherwise than God's Word doth allow are not joined together by God; neither is their matrimony lawful."

He pauses here, clears his throat and appears to be reading ahead in preparation for the next lines. Well, thought Charlotte, there is no impediment on account of marriage, and there's a blessing, I suppose.

"John Blake, wilt thou have this woman to thy wedded wife, to live together after God's ordinance in the holy estate of matrimony? Wilt thou love her, comfort her, honour, and keep her in sickness and in health; and, forsaking all other, keep thee only unto her, so long as ye both shall live?"

"I will."

Charlotte casts a sideways glance at Blake, where he kneels beside her on a rough wooden stool Walker had covered in a beaver pelt. He is a handsome man indeed, but she's still taking the measure of him. He has the face of a man who can't be surprised. His wary eyes tell her trust doesn't come easily. He's older than she is—a lot older, she thinks, but younger than the commodore. His eyes are as brown as the earth, but his ruddy, sun-darkened face, weathered by years at sea, and his brown hair flecked with grey, give the impression of grave intent.

"Charlotte Taylor, wilt thou have this man to thy wedded husband, to live together after God's ordinance in the holy estate of matrimony? Wilt thou obey him, and serve him, love, honour, and keep him in sickness and in health; and, forsaking all other, keep thee only unto him, so long as ye both shall live?"

"I will."

His low voice now rumbles out his vow. "I, John Blake, take thee, Charlotte Taylor, to my wedded wife, to have and to hold from this day forward, for better for worse, for richer for poorer, in sickness and in health, to love and to cherish, till death us do part, according to God's holy ordinance; and thereto I plight thee my troth."

Blake releases her hand and she takes his and says her own vows in response.

Charlotte had not sought Walker's counsel on Blake's suit because she strongly believed the match to be of his design. Since it was clear to all that she would not be returning to England in the near future, and since she could not be expected to remain with the Mi'kmaq indefinitely, a husband was the only solution and this husband the best husband available.

Blake takes from his pocket a simple, heavy gold ring.

"Place it on the Book," Walker instructs in a quiet voice. Then he picks up the ring and returns it to Blake's hand and Blake slides it on the fourth finger of Charlotte's left hand. He holds it there.

"With this ring," he says, and his usually dark-toned voice falters a little. He starts again. "With this ring, I thee wed, with my body I thee honour, and with all my worldly goods I thee endow. In the name of the Father, and of the Son, and of the Holy Ghost. Amen."

At this moment, Elizabeth, who had been nestled asleep in her cradle in a corner of the room, sends up a strenuous howl. She shushes when Charlotte picks her up, but howls again when she tries to set her down, so finally her mother carries her to where Blake still kneels, bringing the baby into the circle of their vows.

George Walker says, "Let us pray," and recites the Lord's Prayer, with all the assembled joining in. And when that is done, he joins the couple's right hands.

"Those whom God hath joined together let no man put asunder," he says. He closes the book, having determined in his own mind that God would not expect more. The small congregation stands for a moment in awkward silence. Then John Blake reaches over and takes Elizabeth into his own arms and rocks her.

So now I have a husband, Charlotte thinks.

"If this ain't occasion for a tot of rum, I don't know what would be," calls out Dan Crocker. Loud hurrahs are sent up from around the room. George Walker beams and by common consent everyone adjourns to the clearing, where a table had been laid for a good noontime meal, if not precisely a wedding banquet.

JOHN BLAKE is a man of few enough words. But his men had seen to it that his new wife was told of his reputation, told of his youth in the British navy, told how he had retired, like Walker, to captain cargo across the Atlantic—lumber and fish from Nova Scotia to England and Spain, European guns and tools to the West Indies, then molasses, sugar, spices and rum back to Nova Scotia. But, oh, they boasted, there was a fierceness in the man that would not be contained. He had volunteered to fight under Amherst and Wolfe at the siege of Louisbourg. He'd almost lost a hand there to a French musket ball—you could see the scar to this day—then fought on, covered in his own blood. When Wolfe was promoted to general and struck against the French in Nova Scotia, Blake served under Murray on the Miramichi and witnessed the destruction of Eskinwobudich and the dispersal of disloyal elements—Acadian and Mi'kmaq—from the area.

When the soldiers were stood down for a fortnight, his men knew for a fact that he'd paddled alone up the river and liked what he saw there: the fish, the empty land. Murray had granted him permanent leave and he'd begun to clear the forest he had chosen beside a dark brook he named for himself. He'd worked alone, they said, until he could hire a crew. Yet within a year, news came that Wolfe would move on Quebec and, such was the intrepidity of their man, he'd volunteered again. On the night of September 12, 1759, he—though a navy man—had managed to be among the eighteen hundred redcoats who'd left the warships and climbed the cliffs to take control of the Plains of Abraham. The next day they were joined by three thousand more and forever broke the back of the French empire in North America. And they swore it to be true that he'd served on the pilot boat *Gremlin* when it guided the *Royal William* down the St. Lawrence as it carried Wolfe's embalmed body home. Several fellows maintained absolutely that Blake was recommended for dramatic promotion. But within a few months, he was piloting ships on the Miramichi and cutting trees again on Blake Brook.

Whatever his history, Blake the groom is the centre of attention at Charlotte's wedding. When pressed to tell his story, he declines, but leaves no doubt that acquiring and clearing more land on the Miramichi is now his aim.

"A man might earn a fair living as a captain," he says. "The commodore here will tell you that. A man may have a proper business, own his merchandise and determine his own affairs and do well enough."

"We'd like to do as well as you, John Blake," says Dan Crocker.

"Nay. Nay. You but think it so." Blake tears off a piece of bread. "To be sure, I may continue on the Miramichi as a pilot. But you cannot find a proper life at sea, lads, not for a lifetime, and I'll be damned if I'll be as some old captains are, who are lost on the very land men were meant to walk on. It's the land, lads, clearing it, owning it, that's what will see a man through."

"Would I be one of those old captains, John?" Walker asks, a smile playing at the corners of his mouth.

"No, damn you." Blake laughs. "You're too canny a Scot for such a fate, George Walker. You're well set here, *and* in the old country, wa hai ye're bred."

Walker's smile fades.

"Indeed, John, but we cannot be certain, not any more. The American rebellion is an earthquake that now shakes us all."

"They may shake us, damn them, but they will not shake us *out!*" Blake's dark brow furrows and his hand clenches in a fist. "His Majesty will not permit Nova Scotia to fall to those rogues. No, he will not—the comfortable swine at headquarters in Halifax are safe enough. But who, I ask you, protects us now on the Miramichi or here at Nepisiguit? Who will defend us from the treachery of the savages? Already they are guiding the damned rebels up and down the river. My own house might be burning at this moment. From here to Pennsylvania and far past, we've sacrificed good British lads to keep our promises to the savages. And how do they repay us? By joining with the rebels in New England and massing against our women and children. By creeping toward us in the woods, even today as we sit here talking among ourselves."

"Aye, aye," grumble several others.

"Mark me, sirs," says Blake, his voice a rumble. "It is not until every savage has his scalp cut from his skull that we may rest here. Scalp them and leave them to die, as they would us. *That* must be British policy. It is *my* policy certainly."

There is quiet for a moment.

In the weeks she had known him, Charlotte had never heard him so vehement.

"Are not some of the Indians our allies, John?"

Her new husband looks at her sternly, and Charlotte holds his gaze. "Do we not have our friends among them?" she asks.

Blake's eyes drop to the table. "How shall we tell who among these Indians our friends might be? It's too late when they tie you at a stake and roast you like you were a damned pig. It's too late then to be asking them!"

"We are well advised, John," Walker interjects softly, "to cultivate friends among the tribes. Your warnings are well given. I myself have but recently lost a fishing station across the bay at Restigouche to the rebels. Yet we must know what our enemy is thinking and the American generals are unlikely to tell us. It's for this reason—not just for trade—that I maintain my relations with Indians such as those here at Nepisiguit."

Blake shifts a piece of venison with the point of his knife.

"Be remembered," he says, "that they hear what *you* say just as you hear what *they* say."

A longer and more uncomfortable silence descends on the table. Then Jack Primm rises from his chair. "I believe it is time," he says—and he gives his head a small waggle to suggest a merriment that did not come easily to him—"to remind us all that we are witnesses to a day of joy and promise. May I propose we drink to Mr. and Mrs. John Blake."

Bob Simpson, a reticent man on most occasions, also rises and says, "To the most beautiful woman who ever set foot in this place."

"To the only damned woman who ever did!" growls Dan Crocker, who also stands, as does every other man.

—

THE MEN BEGIN TO LOAD that very afternoon so they can make an early start the following morning. The six men who came here with Blake in three canoes laden with oats, flour, salt pork and a new bride and her baby would require two days to reach Blake Brook on the Miramichi. The post is filled with the busyness of saws and hammers, the huff of the forge, the babble of working men's voices, the neighing of horses, bawls from the three new calves and occasional instructive moos from their mothers. About noon, men from the Salmon camp arrive at the post. Their trappers were just in off the distant lines with pelts of beaver, fox, lynx, bear and the long-haired hide of a young moose. Their fishermen roll down a barrel of fresh cod and trading starts in earnest, with Jack Primm calling for the molasses, rum, beads, jewellery, iron pots and knives. Six dozen fox pelts are traded for arms at a rate of one dozen pelts a musket.

"He may pay a dear price for those skins," John Blake mutters.

Charlotte sees Henri, a friend from the camp among them. She looks down to the water's edge where Blake and his men are working.

"Kwé, Henri," she greets him.

He smiles shyly. "Kwé, Charlotte."

"Mé talwléin?"

He laughs and replies, "We're all well. Is it true you are leaving us?"

"I have no desire to leave, Henri. But my new husband's home is elsewhere."

"The People will remember you, Charlotte."

"I shall never forget the People. But, Henri, perhaps we shall meet again."

He smiles at her and lifts a bale of furs to his shoulder.

"Charlotte, it is a wide country and you will be on the Milamichi."

"My husband calls it the Miramichi."

"That is the English name."

"Have you seen Marie?"

"Your leaving is sad for Marie, Charlotte."

"I said goodbye."

"She is sad still."

Charlotte looks down to the water and feels a creeping remorse. She was leaving the kindest women she had ever known, and yet had only made the most awkward of goodbyes so reluctant was she to even think she might not see her again.

"Is she in the camp at this moment, Henri?"

"Yes she is, Charlotte."

CHARLOTTE WALKS QUICKLY away from the post, without looking back, afraid she might hear her name called at any moment. Elizabeth in her bunting bag seems as light as down and when Charlotte is over the log bridge that crosses the bog and has begun to climb toward the camp, she is near to running. Marie is outside her wigwam as though she had been waiting. When she sees Charlotte she beams that beautiful smile of hers. A moment later they are hugging fiercely. Charlotte can't tell whether the small woman is a mother she clings to or a sister she holds.

Other women gather around and Charlotte embraces each in turn. They all walk together to Marie's wigwam, where they sit in a circle in the spring sunlight and wait for water to boil for tea. Elizabeth is dandled and cooed at, as is Jeanne-Marie, the infant daughter of Antoinette, and Bertrand, the six-month-old son of Marie-Louise Kagigconiac. They marvel at the gleam of Charlotte's wedding ring and bounce it in their hands to feel its weight.

As they finish their tea, Charlotte speaks quietly to Marie. From her pocket, she withdraws a handkerchief and opens it to reveal a single strand of silver from the bracelet Pad had worn.

"This is for you," she says, holding it out to Marie. "It once belonged to someone I loved." She thought to herself that it was fitting that Pad's memory should rest with this lovely and loving woman.

Then Chief Francis Julian approaches and Charlotte stands.

"I am happy to see you now," he says, "though it is only to bid you adieu."

"I am happy to see you, too, sir."

"Charlotte, your child was born here by the Baie and the Great Spirit will watch over her wherever she goes."

All of them then walk with her to the end of the clearing at the top of the hill. She again embraces Marie and the other women.

"This nation of the People stay on the Milamichi too," Chief Julian says. "Never live in fear. You will always be near to the People."

"I'm glad of that," says Charlotte.

With great reluctance she starts down the hill with Elizabeth.

"Charlotte," the chief calls after her.

She stops to look back at him.

"From here the Nepisiguit will carry you all day until dusk," he says. "John Blake will then enter the stream from the south that the English call Nepisiguit Brook. He will make his camp at the point of portage. The mosquitoes are bad at the portage, bad for a baby. But before you enter the Nepisiguit Brook, where it meets the Nepisiguit River, keep watch. There is a soft meadow there by the tallest pines on the right hand. That is a place where your party can make good beds of spruce boughs in long grass. The water in the stream is good to drink and the mosquitoes are few. The next day you will paddle up Nepisiguit Brook to your portage, then paddle down to the Milamichi to your new home."

BLAKE IS WAITING for her in the company of three other men, who melt away at Charlotte's approach. His expression is fixed, impenetrable.

"Sir?"

"Madam, I would have you follow me, if you please."

He turns and walks quickly ahead of her to the Walker house. Inside, he leads the way to a back room, a storage area filled with sacks, tools and assorted lumber. He shuts the door.

"Set the child down, please. Set her here. It is clean and dry."

"Why is this, sir?"

"Will you set down the child, woman?"

"If you will press me to do so."

She lifts the bunting bag from her shoulders and lies Elizabeth on the low heap of sacking. She touches her daughter's face and the child stirs in her sleep. Blake crosses the room to the window and looks out a moment, then turns.

"It seems we are not well begun."

"How so, sir?"

"How so? We are married but three hours when I must learn that, while I am engaged in business, you have fled to the savages on the hill, and perhaps to one savage especially. Am I well informed, madam?"

Charlotte steps back involuntarily, her whole being suddenly chilled.

"You are not, John. You are not well informed."

"Am I not? On which particular am I not well informed?"

"On all."

"You have not been to the camp of the savages here at Nepisiguit?"

"Why do you call them so?"

"Tell me simply, madam, and do not run me about. Have you not gone to their camp?"

She sees his fury is barely contained. "Yes. I have gone there. It has been my home."

"Has it, indeed? And is it still your home?"

"I have no home now, John Blake, except that you provide me with one."

"And will you bring my enemies into my home?"

He is speaking loudly now and Charlotte is ashamed to think that others might hear what is befalling her on her wedding day.

"Why do you speak to me so?"

"Answer me, woman, or by God, I shall see you make answer in future!"

"Answer you?" Tears of fury begin coursing down her cheeks and she brushes at them as though they were not tears but mosquitoes that annoy her. "How can I answer you about your enemies? I know no enemies of yours, sir. Why would you importune me about enemies?"

Blake turns suddenly from her and walks across the room, stops, looks at her again.

"Where were your ears at table today, but hours ago? Would you have me believe that you heard nothing I had to say?"

"I heard all, John. I attended carefully to all."

"And did you not then go straight to their camp and there, for aught I know, remind them that their enemy is alert to their schemes?"

Charlotte stares at him in amazement.

"You . . . you would accuse your wife, who has given herself to you on so little evidence of your own intentions, who has placed herself in your power, you would accuse her of treachery? Is that so, John?"

"I ask only the truth."

"You would condemn me for treachery because I wished only to bid farewell to the kindest women who have ever entered my life?"

"I don't speak of women."

"You speak *to* a woman, John! You speak to your own wife and call her something foul."

"By God, I do not!"

"What do you do then?"

He is silent, his breathing hard, his brown eyes wide, staring at her from under dark brows.

"You spoke nothing of my affairs then?" he finally says.

"I did not."

"I am monstrous glad of it."

"I am monstrous glad, sir, that you have some faith in your new wife."

She sees some confusion in him now and her own fury begins to abate.

"And this Indian who was said to court you. Did you have conversation with him?"

"Who has told you of courting, John?"

"Some here, at this post."

"Give me their names."

He blinks without speaking.

"John, I accept that you will not. But just this morning I pledged my love and obedience to you for all my life, and I find it hard that any of these rough gentlemen should carry the day against me."

At these words, Blake looks down at the floor. It is for only a moment, but Charlotte at last knows that the hell that had suddenly opened up before her has closed.

"John." She speaks quietly now, controlling and calming herself. "John, these jealousies and discontents that are urged on you by others have no grounds in me and never shall. I am your loyal wife."

He nods slowly.

"Charlotte," he says, "I've not been much in the company of women. I have judged them to be inclined to faithless conduct and this—I confess it, Charlotte—this I fear more than any fate. If I've been quick to anger, I repent it. It's a fault in me and in truth, you've given no cause. I'm not schooled in the ways of a gentlewoman, and you can tell by my speech that I know little enough of your society. But, Charlotte, I entreat your understanding. This land rewards the strong and I intend to thrive in it. I'm accustomed to command and I require obedience in the execution of my plans. Will you give me that obedience?"

"I have pledged it before God."

"For if you will not, Charlotte, it shall be a hard life for you with me."

"Indeed, John, but you have my pledge already."

Elizabeth chooses that moment to stir and cry. Blake goes to her and picks her up.

"This child is ours," he says quietly and passes the baby to her.

—

THE COMMODORE has offered them his own wide bed for their wedding night and has a piglet roasted for their wedding feast—a rare spring treat. Charlotte makes her excuses while the men's plates are still heaped up and retires with Elizabeth to the bedroom. She places the cradle beside her. The sky is still light and the voices of the men in the dining room grow more raucous as they sink further into their rum.

Sometime after dark, perhaps after midnight, she wakens. She had dreamed, she thought, of voices—of fires and alarms. She lies still. Then she hears real voices, some low and steady, others tinged with excitement, fear perhaps. Her candle still burns on the shelf and she looks to Elizabeth, who stirs a little and then sleeps. Charlotte gathers her nightdress around her and dons a coat. The house is empty, the candles still burning on the table. She opens the front door and sees immediately that the men are together in the clearing. They are staring out at a most astonishing sight in the vast bay beyond them.

"Come, Charlotte!" She hears the voice of George Walker. "Come and behold a spectacle all speak of but very few ever see. Come!"

On the distant horizon, a fire casts its ghastly reflection on the clouds above it. Charlotte draws near to Blake.

"What is it?" she whispers. "Is it the Indians?"

"Not this time," Blake answers. "This is no ordinary fire."

"It's the burning ship," Walker says from where he stands at some distance, three or four men at his side. "Strange we should see it now, when no storm has passed."

"No." One of his men turns his face to Charlotte. "But they say it comes sometimes before a storm."

"Or when there's no storm at all," says Jack Primm.

"Aye." Walker studies it through his glass. "It seems a whaling ship this time." He looks at length. "But I have seen it once before, when it was a three master and all its sails ablaze."

Charlotte stares across the water and thrills with the horror of the thing. "Can we not save the poor souls aboard by anything we do?"

There was a scattering of humourless chuckles.

"There are no souls to save on that ship," Blake says. "No souls I would care to meet."

Walker takes the glass from his eye and clears its eyepiece carefully with his handkerchief. "It's been seen from Restigouche, from Paspébiac, from Miscou and many places beside."

"But what is it?" Charlotte repeats.

"A ghost," says Dan Crocker.

"An omen," says another man.

"We do not at present know its true nature," Walker says. "In time, its mysteries may be revealed to men through study and reason. For now"—he passes the glass to Blake—"for now it's the phantom ship."

"It's fading," Blake mutters, "as they say it does."

"The Salmon People will tell you of it," Walker says. "They'll tell you it's been burning in the bay since their grandmothers' time, indeed, since their grandmothers' grandmothers camped on these shores."

"Gluskap," adds Jack Primm. "It's all Gluskap—or else the Great Spirit."

Several of the men laugh at that.

"Aye. But their Great Spirit is but God," says Walker. "It might become us on occasion to be humbled by his works, whatever they be and whatever He may be called. We're a proud lot, we men. A day may come when we shall be glad of mysteries."

"It's a sign, for certain," laughs one of his men, "of something."

"Sign you've drunk too much to be clever, Harry Gough," says another, "but not enough to be wise."

"I still wish I knew its nature," says Gough as the ghost ship fades to black. He wags his head in grave contemplation and steps unsteadily toward the house.

"Aye." Walker, too, laughs as he turns back to the house. "But mynd ye, Harry, need ye or the warld ken awthing?"

"Oh, commodore, don't baffle me now with your Scots," says Harry. "I'm just an Englishman, I am, tryin' to make my way in this here Scots country."

Charlotte heads back to the house and climbs the stair to her room, but her new husband does not follow her.

THE MOON'S COOL LIGHT filters through the narrow window of the bedroom and falls upon the bed where Charlotte lies asleep. Blake enters with a candle, and she wakens but makes no response. She lies on her side, her face to the wall, feels his weight on the bed behind her and hears him blow out the candle. He is still for a long time and she thinks him asleep. Then she feels his hand on the calf of her leg—warm and rough, like the bark of a tree in sunlight. She lies perfectly still. The night is filled with the high, piping, joyful calls of the spring peepers in the nearby marshes. These frog lovers are gentlemen indeed, she thinks. They perch and sing in countertenor and their ladies come to them when they are disposed to do so. Men could learn much from such creatures. Blake moves his hand along the curvature of her hip, her ribs, her shoulder. She can feel the sinews of his arm along her body and then the bulk of his thigh as his right knee works its way carefully between her thighs, lifting her right leg and opening her body to him. She had not intended to allow love making until such time as she determined her heart to be open too, but her body offers little co-operation with this strategy. The heart has its own ideas and insists on beating eagerly, the limbs surrendering resistance with only a token show, the belly revelled in heated sensations that ripple downward and inundate every former intention. She arches her back to receive him and when he has established his rhythm, she meets it with her own. He spends himself silently, holding her in a fierce embrace and keeping her there long afterward.

Charlotte listens to Blake's slow, heavy breathing. This great blunt creature has much to learn of love, she thinks. But I shall teach him.

IT RAINS BEFORE BREAKFAST and Blake hesitates to set off with Charlotte and the baby in the open canoe.

"Why should we delay on my account?" she asks. "I cannot see any assurance that we shall have no rain on this journey."

"You're prepared to endure it then?"

"I am prepared to endure far more than that, Captain Blake."

"Indeed, Charlotte, you're a woman of rare courage, if I may believe George Walker. You must be so, to have married me."

At that moment the shower passes and the sun comes out and touches Charlotte's face and splashes across a lock of red hair than had fallen across her forehead. Blake brushes it carefully aside and smiles, the truest smile she had yet seen from him.

The fog burns off the bay and the sky turns a misty blue. Blake stows the last of her possessions by size and weight in their own canoe, with Harry Gough in the bow. When the farewells are said and Charlotte turns to the canoe with Elizabeth in her arms, Walker comes to her side.

"This then is but temporary, Charlotte," he says. "We shall meet again soon enough."

"That we should not would be insupportable, George."

"I've made every provision for you in my power."

"I know you have."

"And you are in strong hands."

She laughs and surprises herself with tears. "As strong as my own, George."

Walker lays his hand on her shoulder. "When you have need," he says, "you have only to send word."

She bites her lip and her throat swells with a loneliness that seems for a moment unbearable. "Thank you, George," she says, regretting the insufficiency of her words.

THEY ROUND ALSTON POINT and head across the harbour and southeast to the mouth of the river. There is little by way of wind and the strong strokes of the paddles carry them forward as gracefully as swans and swifter. Charlotte looks up toward the Salmon camp on the hill, conscious of Blake's eyes upon her. Then they paddle away from the wooded shore, falling for a few moments under the dark spell of the tall firs. Charlotte holds Elizabeth closely and a bird calls from the forest.

"Whippoorwill. Whippoorwill."

Her breath catches and her body seems to freeze where she sits. The canoes glide forward out of the pellucid water toward the mouth of the Nepisiguit. She searches the shadows for his face.

"Whippoorwill. Whippoorwill."

Now she turns and looks back to her husband. His face is calm. He smiles at her and she returns the smile.

"Whippoorwill."

No bird had the power to distract John Blake from his thoughts of the work that lay ahead.

THE RIVER BECOMES A TUNNEL of giant spruce. Only the far shore catches the morning sun, where the roots of cedars cling to the plunging bank. The water is clear but as dark as obsidian with an occasional reflection of red earthy tones coming from the muddy bottom. Now and then fish, some of them four feet long, breach the surface to hang in the air a moment, catch the light and splash back into the water.

At first, the men call from canoe to canoe, but with the passing hours they fall silent and the stillness of the river envelops them. They put in at noon where the bank is low and a grassy verge offers a place for Charlotte to wash and change the baby. They eat bread and salt pork and drink beer, but the blackflies gather in the still air and they push off into the river soon enough.

"What is that you put on her face?" Blake asks.

"A balm that keeps the flies from her," Charlotte answers. She squeezes a little more of the yellow potion from its small pouch.

"Where have you come by this balm?" Blake asks.

Charlotte replaces the pouch in her basket.

"It was a gift from the friends who made it," she says.

He falls silent. The quiet of the river is comforting. The rhythm of the paddling is soothing; the dipping and swinging of the paddle lulls Charlotte into a daze.

—

As THE SUN SINKS before them on the Nepisiguit, where to make camp for the night becomes the question. Their usual site is on the far side of the portage, but there is general agreement that such a hike is not the thing to inflict on the mother and child at the end of a long day. They paddle in silence some minutes more.

"Decide as you will," Harry Gough says from the front of the Blake canoe, "but my belly is speaking to me of empty feelings. Lonely and empty feelings."

"Your belly speaks loud and often, Harry Gough," says Blake. "You pay it too much mind."

As Elizabeth begins to cry, Charlotte speaks. "Just ahead, where the Nepisiguit Brook meets the Nepisiguit River, there is a soft meadow by the tallest pines on the right. We can cut spruce boughs there for beds and stay until daylight. The water in the stream is good to drink and the mosquitoes are few."

Elizabeth protests again and her mother strokes her brow, greasy from the ointment.

The deepest silence of the river that day could not compete with the silence that now befalls the party, but when they reach the spot, they head their canoes into the bank, and the place is just as the new Mrs. John Blake had described it, a meadow of soft grass stretching away from the banks of the Nepisiguit and a clear stream tumbling into the shadowed waters of the river.

The portage, which begins soon after dawn, is long and arduous. But the journey that follows on the river to the Miramichi is a wondrous panorama. The woods are alive with the season. A moose with a calf, on still-wobbly legs, is drinking at the water's edge; a bear with three playful cubs cocks its head at the passing convoy. The melody of birdsong is everywhere, flowers are bursting with white, violet and red blooms and new green leaves are filling every branch. The Miramichi comes into view late in the afternoon, drawing them out of the forest, pulling the canoe ever faster as though they are paddling downhill. "There she is," Blake announces. "It's just a short run to the brook now."

The river surges like an artery, pulsing to the sea, walled with tall stands of timber and teeming with salmon. As he steers the canoe onto the Miramichi, Blake tips his head toward the smoke coming from stacks farther up the river to the west and says, "Up there is where William Davidson and John Cort have a fishery with as many as twenty men working." They paddle east, the sun at their backs now, and Blake points to the north side of the river. "The Wishart brothers, Alexander and William, live there." The names mean nothing to her, but she's reassured that they are not alone. Her legs are cramped, Elizabeth is squirming, she can imagine the strain on John, but there's an air of excitement as he plunges the paddle into the water like a rudder and turns them toward the brook, cutting through the current to the landing. The other canoes stay in the centre of the river and call their farewells with intentions to gather the following day at some point of land she's never heard of. Closer now, the water in the brook is dark as ink—more Black Brook than Blake Brook, she thinks. The stream winds up into the woodland just above the cabin; she's wondering how far his claim stretches when the canoe slides onto the shore and the Blake family is home.

CHAPTER 6

The Miramichi

1776

*A*s soon as the breakfast of fried fish, bread and cheese is consumed, Charlotte goes outside to take a measure of the place. The interior, she'd already discovered, is plain, damp as dew and untidy, but there are two rooms, a window and a hearth that takes up most of one wall. There are hand-hewn chairs and a table as well as a long board under the window for preparing food, a large bed and, thanks be to God, an oil lamp.

She walks along the brook to see what can be procured from the land. Strawberries colour the soil at the back of the cabin. Blueberry patches that spread all over the bank to the river promise a harvest later in the summer and a bramble of raspberry cane twisted onto the trees at the edge of the clearing will be ripe in August as well. The water in the brook is clear, sweet and plentiful.

The plot John told her about is a woeful heap of lumpy earth that might have posed as a garden, or at least the plan of one. She goes at it like one possessed: whacking the brush out of it, tearing at the roots and turning the soil. She plants the seed potatoes André gave her first. There is evidence of onion roots that she carefully separates from the choking weeds and sets them in a row near the potatoes. Blake says there are turnips to be had from the Wisharts, and she resolves to get them and plant another row into the ground.

Ticking off her survival tally, she wanders along the edge of the woods looking for sarsaparilla as, courtesy of Maria, she knows it will serve a dozen purposes. She follows the property to where the Miramichi runs across the front of the land and finds herself on a sandy beach that rolls out of the wake of the river onto the shore—and in spitting distance of a big black bear. She wants to scream but catches her breath and backs away slowly, hoping Elizabeth, who is riding along on her back, will somehow understand the desperate need to be quiet. When she gets to the cabin, all she can utter is "Bear, bear." Blake reaches for his musket and moves to the door in a single motion. The bear is gone but serves as a reminder to Charlotte to be wary.

Then she takes on the washing, insisting that Blake bide nearby. She hauls a tub outside, makes a dozen trips to the fire for hot water and slices off a chunk of what Blake calls river soap—strong lye mixed with tallow—and begins the task of scrubbing the filth from their clothes as though she is beating the past out of their lives. She pounds his trousers against a rock with such ferocity she is surprised they don't fall to pieces. She pummels the shirts and skirts with her reddened hands, and flogs the socks, stockings and drawers with a stick. Blake, amused with his new wife's tenacity, watches the frenzy with Elizabeth, who is learning to crawl now and inching her way around a piece of moose hide spread on the ground. Charlotte drapes the clothes over boulders and bushes close to the cabin, then refills the tub and, demanding that Blake stand by with his back to her, strips off her clothes and immerses herself in the water. It's so hot she can hardly sit still while she scrubs herself hard with soap until her skin tingles.

That done, she dons a clean frock and sits down to discuss the tasks that remain. "As far as I can make out there's lots of black tea, pork fat and fish, John Blake." By the look of the animal bones out back, he has also survived on game. She has a plan for more.

"You need to get a cow, some chickens, a sheep and maybe a goat," she tells him.

"Is this the proper comportment of an Englishwoman—to strip off her clothes in the broad daylight and then give orders to her husband."

She's relieved to see he is smiling. "You're not offended, are you, John?"

"To the contrary," he says, sizing up her stamina. "You will need to spend a good portion of time alone while I'm away at sea or on the river. Your manner will serve you well."

His smile fades when he starts to talk of the lay of the land.

"It's more than bears you need to heed. The scoundrels from the colonies are nothing but pirates and marauders. You need be mindful of them. And hearken well, there are those who would aid them in the dastardly work they do."

She assumes he means the Indians. There's more.

"I cleared the bush from much of this tract and want to do more. Those Halifax governors know nothing of these parts. They ignore us here on the Miramichi. But signed deeds for this lot there must be. The land, Charlotte, it's the land that will make a man prosper."

The weeks that follow are consumed with the task. She works the garden while he splits downed trees for firewood and chinks the gaps in the cabin with moss. She suggests he use birch bark to cover the open spaces and shows him how to strip the bark in large sheets by rubbing the trunk with warm water. In the marshes between the brook and the river she finds sarsaparilla and gooseberries just like the ones at the Baie and, remembering Marie's advice, plans to dry and store them for winter when they'll need the nutritious plants to avoid scurvy. She saves ash from the fire to use as fertilizer in the garden. And again recalling Marie's instructions, mixes the ash with water and animal fat, boils it and leaves it to harden to make soap that's a little less harsh than the lye-based one he's been using.

And she ferrets out the inside story on some of the settlers.

"Davidson and Cort have nearly one hundred thousand acres up at the forks of the river," John says. "Had it for more than ten years, I reckon. Some of it worked by Acadians before we rid the land of them."

Charlotte grimaces at the slight to André's family but only asks, "What do they do with all that land?"

"It's a salmon fishery they run up there and the shipbuilding they want. They've nary a care to clear the land."

On the other side of the river and not far from their own place, the Wishart brothers have set up a business to cure salmon.

"They use a method of curing they brought with them from Scotland," he says. "But it's my belief they haven't registered any of the lots they occupy."

There's another man called Alexander Henderson who arrived just weeks before they did. John doesn't know him yet as he's been away for more than a month, but means to find out what his business is here on the Miramichi.

By fall the revolution in the thirteen colonies to the south is truly creating havoc for settlers on the river who depend on the ships that come to the mouth of the Miramichi for supplies. Oil, flour, occasionally butter and fresh vegetables, cheese, sometimes fruit, and whatever manner of provisions that might be available—iron pots for cooking, kettles, even a few head of cattle can be had from traders who dock in the Miramichi Bay. Now the supply lines are often cut by the privateers.

"These thieves don't even want the goods, they just don't want any of us to have them," her husband tells her when he returns in a rage without the cow she had hoped he could procure.

"Davidson and the Wisharts can't export their goods for fear of attack on the river." She hears brutal tales of burned houses and looted businesses from all around the region, especially along the coast. She also hears that the Indians are helping the privateers. Blake, who still pilots whatever ships dare to sail up and down the river, invariably comes back with accounts of violence and even murder.

He's been toiling at a particularly feverish pitch the night they sit down to supper and he announces he must leave for the West Indies. A ship has been readied. They want him to captain it. He must go. He thinks it will take five or six weeks.

"We have no sooner settled and you leave," she says. And he's no sooner gone than she realizes from the telltale signs that she is once again with child.

HER TASKS, as she sees them, are to keep Elizabeth out of harm's way and to keep the squirrels and deer from consuming the ripening garden crop. She prattles away to her daughter while she tries and fails to win the nightly contest with the animals. Then while walking by the shore she discovers a peat bog. "What do you think, my girl? Could this peat moss be good for burning and making a smoky shield for our potatoes?"

Being cautious to avoid falling into the bog and with one eye on Elizabeth, she uses a knife to cut out a square piece and sets it to dry near the cabin. On the way back to the house, she spots the familiar sleek canoes of the Mi'kmaq paddling by, flying the flag of the revolutionary patriots. She wonders how the people she knew at the Baie could be doing the things Blake speaks of here on the Miramichi. Her intuition tells her he's right, while her heart wishes he were wrong. The other boats belonging to Davidson or the Wisharts, she presumes, that ply the water in front of their lot give no indication of stopping to visit.

The peat-moss experiment seems to work. Once it's dry, she lights it and the smoke it produces rises a foot and smoulders for hours. It takes a whole day to cut the squares from the bog and arrange them around the plot. That night she lights each one before she retires. In the morning, the peat is still smoking. A triumph.

It's a lonely life, though. Fog rolls along the river sometimes for days at a time, smothering her in an unsettling isolation. It's so thick some mornings she meets it at the door and can't see the river. Sometimes the sun burns it off by midday. Other times the soundless cloak is so consuming she thinks there's nothing else out there, except maybe trouble. One day when the fog is gone and sparkling sunshine gives her a view up and down the Miramichi, she spies a dory cutting through the main channel toward Blake Brook. There's a man rowing the little grey boat. With his back to the landing, he deftly strokes the boat to shore and slips in beside Blake's canoe. He calls to her from the dory. "William Wishart," he says by way of introduction.

"Welcome," she calls, "I'm Charlotte Blake," and walks to the shore to meet him.

"There have been more attacks on the river. I'm wondering how you and the wee bairn are faring," he says.

"We're fine. Only the squirrels are threatening our survival," she says, hoping to explain the smoking peat that surrounds her plot.

"I can see you're an inventive lassie. You'll need to be. The war in the colonies is ever more fierce."

"How do you learn these things?" she asks.

He explains a system that fascinates her, like the post being carried wave to wave along the river rather than by horse-drawn carriage as it is to her father's home. "The ships all stop in Liverpool on the coast of Nova Scotia," he begins. "Whether from the Baie de Chaleur or the West Indies or Britain, many trade their cargo on those docks. Simeon Perkins gathers the news and passes it to every ship's company. He writes down all the comings and goings and gives the account to the ships that follow."

"So this Perkins man is like the post master?" she inquires.

"Nay, Charlotte, he's the commissioner of roads but keeps his office at the wharf. It's Simeon who told me that Captain Blake had sailed away and that you were alone on his lot."

She enjoys the visit, as she hasn't set eyes on another adult since Blake sailed away more than three weeks ago. He's tall, with hair as black as coal, searching dark eyes and oversized hands. He seems a calculating man, watching, listening and only sharing a portion of the story she's sure he could tell. After a cup of tea and as much news as she can get from him, he turns to leave, promising to return with turnips from his own garden just as soon as they are ready for digging.

By the time Blake sails back to the brook, the garden is flourishing, the cabin is rearranged and an outdoor oven has been patched together. Charlotte is happy to see him. Happier still with the gifts he brings—spices from the West Indies—salt, pepper, cinnamon and ginger, as well as a tiny bracelet of beads that he slips on Elizabeth's wrist and two barrels—one full of molasses, the other, sugar. It's been a successful trip. She waits until supper is over and Elizabeth is sleeping to tell him her news.

"We will have a child, in February, I reckon," she says. No reply.

"Have I encumbered you with my poor plain speech?" she asks, mimicking his remark to her when he asked her to be his wife.

He stares at her, speechless. The hard-driving bargain of the sea for a man who takes to the water has shaped him these eighteen years since sailing away from childhood. Now this woman sitting before him is telling him that his hearth will be tended, his home filled with family. He'd only ever hoped to avoid the worst. Now his expectations are high.

"It is very fine news, indeed," he says.

He, too, has news, gathered from Simeon Perkins when his ship sailed into Liverpool on the way home.

"George Walker's establishment at Nepisiguit is destroyed utterly."

"How?"

"It's the work of the American pirates and the Indians who think them friends. They say the loss is ten thousand pounds or more."

Charlotte looks down to her feet and the beaded moccasins she wears.

"And, George, how does he fare?"

"He's a wily old pirate himself, Charlotte. Escaped and safe. He's one of those who is always standing when the smoke clears."

More disturbing because of its proximity is the news that John Cort's store had been ransacked, his cattle stolen and his house burned to the ground. "The privateers have us in their sights," John warns. But autumn is upon them; anxiety about the onset of winter is greater for Charlotte than these robber barons of the sea. "Look," she says while he continues his denunciation of the Indians, "the birds are flocking up; it's as sure a sign as I know to be getting ready for the cold."

Fall brings the months of dawn-to-dusk travail. The clock ticks against the coming freeze while she's as industrious as the squirrels plucking their own moveable feast from whatever falls from the trees or is left in Charlotte's garden and digging furiously to bury the bounty for later. The wood is cut and stacked. The slender cedar that sparks but gives no heat is good for kindling and goes in one pile while hard wood, especially maple that burns slowly and produces a fine heat, is stacked in another. Her husband brings nets full of fish when he returns from his piloting duties; she tries to remember how they were dried at the camp. She guts and cleans them, lifts out the backbone and soaks them in brine for half the day. Then she lays them on the flat side of wood John has cut and leaves them there all day, turning them so the cut side is down before the dew gathers at dusk. She repeats the chore every day until they are as stiff as the boards they lie on. Cod, salmon, mackerel are laid out like slivers of wood and stacked for winter. She worries about the livestock that never appeared. "We need a goat at least to have milk for Elizabeth when she leaves my breast," she complains.

He's away piloting a ship up the river when her ear is tuned to the call of the whippoorwill—it's unmistakable. She is overjoyed to see Wioche, rushes to where he stands among the trees and stops herself from reaching out with her arms. She is tongue-tied, but a thousand messages pass between them in silence. He speaks first. "Charlotte, Elizabeth—good on Milamichi?" Her reply is so convoluted with bits about her life these last few months on the river, the baby's antics and her questions about the camp on the Baie, Marie, Walker's troubles, he's soon laughing with the pleasure of connecting again with the unpredictable Charlotte.

"What brings you here?" she asks.

"Chief Francis Julian is visiting the Mi'kmaq camp in Taboosimgeg," he says.

"Why would he travel there?"

"Trouble is coming. You must be careful. Your friend Commodore Walker is not safe. Many more privateers sail on the Baie."

She tells him she knows and although wants to ask what part his people play in this trouble she asks instead about Marie. They walk toward the cabin while he tells her the news of the camp. He doesn't stay long, explaining that he must join the chief at a grand council meeting that is bringing chiefs from all over the district together to talk about the warring colonies south of them. On his way out of the cabin, he smiles at the sleeping Elizabeth, notices the braid of sweetgrass hanging on the hearth and says softly, "Baie de Chaleur stays with you." Then as though to put his own stamp on the land where she lives, he adds, "Here it is called Mtaoegenatgoigtog." It means Black Brook—the word she thought appropriate when she first saw the ink-coloured brook that has become her water well, wash basin and fresh-water fishing hole. Without another word, he is gone, having promised to bring a new braid when the sweetgrass grows again in the spring.

She's unsettled as much by the brevity of the visit as the plain fact that John Blake would not have appreciated the Micmac man on his land. Feeling a pang of guilt, she decides to make a special dinner for her husband and throws herself into preparing pommes de terre rappée, a favourite repast of André's Acadian family. She digs up a hill of potatoes grown from André's seedlings and sets the pot to boil while she grates the earthy-smelling vegetables, mixes them with diced pork fat and rolls the mixture into balls that she drops into the boiling water. By the time he gets home, the hearth is as he likes it.

His tales of piloting ships up and down the Miramichi become daily thrillers. The journey is invariably fraught with potential mishaps—the changing tide, the treacherous shoals and the possibility of attack. The Blake cabin is above the sub-merged sandbank that separates Miramichi Bay from the river, so Charlotte can only imagine the tricky manoeuvres her husband tells her about. But she's always relieved when he returns and relishes the stories he brings that knit the strands of their pioneering life together.

There's something else she notices that plays like a subplot in his stories. He seems to know a lot about the patriots, even calling some of them by name. It makes her wonder from time to time if piloting ships is all he is doing out there on the water.

The cabin is readied for winter with extra boughs, and Charlotte suggests they line the walls with animal skins. "This is not a Micmac camp," he says with more judgment than she cares to hear. Then he adds insult to injury by declaring, "The sweet-grass won't keep you warm either." She ignores the comment and instead calculates the stores: potatoes and onions are buried in a deep pit at the back of the cabin. There are spices and tea, molasses and sugar and enough flour and oil, she thinks to see them through. He's brought whale oil for the lamps and to use as butter as well. Blake reminds her that livestock cannot survive the winter on the river, they are usually slaughtered in the fall and unless she wants a goat living in the cabin, she better look to other sources of drink. There's tea, rum, spruce beer that he makes himself in a still behind the cabin and the brook is a source of fresh water even if they have to cut through the ice to get to it.

The brook is the first to lock up, then the river; it freezes solid within a week of being covered with a thin layer of ice. The siege that is winter is upon them.

Save for the happy February day when the lusty cries of their first-born son—John Blake Jr.—fill the cabin, winter is long, harsh and punishing.

CHAPTER 7

The Miramichi
1777

*J*ohn Blake is away—again—sailing to the West Indies. And again Charlotte is left to bargain with the critters in the garden, the size of the woodpile and the threat of privateers, this time with two children at her side. It is a warm clear day when she spies a familiar dory crossing the river to her own small dock.

"Pray!" she calls to the approaching boat, "How does William Wishart do?"

He throws out the bow rope and she holds it as he climbs ashore. Together they pull the boat up.

"Well enough, I suppose, Charlotte. I hope *you* are well, and the wee children."

"I am, William. But why do you answer me indirectly?"

"Och, Charlotte, let's not speak of me. Where's the new bairn?"

"Asleep in the house and let him remain so."

"Indeed. A sleeping baby—a blessing to all mankind."

"Indeed, indeed. Have you come to visit me?"

"I have, Charlotte, and I've brought you a few things."

"What things?"

"Aye. Many things." He leans into the boat, where two bulky hempen sacks lie on the boards. "And I've brought you news," he says.

They sit in the kitchen, their voices softened on account of the baby.

"I'm afraid for you, Charlotte."

"Are you so, faith?" She fans her cup with her hand and sips the tea cautiously. "What do you propose?"

"There is worry of an attack. I think you ought to join the Murdochs. Just awhile. Until John returns."

"I see. And what do you propose I do with my own house, left open and unguarded? And my garden. What shall we eat, come winter?"

"It would not be easy, I know. But I've brought you a large store of potatoes and what onions and cabbage I have and a bushel or two of good turnips. These, with what you have, will make a contribution for your keep. You may work with Janet Murdoch, who has barely a notion of how to begin the business of settling a homestead."

"William, if I were to follow this course, what would you and your brother eat? You cannot live by salmon alone."

"Aye. That's so. I've come to tell you, Charlotte, that we are leaving. We'll go to Halifax for now, where Alexander has friends."

Charlotte sits back in her chair.

"It's as bad, then, as I feared."

"New crops destroyed up and down the coast. Cattle stolen. And these losses are attended by events I will not describe. Men killed *and* women *and* children. Raids and burning these several weeks past even above us at the forks. There's no one cares to defend us, it seems. Even if this were not so, we cannot get our fish out in a regular way. Now we'll take what we can, while our hides are still on our backs and our scalps on our heads."

"I am sorry to hear all this."

"And I'm sorry to see it. Sorrier still that John is not here to protect you."

"He thought by this one adventure to give us what we need to prosper."

"Aye. Prosper indeed, when a man returns to find his wife and children all dead."

"Fie, William! You mustn't speak so!"

"I'm afraid for you, Charlotte."

WHEN WISHART HAD LOADED the handcart to the top with his previous year's potatoes and turnips and a small sack of half-grown onions and cabbage, they pull it together from the boat to the house. Charlotte opens the sacks to the air. A pronounced smell of mould wafts out. She pulls out several specimens.

"It appears a little life remains in most of them," she observes. "I'll make a soup tonight with pork and my new parsley. Will you stay to dinner with us, William?"

"No, Charlotte, there is something else to tell ye."

"Is it John?"

"No, the captain is a man at home with hazards and I think ye should have nary a fear for his safety. The *Hunter* is in the bay."

"The *Hunter*?"

"Captain Boyle come from Halifax with all arrangements for the registration of the lands."

"The governor now deigns to acknowledge us here?"

"The governor? Were you not aware then that the rogue, Legge, is recalled to London?"

"I was indeed. But our masters in London have sent us another better man, have they not?"

"You run behind the times, Charlotte. There's more news with every ship. Our masters in London have not sent us another and better man. This Legge remains governor. Though now residing in England."

Wishart sits on the blanket where Elizabeth plays and puffs his pipe into life.

"So Legge governs us from England?"

He nods. "I should think it worth his life to appear again in Nova Scotia. And Whitehall has forced the resignation of Michael Francklin as lieutenant-governor. He was an honest Englishman and one who had nearly won the loyalty of the Indians. Now in his place they've put our lives under one Admiral Aruthnot, a proven blunderer advanced to commander of His Majesty's Royal Navy on this continent. By God, a man might blush to think of these stumblings.

"But for all this there's news for us—or some of us. Captain Boyle has come with the authority of the governor's minions in Halifax. Eight persons here on the banks are properly registered. You and John are included."

"I'm glad of it, then. For aught we knew, with their many high purposes, they might have forgotten us entirely."

"Alex and I are not among the chosen."

"How can that be, William? You have been settled and working your fishery these several years."

"Ay, but we didn't stake an official claim to our lots and this is the consequence."

"Did you and your brother not apprehend that life here is all about these lots? Land and owning land is the constant subject."

"To be sure, to be sure. We thought our presence was enough

for now, as perhaps it might have proved. No matter, we are off and finished with it for now."

"How will it be done then with this Captain Boyle?"

"This river is so dangerous, Boyle must actively patrol the bay, as does Captain Harvey on the *Viper*. He's sent a fellow named Plumnell in his stead. Some have met with him already, but you must meet him at the Murdoch place, since it is the nearest to the bay. That is my chief reason for coming to you now."

"You're most kind, William. When will this Plumnell be there?"

"Tonight. He seems anxious to rejoin the *Hunter* so he can scamper back to Halifax. There's great anxiety everywhere. You can well imagine, no employee of the government chooses easily to risk his skin. We should depart forthwith."

"Let me gather what I'll need for the children."

SHE HAS NO GREAT AFFECTION for the sea, but a boat on the river on a bright, late afternoon with a good breeze is a different thing altogether. She looks back with unalloyed pleasure at the house as it diminishes with distance, admires the broad swath of cleared land, the tidiness of the garden, the woodpile, the outbuilding, the seemly rise of wooded slope beyond. There is my world, she thinks. There is what I have made with my husband and there is where we shall build and grow.

In midstream, they drift downriver until the Murdochs' house comes into view. It is a grand if ramshackle affair—the brief shelter and place of work for a company of departed loggers—and it perches on a considerable lot of five hundred acres on the curve of land where the river debouches into Miramichi Bay across from Bartibog Island. John Murdoch himself—with his mild, thoughtful eyes, ruddy, red-veined cheeks, high brow and fair, thinning hair—was quickly recognized as a steady and upright individual. The jutting nose of land he occupies was soon called Murdoch's Point in recognition of this—and of the size of his family.

Past the house and around Murdoch's Point is a Mi'kmaq summer encampment. When the Murdochs had first arrived, and before the recent commotions stirred by rebel privateers, Janet Murdoch had made it clear to any who would listen that there was much of value to be learned from the natives. This was hardly lost on Charlotte, but though she had longed to visit the camp, the strong opinions held by her husband, and the fact of her having no grown children at home, had kept her from doing so. Janet had gone herself with her daughter Mary and Mary's husband, John Malcolm. They reported the natives cautious but friendly and that there was nothing to suggest they intended mischief, though they had complained of mistreatment by British soldiers and sailors. Yet as news of Indian attacks spread along the river, less heed is paid to Janet Murdoch's soft regard for the Mi'kmaq, and Charlotte sees little wisdom in making her own opinion more widely known.

John Murdoch had done much to improve the house, with bedrooms in the upper storey and glass windows in every wall. And in fairness to Janet Murdoch, Wishart's reservations notwithstanding, she had played her part despite a most unpromising beginning. Her appearance upon their arrival the previous year had remained a source a covert mirth in the vicinity of Blake Brook: the polished riding boots, the quilted dress—admittedly a very good dress—with its embroidered apron of what may actually have been Spitalfield silk, topped, as it were, with a properly plumed bonnet. But poor, thin-lipped Janet Murdoch was not seen in those clothes again.

The Murdochs had not been long on the banks when stories of their origins caught up with them. Janet, the daughter of a good family in Banffshire, had eloped with her father's coachman, a bit of gossip that secretly thrilled Charlotte. They had first kept a store on St. John Island, but John Murdoch wanted land—the preserve of privilege in the Old World and the birthright of the poor in the New World. The Murdochs brought nine children—three sons and six daughters—to the settlement, and Janet did indeed lift a hoe to feed them.

ALBERT PLUMNELL has made himself comfortable at the Murdochs' expense, an arrangement in which John Murdoch apparently sees some advantage. Plumnell is a rotund, bespectacled man who might have been groomed for his role as official errand runner and clearly relishes the dispensing of fates. Eight families are recipients of official allocations, with each to receive a half-mile of river frontage, the depths to vary according to the allocation.

"Ah," says Plumnell when Charlotte enters with the baby John asleep in her arms and Wishart behind her, carrying Elizabeth. "This then is the renowned Mrs. Blake."

Not one to dodge a challenge, she replies curtly, "I hope my renown is of the proper sort."

Greetings are exchanged between neighbours and the necessary introductions completed. The whole Murdoch family is present except for the eldest child, Mary, who had recently married John Malcolm and they had built their own small cabin farther along the bank and at a distance from the water. In their place are two dewy youths just come up from New Hampshire to work for them, James Doone and Douglas Rose.

Plumnell makes much of opening ledgers and shuffling documents, then adjusts his spectacles.

"As I have informed the others, Mrs. Blake, I act here for Captain Boyle and on behalf of His Majesty's government at Halifax. I have John Blake, who is your husband, registered as the first settler on the Miramichi. Mr. Alexander Henderson, whom I understand I am to expect presently, is the second." He shuffles some more, looks up. "Captain Blake is absent, I gather."

"He's in the West Indies," Charlotte says.

"Is he? I had thought otherwise, madam. Well, you shall convey all to him, I'm sure. Three hundred acres are registered to Captain John Blake and to yourself, madam, as his wife. You are listed here as the third settler on the banks."

"I was so."

"In my opinion, madam, the Miramichi River is unsuitable to be inhabited by women."

"Is that what you think, sir? Whom shall it be inhabited by?"

"By men equipped for its dangers. Women should find their place only when these wildernesses are tamed. I have told these others so."

"Have you consulted with the men in this matter, sir?"

Plumnell looks at her sharply over his spectacles.

"Madam?"

"Are other men in agreement with you, that they should be without the company of women so as to comply with your theories?"

"I do not understand you, madam."

"Here, Charlotte." John Murdoch intervenes. "See the maps Mr. Plumnell has brought."

"Hush!" Janet Murdoch says suddenly, a plate of boiled eggs

and green onions still in her hands "There's someone at the landing."

"Is there?" William Wishart laughs, though thinly. "How can you tell? 'Tis getting dark, Janet."

John Murdoch laughs too.

"Oh, she's a hare, she is, our Janet. She can hear the birds break wind in the trees, can you not, my dear?"

But Janet remains where she had first stopped. "They're coming up," she says.

The men push their chairs back from the table. John Murdoch crosses to the hearth and takes his musket in his hand.

"I'm quite certain 'tis none but Alex Henderson," Wishart says, but he looks keenly from face to face.

Murdoch opens the door. They all see the lantern approaching from the river.

"Halloo!" Murdoch calls.

"Halloo!" a voice responds.

"Ha!" cries Wishart. "'Tis the bold gentleman himself! Throw wide the door and hide the rum!"

"He's running," says Janet Murdoch.

They gather at the door as he bursts into their midst.

"Shut the door, by God!" he pants. "Let no light from the window to the river!"

"What is it?" Murdoch and the whole company stand back a pace and look as Alexander Henderson slumps into the first chair.

"Alarm, gentlemen! Alarm!"

"Children!" Janet Murdoch sweeps around the room like a brood hen. "Quickly," she tells them. "Extinguish the light."

"To the river," says Henderson. "They'll come on the river."

"Is it the rebel privateers, man?" Wishart asks.

"I think not, Willy. I think not. I was just returning by boat from the forks when I came upon them. They were burning Robbie Buchanan's mill and I saw their bodies painted and saw the dancing devils and the fire. I drifted by, my heart almost stopped in my breast, but they ne'er saw me, they were so intent."

"My God!" Charlotte steps back. "What of Robbie?"

"I know not. Fled, I hope. I came here straightaway."

"Oh," cries Janet. "What of Mary and John!"

"George!" John Murdoch turns to his twelve-year-old. "Run now to the cabin and tell Mary and John to hurry here. Tell John to bring his musket. Run now!"

"This is intolerable, sir!"

All eyes turned to Albert Plumnell, who had spoken from his place farthest from the door. "I am the representative of the governor of Nova Scotia, gentlemen. I cannot under any circumstances be subjected to these dangers and indignities. What action can you take that Captain Boyle should know the danger I am in?"

Charlotte cannot help herself. "We'll do what we can to save ourselves, sir, and if you be saved as consequence, God be praised." She turns to Murdoch. "How many weapons have we?"

"I have two muskets here, and two swords."

"I have my pistols in the canoe," Alexander Henderson says.

"The weapons belonging to my brother and myself are in my boat," says William Wishart. "I'll fetch them now."

"We each have a pistol," says Douglas Rose.

Murdoch, Wishart and Henderson go out to fetch the arsenal, staying low to the ground and scanning the river for evidence of approaching canoes. The young Glasgow men go into the back room, where they had stored their baggage.

"Janet, have we other means to defend ourselves?" Charlotte asks.

The Murdoch children look from one to the other.

"Knives?" Charlotte asks. "Axes? Pitchforks? We cannot stand helpless while the lives of our children are imperilled, Mrs. Murdoch. What have we?"

Janet is suddenly animated, though her voice is calm.

"We have forks in the barn."

Albert Plumnell meanwhile feels his limbs weaken and believes he might suffer a spell such as he had suffered two months earlier. He sinks into the largest chair and applies his handkerchief to his brow. Charlotte regards him a moment, then goes to the west window. Blake had said they came by night, but were often poorly armed. She would not huddle in fear while the house was burned around them, as had happened to the Camerons and now Buchanan. These windows facing the forest are a poor business. Attackers who come by water cannot be relied upon to attack from the water.

"Abigail!" The girl stops following her mother. "Help me here. We must watch from these windows."

Even as she crouches by the window, her mind shrinks from the notion that the Mi'kmaq could play a part in these desperate events. Nothing she had observed when she had lived in the camp of the People suggested any capacity for such brutality.

"Charlotte, there's a light in the woods."

A prickle of fear runs along Charlotte's shoulders and climbs the nape of her neck.

"Where is that?"

"I saw it up the slope, in the woods."

"Stand back from the window, Abigail."

It is a moonless night but enough light remains to make the sloping land behind the Murdoch house dimly visible. Murdoch had cleared it quickly enough, but the drudgery of uprooting stumps was still in progress. Beyond the open ground, the wooded land rose a little more steeply. It had been cleared of brush for firewood, and she is able to see the contours of the hill for some distance. Above the grey silhouette of the forest, a few stars twinkle in a black sky. All is otherwise still.

"Perhaps I saw only my reflection," Abigail ventures.

"I must hope so."

Charlotte begins to turn from the window, and in the same instant she sees the torch. A second torch flickers.

"Go tell the young men to come in here now," she says, her tone flat.

"What is it?" Albert Plumnell croaks from his chair. "In faith, I believe some fit has come upon me, madam. Can you not help me?"

The back door opens and Janet Murdoch and her brood enter, their arms bristling with tools from the garden and barn. Charlotte puts a finger to her lips.

"I shall be obliged if you can remain quiet and calm," she says, careful to keep her own voice so. "There are persons approaching from the woods to the east."

"Oh Lord!" Janet Murdoch holds her hand to her mouth. Several of the children begin to cry. She muffles their mouths with her hand.

"Mat." Charlotte turns to the nine-year-old Murdoch boy, who stands dry-eyed among his sisters. "The men have not returned. Go quickly to the shore and tell them. Quickly now!"

"James? Douglas? Do you have your pistols?"

"Here they are." The young men put two pistols on the table, with their powder, balls and tamping rods. Douglas picks up John's musket.

"I believe this to be charged already," he says.

The door opens and Murdoch, Henderson and Wishart follow Mat into the room with four muskets and two hempen sacks. Behind them come a wide-eyed Mary and her young husband, John Malcolm. They shut the door quietly.

"We have seen them," William Wishart growls.

Doone rushes to help with the weapons. "How many are there?"

"I canna tell. They have no doubt seen the house and extinguished their torches."

"What shall we do, John?" his wife begs, her arms about two of her children.

"'Tis of little consequence," Wishart says. "They know we are here withal."

"Aye, they do," agrees Murdoch. He peeks from the east window.

"Who are they?" asks Doone.

"Indians," Murdoch says simply.

"Could they not be rebel privateers?"

"Nay. Privateers would have come by ship lest they had need of a hasty retreat. They have sent these savages in their place, as is the fashion now among them."

"John, hear me if you would." William Wishart has finished laying out the weapons on the table. "We must see these weapons are loaded and devise a plan. We shall be taken otherwise."

"By God, we shall not be taken," says Murdoch. "We shall defend this house with our lives."

Wishart shakes his head slowly.

"We can choose only between defence and attack," Wishart says, looking around at the whole company. "The house is indefensible, so we must attack."

"What, man?" Murdoch's urgency seems about to translate to anger. "Leave our women and children and attack a band of savages with but six men and as many muskets? I cannot condone it."

"Aye, you're right, John." Wishart nods. "But consider that they are likely to be but few themselves, coming alone along the river and picking off undefended places. Alex saw them at Buchanan's mill just hours ago. If they are many, we are without hope, but John, we must believe they are few."

"But how shall we attack them?"

"Let two men go separately toward the river, and two or three more climb through the garden above the house, and one stay here with the women." He makes no reference to Plumnell, who now stares mournfully from his chair.

Charlotte watches Wishart while he speaks. He takes easy control of the room as he sets out his plan. She could not help but wonder how her own fierce John Blake might have conducted himself in these circumstances. Certainly without fear, she thinks, and equally without caution.

John Murdoch speaks, "Agreed then, Douglas, you and James go out the back with my son-in-law, John. Keep low and enter the woods above the house where you may hear us. Alex, you and"—he hesitates, turns to Wishart—"Shall I stay here, William, or you?"

"You will protect your home best, John," says Wishart.

The four men go to the table and load the muskets carefully, each providing himself with his shot bag and powder. Then they steal out into the night.

"We have these." Janet indicates to her husband the forks and axes against the wall.

"God grant that we shall have no need of them," Murdoch says. "But take them and the children up."

"Take Elizabeth too, Janet," says Charlotte, "and little John." She carries the cradle to Abigail.

"Will you be coming up?" Janet asks. Charlotte looks at her directly. For all their kinship of circumstance, she has never liked the woman much. But in that moment she sees past the brittle manner to the mother and wife that Janet is. I shall not go to my death, she thought, burdened with casual contempt for another.

"Not yet." She says. "I shall stay here awhile, Janet."

"Charlotte?" Murdoch is by the table. "Have you fired a pistol?"

"I have had no need, John."

"You have need now."

He shows her the quantity to pour in at the muzzle as a charge. He wraps a ball in its cloth and tamps it home with the rod. He slides back the cover of the flash pan and trickles a small quantity of powder into it. He shows her how she should draw back the flint arm to cock the mechanism. For the moment, he releases it gently with his hand and lets it rest against the steel strike plate.

"Have you understood?"

"I believe I have."

"Aye, 'tis loaded now and deadly. You need only cock it, aim it and pull the trigger. Now do this other for yourself."

"This smaller one?"

"Aye. Use the larger as we have planned. But discharge this smaller one only at the end, if your enemy is upon you. Do not hope to strike him from across the room. You will have time for but one shot."

She loads the second pistol with care, then takes her place by the east window, both pistols in her lap. She looks out—all is dark.

Murdoch goes to the bottom of the ladder. "Mat?" he calls softly.

"Nothing. Nothing." It was the voice of his wife, calm now.

"Keep watch from the south window also. And light no candle."

He moves silently from window to window. Upstairs the children fall quiet. There is no sound except the steady pulse of the crickets.

Plumnell whimpers softly from the chair where he sits, head back, eyes closed.

"Mr. Plumnell?" Charlotte whispers.

He stirs. "A terrible bad spell," he says quietly but clearly.

"Never fear, Mr. Plumnell," she whispers again. "We shall all be well. Take heart."

They wait. The crickets stop.

Mat's small, urgent voice comes from the top of the ladder. "Papa! Abigail saw a light!"

"Where is it?"

"Abigail! Was it where you saw it before?"

A pause.

"Yes." Her voice trembles with fear. "But closer, by the broken oak."

"By the oak?" her father asks.

Then Charlotte sees the torch. It flares and she sees the naked arm of the man who holds it. Immediately it dims. She gets up, pistols in her hands, the hair erect on her neck.

"John! They are there! I have seen them!"

Murdoch steps to the door.

"Now then! Now!"

Charlotte rushes out the door behind him. As she does, Murdoch lifts his head back and emits a terrible bellow.

"Kill them!"

"Fire!" Charlotte cries out as harshly and deeply as she can.

Murdoch discharges his first musket. He knows where in the dark the broken oak stands. Immediately the other muskets begin to fire, not in a uniform volley but with a slow, steady rhythm—one, two, three, four and another, then again.

Charlotte steps forward and shouts again with all the force she can project. She raises the big pistol with two hands. Even as she does, a torch flares again and she hears a voice cry out from the woods, then another. She holds the weapon and looks along its top to the torch, which still flickers visibly. She fires and the force almost throws the pistol from her hands.

"Stay!" Murdoch shouts. "Stay."

Charlotte, too, can hear it—the sound of running in the dark woods, stumbling through the brush beyond the cleared area. Nearby, ahead and to her right, she hears Wishart's and Henderson's shouts. They are well advanced into the woods.

Murdoch goes back into his house to fetch three pitch torches. He holds one to the embers of the fire until it begins to burn. He lights the others from it and walks out the door.

"Papa?" Mat calls from the stair.

"Stay, Mat," his father says. He hands a torch to Charlotte and they walk through the clearing. She holds a pistol, Murdoch his musket. By the light of the torches, they see Doone, Malcolm, Rose, Wishart and Henderson. As they advance into the wood, they can see the faint glow of the torch where it lies in the brush. A fire has started in the leaves around it. The man who had held the torch lies beside it on his back. His bow is still slung on his shoulder. He wears a vest of buckskin that's soaked by the blood that pulses from the hole in his right breast where the ball had entered. They gather around him in silence. From the house, a procession advances with Janet at its front, a candle lantern in each hand.

Charlotte looks at the man on the ground as the others stamp out the fire around the torch. He is her own age, a year or two younger perhaps. His smooth complexion is daubed with paint, his strong arms circled with bracelets of beads.

"Is it a real Indian?" Mat asks.

"It is," his father says.

"Where are the others?"

"They're gone, Mat. They thought us too many, as indeed we might have been."

"We are fortunate that these were too poor to possess proper weapons," Alexander Henderson says. "It might have turned out differently, had it been otherwise."

"Aye," the others agree.

"Come, children," says Murdoch. "Return to the house with your mother."

Charlotte Blake sinks to her knees. She sees the boy's eyes are open just a little and glinting at her in the light of the torches. She touches his shoulder and her heart breaks.

"What's the matter with Mrs. Blake, Papa?"

No one speaks; Charlotte's weeping is the only sound.

"She has been brave, Mat, as have you all. Very brave. That is all. Come, Charlotte."

They walk all together back to the house and after much talk the children settle down and the men stop peering from the windows. Albert Plumnell avows he is much better, thank you, 'twas but a spell such as he was accustomed to. Doone and Rose keep watch and the others find places in beds or on the floor and let sleep claim them. Later John Murdoch and William Wishart go to the woods, then row to midstream and set the body to drift on the Miramichi.

In the morning, when Janet goes out to milk, she finds both cows and a calf on the straw on the stable floor. Their throats had been cut.

A WEEK LATER, the Davidson migration deepens the dread and melancholy. Murdoch and the older children continue to tend their field, Janet Murdoch continues to tend the house, Charlotte, home again at Blake Brook, tends her babies. William and his brother Alex bid Charlotte farewell and leave the river for Halifax as they said they would do. The sun rises. It sets again. But when the line of Davidson boats passes, with the tall *Miramichi* at the fore, the meaning is clear enough.

"Who am I," John Murdoch asks aloud from the bank of the river, "to keep a family here when a man as shrewd as Davidson takes all he owns and the thirty souls he supports and moves the lot of them to the Saint John River?"

"All his animals are killed," Janet Murdoch says.

"Aye. He's no farmer, so the loss is not so great, but warning enough, I warrant."

"Shall we go too, then?"

Three of their children look from the passing flotilla to their parents' faces and back again.

If William Davidson was no settler in the sense understood by men like Blake and Murdoch, if he had no taste for the plough and claimed the smell of manure disagreed with his digestion, the Davidson-Cort establishment at the forks was still the undoubted heart of the Miramichi. Davidson had arrived from Scotland first—and Cort had followed—to found a salmon fishery and they'd calmly taken receipt of one hundred thousand acres including the old fort built by the Frenchman Nicholas Denys. But by the time John Blake was beginning his house, Davidson and Cort were constructing their *Miramichi*, three hundred tonnes and the first seaworthy keel put on the river. It was loaded with salted salmon and furs that first season, but long straight pines for the masts of the British navy had made their fortune.

The *Miramichi* passes sombrely that day, The week that follows passes sombrely as well. There is no further news of attacks and no word from Blake.

She watches the river every day seeking a familiar sail, burdened by images that play on the back of her eyelids.

"It will be the Indians who will kill us, of course," John Murdoch had said the morning after the dreadful attack. "Indeed, it will. Their memories are not so short, Charlotte."

His words turn her mind to the sandy shelter, the icy water of the Baie de Chaleur, the blue of that winter sky. "We fought them and we killed them," Wioche had said. "My father, Amoq't, killed many in Chebucto and Canso. I, too, have killed."

From there her thoughts drift to Walker, and she fights to keep them and their burden of sadness at a distance. How curious that she should retain so little affection or remembrance for the settings of her childhood, but had come by degrees to think of Nepisiguit—a wilderness outpost, a place of commerce filled with frank uncouthness, a stretch of water, a little hill, an encampment of tribal people—as her home, her refuge.

—

A few cicadas speak from the trees behind the house. The crickets chirp cozily in the grass. Little John is awake and playing with his fingers. Charlotte stands her daily vigil on the shore.

"A sail!" Charlotte cries. "I see a sail! 'Tis Blake, I'll be bound!"

It isn't. An American privateer approaches flying the colours. "God help us, she'll soon be upon us."

She grabs the children, starts up the bank, telling them softly, "We shall fly to the woods until someone comes to help us."

The ship slackens sail. Now two boats depart the shore and row out toward her. One of those rowing is John Murdoch.

Captain Simon Harvey scowls as he listens to the report and can hardly credit what the two men are telling him. They're aboard the *Viper*, a sloop of war: three masts carrying ten six-pounders and two twelve-pound carronades. She is classed as a Sixth Rate and would shy quick enough from a bigger ship, but Harvey's battle here in Miramichi Bay is one of credibility.

"If what you are telling me is so, gentlemen, we are discussing one of the greatest crimes contemplated by savages in British North America."

John Blake looks steadily at the captain.

"There can be little doubt what they contemplate. They accepted readily enough that we were rebels and were eager enough to impart their plottings."

Harvey looks at Blake and then at Ross and weighs their story. This Blake seems sound enough and his reputation as a ship's captain and pilot on this river go before him. But Ross, despite his English name, speaks with a curious inflection, claims he captains "Le Vairon, out of Perce, Gaspé," how does he come to be here in Miramichi Bay?

"You say you blundered but three days ago into a meeting of a council of chiefs on Bartibog Island and, as you claim, they confided in you their intention to slaughter every man, woman and child in this Miramichi settlement?"

"No, captain." Blake looks at the three officers in turn. "They intend to massacre every settler in the whole of western Nova Scotia."

"Oh, sir," Ross interposes. "They were so ill-disposed, they would have slaughtered *us* and our crew had they not accepted without question our little flag."

Harvey snorts, recalling the flag he calls "the stripey thing," the patriot flag of the rebellious colonial union that Ross and Blake claim they flew to gain such access.

"I marvel that such a rag should have fooled even a savage."

"Your help is much needed, sir," Blake tells him. "The settlers of the Miramichi have only their own arms to protect them. Nothing more. They can expect no support from Halifax or His Majesty's government anywhere in this land."

Harvey shakes his head slowly.

"It's preposterous that these natives should conceive of such a project." Harvey rubs his eyes and forehead in contemplation. "I cannot disregard your damned intelligence, however you came by it. And in truth it confirms suspicions we gained from the rebel pirates we so recently captured. Tell me more of these beasts you encountered."

"They were chiefs," Blake says. "They'll have dispersed to their several camps and peoples in preparation for the attack. I have no doubt, captain, that they are encouraged in this by rebel elements such as those you took captive. The Mi'kmaq especially, with the loss of their French friends, spy new friends in the Americans."

Harvey growls again.

"Blast their eyes. There's nothing to support their assumptions. His Majesty's government—I meant the army—has attempted to deal fairly with the savages."

"The New World is an untidy place, sir," Blake says. "Much like the Old World."

They sit a long minute. No one speaks.

"Very well, gentlemen. This vessel that accompanies us is the American privateer *Lafayette*, christened so by the rebels for that jumped-up French fool who has crossed the ocean to join in their adventure. We took her captive in the Gulf of St. Lawrence and now I see she may serve a purpose we had not looked for. You are pilots, both with knowledge of the Miramichi."

"There is no one more familiar with these waters, sir, than John Blake," Ross says. "There's no shoal or snag he has not committed to memory."

"Hm." Harvey locks his fingers and presses his thumbs together. It would not do to squander this opportunity. "Very well. You shall go then. Lieutenant Randall and fifteen armed men here shall accompany you. The *Viper* shall lay here in the bay. I shall see the *Lafayette* reappear in five days time."

"Where are we to take the ship, sir?"

"Up the Miramichi, man, up the Miramichi to meet with your Indians and *not* to trade them *rum!*"

"It will be done, captain," John Blake says.

"You've practice already as rebels, have you not? Now you may play the part in earnest and full dress."

"It will be a pleasure, sir!" Daniel Ross beams.

Simon Harvey scowls.

"Did not these savages recognize you, Mr. Blake, living as you do up the river from Bartibog Island?"

"I saw none I knew, captain, so none knew me."

Simon Harvey relaxes his scowl and sniffs, "I hope so for your sake, Mr. Blake." He turns to his officer. "Mr. Randall, have the boy bring us brandy."

THE INDIANS' CREDULITY is surprising. They board the *Lafayette* without weapons when Blake drops anchor off their encampment on Bartibog Island. They seem at ease, even enthusiastic at the prospect of examining an American warship, albeit a minor one. There is a good deal of general babble on the deck, with sailors in studied and complaisant postures exchanging words and hand signs with a dozen braves. The rum had gone round for a second time when Blake hears Louis, a tall, handsome fellow of the Goneishe family, speak in English.

"This, good, strong ship," he says to the men around him. "Before now one year, we dance on this deck at Kouchibouguac. War dance and many many dance."

Other Indian men laugh and so do the two young tars talking with them.

"What?" Jim Rompole marvels. "You danced here on the *Lafayette,* did ya?"

"Yes, dance," avows Louis. He stamps his foot on the planking and smiles. "Here."

"Well, who mighta guessed?" says the sailor. He shoots a merry look in Blake's direction. "That musta been 'fore my time. Yes, yes, that was before I came on her."

"Many dance," Louis says. "Boston men too."

"Yes, yes. Plenty o' lads from Boston. That's our port, Boston. They were good dancers, I wager."

"Good drinking rum," another brave volunteers.

"Oh indeed!" Rompole cries. "Good then, was it, at Kouchi-where? Or good this time here?"

"Good," the young man says.

Blake surveys the crowded deck. So this is the explanation behind their ready acceptance. He chooses this moment to intervene.

"Will you and some others come with us then, Louis?" he asks. "We're going up the Miramichi to put the fear of God in these English."

Louis's smile vanishes. He looks at the other Mi'kmaq men.

"Very bad for Englishmen," he says.

"Precisely," Blake nods. "Louis, I invite you and your men to honour us by sharing a meal—some food—with us, then you go back and speak to your chiefs. Your chiefs, perhaps they'd meet and speak of war. Perhaps they'd join us up the Miramichi."

Daniel Ross appears on deck. Behind him, a lad carries a small keg.

"Don't go! Don't go!" he cries. "We've but just now opened another cask!"

"We must speak about the English, Daniel," Blake admonishes him. "Rum is for later."

"Rum and talk," says Louis Goneishe.

"Rum and talk, rum and talk," the men behind him laugh and chant.

"Rum and talk, rum and talk," join in the tars, their eyes sparkling with mischief.

"At Napan Bay tomorrow then," Blake tells Louis Goneishe. "When the sun is high."

—

AT FIRST LIGHT, Blake orders, "Weigh anchor. Furl the sails." The *Lafayette* flying its rebel flag heels a little and catches the incoming tide to the shoals. Blake tacks the ship around the submerged banks to the river. He stands at the helm. The leadsman chants quietly from the bow. "By the deep three," he calls. "Left full rudder." Then, "Back the topsail." Over the shoals they sail straight up the channel and a little beyond Napan Bay.

It's mid-morning when John Murdoch and John Malcolm slip off from a concealed shore in their own boat and come aboard. From the deck of the *Lafayette*, Peter Brown, Alexander Henderson and his five sons look on as the two men climb aboard.

John Blake comes forward from the wheel.

"John Blake." Murdoch extends his hand. "If any man might manage this, it would be you."

Blake hastens to his side. "I understand my wife and children to be well."

"They are, John."

From where they lie, Blake can see along the bank to where the brook cuts out of the river. But his cabin isn't visible, not even with the glass. He averts his eyes from it.

"I believed she was to take refuge with *your* family," Blake says, frowning.

"You've been acquainted with the troubles here, John, and know your wife to be welcome in our house. But Charlotte feared her crops would go to ruin. She chose to return home."

Blake looks one last time down the shore.

"That's Charlotte," he says and turns away. "Weigh anchor, Mr. Smith."

They drift back to midstream. Blake tacks the ship around. A good breeze comes down the Miramichi from the west and the water turns choppy. When the sun is overhead, they run before the wind into Napan Bay. Ahead, to left and right, the sun shoots out from under a slate-grey swath of western cloud and gilds the wooded shores of the bay. The smoke of the encampment is straight in front of them.

"THEY'RE PAINTED UP PROPER, are they not?"

Ross stands by Blake staring at the figures in the six canoes that are approaching.

"This is much as I expected," Blake says. "We must show as much spirit as do they. Gather our committee."

As the canoes draw alongside, Randall, the six Hendersons, John Murdoch and John Malcolm stand at the rail and lift their arms in one shout.

"Hurray! Hurray!"

Fifteen marines wait unseen in the cabins beneath the quarterdeck.

The rope ladders go over the side. Blake studies the faces of the men who climb them. The chiefs wear no visible expression under their war paint, nor weapons at their sides other than knives. When they are on deck—twenty-eight in all—the regular and irregular sailors of the *Lafayette* back off and the two groups stare unblinkingly at one another.

A dozen of the Indians are as young as Louis Goneishe, who has returned with them. It seems plausible to Blake that these are a bodyguard and the others leaders of the local tribes, or leaders accompanied by elders. Regardless of age, all twenty-eight men had painted their faces as though for battle, and even the older men's bodies are taut and strong-looking.

"A noble enemy," Murdoch whispers to his son-in-law.

Blake steps forward.

"Welcome, chiefs and men of the Miramichi Mi'kmaq. I am Captain Patrick Cross of the *Lafayette*. Our home port is Boston, the colony of Massachusetts. You join us as allies in this business with England."

From the front ranks of older men, a short, deep-chested individual steps forward.

"I am Jean Renew, chief of the Cedar People of the Lustagoocheehk." He gestures to a man whose features are a weathered version of the young brave Louis Goneishe. "Here is Jean Goneishe, chief of the Metepenagiag people. Here is Sylvain Jerome of Esgenoôpetitj. Here is Phillip Nocoute of Mtaoegenatgoigtog." Just the trace of amusement—not so much as a smile—crosses his features when he turns to a man who stands taller than the tallest Mi'kmaq and a head taller than any of the English. His face beneath his eyes is blacked with charcoal paint. "This is Pierre Martin." Renew announces, nodding slowly. His sombre countenance resumes. "We have come at your invitation."

"Thank you, chief," says Blake. "We wish to make council with you on behalf of the colonies of Massachusetts and Virginia."

Jean Renew says nothing.

"These English, Chief Renew, think us slaves who will labour only to increase their trade. But we Americans will brook it no longer. We must know if the Mi'kmaq of the Miramichi will oppose us now."

Jean Renew looks to his left and right at the chiefs nearest him.

"We will hear more," he says. "More of the English and you."

"This gives me great pleasure," says Blake. "We have prepared a feast below. We invite you to join us."

"Come in! Come in!" Daniel Ross raises his arm in welcome. "Welcome, friends!"

One by one, the chiefs and their retainers descend the ladder to the lower deck. The Henderson boys had set out a long table and laid planks across upended casks as benches. The guns of a naval ketch being on the main deck and there being no openings on the lower deck, the hatches are open to the sky. Light streams down on the joints of meat roasted the day before, a steaming kettle of fish stewed with potato and onion, the twenty loaves carried aboard by the Hendersons. An aroma familiar and inviting wafts up to greet the Mi'kmaq. Thirty rum mugs had been set out and the cask poised invitingly at the table's end. Lieutenant Randall and two sailors are already seated. Two marines lean on their muskets in casual conversation. The chiefs, who look uncertain, take places at the table and the braves stand behind. The settlers, with the exception of John Murdoch, remain on the main deck.

"Gentlemen, gentlemen!" Ross calls out. "You know among us Americans, no one can eat until all are seated. Come! Come! Let us now drink good rum and make good talk!"

There is a short exchange between Renew and the braves in their own language. After some hesitation, all are seated. That's the signal Blake is waiting for. Murdoch, who had stood by the aft ladder, moves to the main deck. Then a voice, a simple statement and Blake's heart turns to ice.

"You were on Bartibog Island."

Blake looks down the table to see who speaks. It is a middle-aged man who wears an elaborately beaded shirt and vest. He is looking directly at Ross, his eyes narrow. The other Mi'kmaq stop eating to look at this man, at Ross, then at Renew.

"Ah, Bartibog Island," Ross says. "What do *we* call that?"

"Yes. We saw you there," Blake interrupts. "Who are you, sir?"

"I am named Étienne Bamaly. You had a small boat then."

"That is so," Blake says. He avoids exchanging any glances with Ross. "But now we have a bigger boat."

"You are an Englishman at Perce," says an older Indian to Ross.

Jean Renew addresses the man sharply in his own language, the tone urgent. A palpable pulse of alarm passes around the table. Blake rises slowly from his chair.

As quick as a blink a dozen young Mi'kmaq are on their feet, their knives drawn. Joseph pulls his pistol from under his shirt. He waves it wildly and it discharges, filling the space with smoke and bringing every other man to his feet.

"Prepare to secure the hatches," Blake bellows.

A marine fires his musket from the third step. A young brave who had risen at the end of the table falls, and in the same moment Ross races to join Blake at the aft hatch. Johnson, the second marine, trapped among the natives, stumbles backward, his pistol in one hand. Two Indian youth fall on him and wrest it from his hand.

"Help me, sir!" Johnson cries. Blake draws two swords from behind the coiled rope where he had earlier secreted them. He turns to pass the second sword to the other captain, but the Indian who had seized the pistol fires it. Ross cries out, grasping at his right arm with his left, blood welling up through his fingers. Blake tries to reach him, but the giant Pierre Martin is almost upon him, a steel hunting blade in his enormous fist. The first slash of Blake's sword is short, though the end of the blade catches the man's arm below the shoulder and cuts to the bone. Martin seems not to feel the cut. He shouts in his own language and lunges forward. Blake holds the longer weapon, but he steps back involuntarily. Immediately behind him, as other men haul Ross to safety, the two marines reappear in the aft hatch and fire simultaneously. The hold, darker now with the forward hatch shut, fills with smoke. Martin seems to hesitate and Blake, still off-balance, strikes again, cutting the man deeply across the chest but missing the thrust that would have pierced the vitals below the ribs.

"Captain! Sir!" a marine calls from behind him.

A musket barrel drops down across his right shoulder and fires. Blake turns to follow the marine up the ladder. Two Henderson boys lift him bodily onto the deck. Joseph had gone before him. It is too late to save Johnson. He lies on the planks with a knife through his neck.

"Close the hatch!" Blake orders.

As the cover goes down, it bursts open again and a bloody Pierre Martin explodes from the hatch, another brave just behind him, a knife in one hand, a table fork in the other. A dozen marines instantly pull them down to the planks. Two seize Martin and struggle to clap irons on his huge arms. He is suddenly subdued, still, almost limp. The irons clatter. The marines turn on the other brave, overcome him and truss his hands and feet.

"Shut the damned hatch," Blake hollers again. Those trapped below begin to ram the hatch cover upward. Alex Henderson, his face a mask of desperate alarm, runs to stand upon it. The others do the same at both the fore and aft hatches.

Without warning Pierre Martin's arms shoot up and his hands close like bear traps on the necks of the men who hold the shackles and flails them to the deck. Other marines stab at him with their bayonets as he and his victims writhe and twist in a widening splatter of the giant's blood. Twenty men surround him, thrusting at him from the distance of a pace. The settlers beyond them have muskets at the ready. Martin struggles to his feet again.

"Shoot him!" Blake orders.

The men look at him in desperation. All have fixed their bayonets in the muzzles of their weapons.

"Stand back that we may shoot!" John Murdoch cries.

Several marines struggle to withdraw their bayonets, but in that moment, Martin grasps one of the blades in his bare hand and pulls it from its weapon. Before the owner can react, Martin tosses it, misses and buries the point in the main mast. Two others thrust their bayonets into the Indian's body. He falls lifeless to the deck.

Blake turns to Ross, who sits against the rail, John Malcolm at his side.

"Daniel, where are you shot?"

Before Ross can answer and when all eyes are elsewhere, the corpse of Martin springs to life. He shrieks and looks about wildly. Every man starts and steps back. Then, eyes still bright and bulging in his bloody face, he wheels to look down on the other brave, who lies on his back on the deck, bound and bleeding. Marines rush forward as Martin falls to his knees and fixes his hands around the neck of the captive man, who only has time to emit the first part of a scream. Martin loudly chants a rhythmic song rocking back and forth, his legs straddling his hapless comrade. The Irish marine Robert Beck drives his bayonet through Martin's back just behind his heart. The man's rage ends in a final spurt of blood.

"God save us," says Beck, still panting with his exertions. "He was the very devil himself."

The deck is crowded and noisy with men. Beneath their feet, the captured warriors rage like damned souls.

"Lay out the mainsail!" Blake calls. "Mr. Smith to the wheel, please."

He stops. The forward deck moves—not the movement of the sea, but another, less familiar movement. It moves again, lifting an inch. There could be no doubt that beneath him, a score of men or more are contriving in the darkness to raise the planking above them.

"John! Alex! Stand here with the boys!" He turns to his bo's'n. "Jack."

"Sir."

"Have the men drag both anchors here and bring all chain forward. The deck seems not so secure as it should be."

"Aye, sir!"

Blake goes back to where Ross remains at the rail. The wounded man looks up and attempts a smile.

"Mr. Malcolm here has stopped the bleeding, John. 'Tis nothing I cannot withstand."

Blake stoops and examines the arm as best he can without removing the bandage of cotton that binds the wound.

"The surgeon on the *Viper* will determine that, Dan. For now, we'll make you a proper place to lie."

The foredeck shakes again and the howls of the men trapped between the decks carries above the sound of water and wind.

"From the noise of it, you might think we'd caged a whole tribe below," John Murdoch calls, not without some awe in his voice. "Perhaps the savage is tamed on the Miramichi."

Blake looks past the bow. They are making near to eight knots. He could expect to rendezvous with the *Viper* before dark.

"Aye," he says. "We do appear to have caught his many heads in a single basket."

LE VAIRON SAILS the next day about noon for the upper banks of the Miramichi River. The *Viper* and the *Lafayette* sail for

Quebec. The captives are in due course transferred in irons to Halifax and imprisonment. Only six ever find their way back to the Miramichi. Louis Goneishe is not among them.

THE MORNING had been dense with fog and now it rolls sluggishly along the river throughout the limp, breezeless day, not troubling itself to lift entirely even when the nearly invisible sun is high at midday.

From the clearing comes the sharp crack of the axe as Charlotte cuts and stacks her firewood and the soft thwack as she splits the cedar kindling. From the house comes Elizabeth's cooing and chuckling as she sits by little John's cradle. Yet the day carries a sense of poignant, shrouded isolation and this, she thinks, is what unsettles her. She walks again and again to the water's edge and stares at the patches of fog. She had observed John Murdoch board an American gun ketch. Heard the sounds of muskets and men's voices raised on the river. Events are everywhere obscured.

'Tis the fog only, Charlotte thinks.

Within a week, the work of harvest and storage must get underway. She, like the squirrels, must begin the gathering, the drying, the burying. Each task she contemplates returns her thoughts to Blake and then to the melancholy fact of his absence. Blake would be a settler, he had said, not a sailor. I'm impatient perhaps, she thinks, but she cannot subdue quicksilver flashes of anger when she takes account of the dangers she faces with their children. Meanwhile he betook himself—where? The fat Plumnell had doubted the West Indies. Where then? Her heart sinks again to think of what might have befallen him and she scolds herself silently for the petty reproaches she administers him in her imagination. For if he remains a stranger in some respects—a man both swift and clumsy, eloquent and mute, strong and weak, open and closed—and if his unfounded starts and fears that she might turn her attention elsewhere had caused them both needless misery—she had witnessed John Blake strive to make of himself a proper husband and provider. He had cut wood and fished fish and hoed the ground for her plantings. He'd sat awake all night in May when the bears had come. And when he'd departed three weeks ago, he'd held her as she'd always hoped he would—as a man should hold a woman—tenderly but strongly—and promised he would hurry back to her. He is her husband and she has given him something more—or perhaps something other—than her heart: she has given him her life's devotion.

And these are in large part the very thoughts she has as she stands by the river in the waning afternoon. A soft breeze springs up and blows the rest of the fog down the river. She sees the far bank of the Miramichi and then a flight of geese and then a big fish leaps. Then a sail appears to the east in midstream and John Blake comes home.

HE ROWS TO SHORE in a small boat alone. *Le Vairon* sets its sails and tacks across the river in the direction of the Henderson homestead. She watches him from a distance. And is suddenly furious. He shoulders his pack and walks to where she waits. She's so angry now she can hardly spit the words from her mouth. "The *Vairon* . . . you've come on the *Vairon* . . . were the winds so fortunate, John, that you could sail to the West Indies on the small *Vairon* and return in but three weeks?"

"No," he says. "I was never bound for the West Indies. I've had business in these waters."

"And am I, your wife, not to have knowledge of your whereabouts these many weeks?" She picks up both speed and voice now with her diatribe.

"Am I to cut your wood, tend your hearth, raise your children while you . . . sail about these waters with your friends on the *Vairon* . . . which belongs in the Gaspé . . . on the Baie de Chaleur. Is that where you've been, John Blake?"

He's flabbergasted. "Charlotte, come here to me. I have much to tell you. There's been a bloody battle with the savages."

She stands before him, her fists still pummelling her thighs, the heels of her boots still stomping the ground around them when he begins to tell her the story. He hadn't known whether the battle would take place so near their lot or even if it would happen this soon. But yes, he says he's been piloting ships these many weeks but as a lookout for the British navy more than as a river merchant. And yes, there has been a mighty confrontation with the Indians; one that was planned these last weeks since the series of attacks on the settlers around them.

It's Charlotte's turn to be surprised. And although she knows full well it would be better to hold her tongue, she blurts out her first concern. "The People from the Baie, were they involved in this fracas?"

"Why wouldn't they be?" he says sharply and turns toward the cabin, asking, "The children, are they well?"

Around the hearth that night she tries to explain her turmoil to her husband. "It is clear that your bravery saved many lives on these banks, John Blake, but I must share with you my utter perplexity about the actions you describe versus the people I lived with at the Baie. They are not warmongering people. They have been invaded themselves by those who came to these shores from away. They are a gentle folk; they treat their children with limitless tenderness and their elders with utmost respect. Even their method of nourishment is a testament to their values. They share what they have—even with a stranger like me. They give thanks to Mother Earth for everything from the fish in the sea to the rain from the sky. How can these people you call savages be the same ones who sheltered me with such goodness?"

He has nothing to say, but there are other unspoken facts for each of them to consider that night. Their cabin has not been attacked as others had been. Charlotte's laundry blows in the breeze untouched while the Murdoch's goods are stolen, burned or torn to shreds.

It's Charlotte who finally breaks the silence between them.

"So you've been busy at war, John Blake."

"I've wanted only to defend us."

"Ah. And are we defended?"

"By God's grace, we may be the better for it."

"The rebels are gone?"

"No. Far from that. But their Indian friends are quieted."

"Have you killed some Indians then, John?"

"*I* have killed none, though they might have killed me—and our children too."

She sits still a long while.

"*I* may have killed an Indian," she finally says. "Though his death has broken my heart, however it came to be."

He walks to where she sits and puts his hands on her shoulders.

"I've heard all," he says.

In those few words he somehow contrives to convey the depth of his devotion and the extent of his pride that he should be the husband of Charlotte Blake. And for her part, Charlotte takes the cue and says, "Come to bed, John Blake."

CHAPTER 8

The Miramichi

1781

*C*harlotte is moved by the powerful beat of her life here on the river. She sits on the bank one afternoon while taking a break from her endless chores and notices sandpipers hopping along the shore, jittery little creatures that move as one when they take flight. She watches them soar over the river, their speckled bodies contrasting with the leaves that reflect in the water below and thinks this ever-changing river has become the rhythm of her life. Its morning mist rising like droplets, the sun's rays turning them into sparkles like fairies playing in the haze. The dunes on the shore are forged and carved by the rising and falling tide. The river rolls and heaves, slips by her land, its waves winking in transit in summer, then freezing into a byway for laughing children snuggled in sleighs. It threatens and warns and sucks unsuspecting souls to its depths. It gives forth food and brings the far-flung world to its exiled shores. This Miramichi has seasons of stillness and vigour, of calm and commotion. It is enduring, suffering, timeless and sustaining.

She thinks back over the four years that have passed since she came here and how the seasons have shaped her.

When spring thawed the Miramichi, the fiddleheads would poke up along the banks of the creek and a new generation of blackflies would come out to torment the hapless harvesters eager for the first fruits of the year. The red-tailed hawks mated and made their nests in the pines and their chicks ate the mice that abandoned the settlers' houses for the greater bounty of the fields and pastures. The bears woke up hungry and shambled to the river's edge to gorge on salmon and stretched out on the grassy banks in the sun and watched their cubs like wardens. In the barns the cows' ribs showed through their hides and their hollow eyes watched until the settlers led them at last to the pastures that sprouted shoots of sustenance.

In the spring of 1778, George Walker died and was buried in the Church of All Hollows, Barking-by-the-Tower. The news wound out from London via Liverpool, Nova Scotia, and on the distant Miramichi there was a woman who wept bitterly to receive it. After his return to England, Walker had always intended to look up General Taylor and plead reconciliation with his daughter but had never found the opportunity. His labours at Nepisiguit had gone largely unnoticed by the administrators in Halifax, and unrewarded by their loftier superiors in Whitehall. But like the proper pirate he was, he eluded his foes or took broadsides without sinking or found a treasure when all was lost and in the end succumbed to apoplexy and sailed off in his own bed.

That same spring, on a particularly soft evening, when John Blake was fishing off the bank, Charlotte had heard the sound of a whippoorwill in the woods above the cabin, and she had responded with her own best whippoorwill call and believed she heard the bird call back. But whippoorwills will do that, she thought.

WHEN SUMMER CAME to the Miramichi, it would bring a rush of growth that was the botanical equivalent of insanity. The stern geometry of trunks and twigs, the curve of hillsides and the sharp edges of riverbanks were swept to bedlam by a mad surge of rebirth. Charlotte would hoe around the hills of André Landry's potatoes, the offspring of the seedlings he had shyly passed to her as she said goodbye to the People that June day in 1776 and passed a last time down the trail to George Walker's now vanished house. She would undertake to hoe as early in the morning as she could, but a woman with two children—one still nursing—could count on interruptions. When the sun had passed the meridian, she would still be in the patch, her clothes soaked with sweat, the deer flies gathered from miles around to buzz her head and whir in her masses of tangled hair. They were good potatoes, as André had assured her they would be, and would have been better if he and his hoe could only have followed them.

In the summer of 1778, Charlotte Blake gave birth to a child she called Mary Ann, whose hair was a blaze of red like her mother's and soon grew to frame blue eyes that were born looking into the distance and were still looking there well into the following century.

That summer, too, Blake built another room on the cabin. Young Peter and George Henderson came across the river to saw lumber and help raise the beam. When they were finished, it was a pretty snug little addition, perhaps more solidly made than the house itself, and would provide a bedroom for the children as they grew.

In the summers, American privateers resumed their customary raiding along the coast. The river traffic brought news of every pillaging and burning, actual or feared. Many families were fled now, following Davidson and Cort, who had gone first, having the most to lose. But Alexander and William Wishart had returned to resume fishing. In the summer of 1779, Mi'kmaq from far upriver, not so easily cowed as had been thought, burned the Wisharts out. The brothers boarded the *Viper* for Quebec, where they were to take commissions under General Haldimand.

Late that same summer, the frantic ringing of a Henderson bell brought the Blakes to the shore at midnight. There were flames across the river at their farm. Blake gathered his weapons and set out by boat. By moonlight, Charlotte could see the boats of the Murdochs crossing too. But the Hendersons, as it transpired, were too many and too alert to lose all and Blake was back before dawn.

"These were no privateers," he said.

AUTUMNS ON THE MIRAMICHI had the poignancy of autumns in all the northerly colonies: bursting with a riot of colour, the fields a bountiful gift of harvest, the time before freeze-up ticking loudly like a warning. Charlotte often thought of the burnished seduction of late fall as a whispering lover who proposed a few more hours together before he was gone forever.

She stooked the dry hay in the field and carried it to the mound and stood with her husband when they were finished to assess whether it should keep a cow alive until Christmas. Inside the house, two casks of John Blake's spruce beer sat bubbling in the larder and the shelves above them were heavy with tea and molasses and sugar loaves and flour and whale oil. Janet

Murdoch had learned cheese making at St. John Island and she in turn taught Charlotte. A dozen hard cheeses joined the other provisions.

When the hay was in and the wood was cut in the autumn of 1779, John Blake made a last venture with Daniel Ross to Liverpool on the sea coast southwest of Halifax. The hull of *Le Vairon* was filled with the best oak and here was a last bounty for the year and, provided they did not cross paths with privateers, a chance to buy better tools.

Wioche had appeared at dusk one day as though he had materialized from the earth. Charlotte had run to where he stood at the forest edge, had taken his two hands in hers but had not invited him into the cabin. Behind the cover of tall timbers, they had shared the events of their lives. She fingered the fresh braid of sweetgrass he had given her while he explained that the raids and attacks had been planned by the American privateers to rid the river of the settlers so they could claim the land for themselves. His people helped because they, too, had been attacked by the British and it was the wish of the grand council to even the score.

"There are many changes for the People," he'd said. "The British are taking our land." The moon was high over the river when he rose to leave and reminded her to watch for the signs— "the rabbit skin is thick, the air sacs on the fish are long, winter will be hard"—and then he'd added, "You won't be alone."

SHE'D WATCHED the seaward stretch of the river anxiously in the days that followed. Then on the second of October, the little ketch had appeared, its boat in tow. And John Blake paddled triumphantly to shore with a nanny goat in the cargo. "We shall have milk even if we lose the cow," he'd told her.

Winters on the Miramichi made a dignified arrival when the land had given up its growth and lay still to await its fate. The air would seem suspended, motionless, as quiet as a settler family at grace until, as the Mi'kmaq tale allowed, Summer fulfilled her end of the bargain and the first skiffs of snow settled on the fields under grey skies. Blake Brook was always first to freeze, then the salty waters of the river took refuge under a thin sheet of ice that thickened every night. Finally, usually in December but some years much earlier, the snows would come and cover the land and everything on it.

Winter was a respite from hard labour and an invitation to gather in houses, sample one another's beer and talk by the warmth of the fire. In the winter of 1779, such talk turned to the rebel war to the south, to the raids now suspended on account of weather, and of course to the Indians. One Dougal Shank, whose claim was that he had been a preacher in Scotland, had constructed a rough shelter on the north bank of the river not far upstream of the Hendersons. He was a humourless man, not easy to warm to, who neither traded nor farmed. His high, beetling brow and thin line of a mouth lent credence to the strictness of his religious beliefs.

"The Indian will come again," he said. "Like the pharaohs of Egypt, we have earned the plague he brings. The Indian is God's instrument."

"The instrument of the rebels, more like," interjected Peter Brown, who lived upstream on the south shore.

"It is not for me to say," Shank intoned, "who deals with God and who with the devil."

Blake turned a black glare on the man.

"It's not for you to say anything, sir, until you have lived among us a season more."

John Murdoch hastily cleared his throat.

"I'm disposed to think the Americans will soon carry the day," he said. At this, many present who might have spoken out in indignation two years before now grunted assent. They knew the frail status of their own holdings and the weak links that connected the banks of the Miramichi with their rulers in Halifax.

Winter offered time to ruminate on the season to follow, on plans to assure that the coming year's crop would diminish the last by comparison. The greatest and most important crop of all was the forest itself. It had to be cleared to make way for the plough, and the trees that the clearing produced meant cash for tools and livestock. In the end, though, the winter provided more opportunity for thought than any settler reasonably required. What would begin as a respite from toil would become a prison in which men and women could only wait in patience for reprieve.

THAT'S WHAT SHE'S THINKING about this brilliant sunny day sitting by the river watching the sand pipers. She's hoping as she does every year at this time that their lives will be less tumultuous in the year to come. It is not to be.

"There's an ox gone," John Murdoch tells John Blake. "And a calf last week."

"You know well enough the import of that," Blake says.

Their wives listen in silence. The two families had gathered as they often had at the Murdochs' house, since it was the nearest house to the Blakes' and the largest dwelling on the banks. They could all recall too clearly the events of 1777, then the animals and bedding stolen in 1779. Now a calf gone and—a more serious loss—an ox.

"Had we a governor of our own in this land," John Blake says, "and not some indifferent fool in Halifax, we might seek some protection. But we have none. Better we attack their leaders, as we did but three years ago, than discover ourselves murdered in our beds."

"I think it wicked that these rebels should employ the native people in this fashion and make them the objects of our revenge," Charlotte says.

"Perhaps." Her husband's brow is creased in deep furrows. "But the wickedness of rebels will be no excuse for our neglect of ourselves."

"Aye, John," Murdoch says. He had been among the loudest in the opinion that the worst had passed and the best course of action—apart from the most pressing self-defence—remained no action at all. Now he seems doubtful. "Let us meet together, every settler on the banks, and agree how we shall best proceed."

"Don't parlay too long," Blake mutters.

"Help!"

At first, the word was hardly distinct from the call of the seabirds that swooped down the river from the bay. Charlotte looks up from the woodpile to the darkening woods above the clearing. The rain had diminished. Being July, there is still an hour of daylight in the sky.

"Help!" The cry again, now more distinct. Mary Malcolm's voice. The girl breaks from the woods and runs stumbling in her soaking skirts toward Charlotte. "Mrs. Blake! Help us! Come all! Come all and help us!"

"Oh goodness, Mary. Is it another cow?"

"They've taken all, Mrs. Blake. All! And set our barn and house afire!"

"God be merciful. Stay here, Mary." She looks up to the woods to her right and sees her husband coming down, axe in hand.

"John! The Murdochs are attacked and their house on fire!"

Blake says not a word; he takes two buckets from the cabin and pushes off in the canoe as the quickest means to Murdoch's Point. He rounds the curve to find the house engulfed in smoke but no visible flames. The family is running a water brigade from the shore in basins and buckets.

"The back! The back!" Janet calls. "John's on the roof!" Several of her younger children are weeping helplessly as they struggle to pass the pails.

At the back of the house Malcolm is receiving and passing buckets to Murdoch, who stands on the remaining portion of the roof tipping water on the steaming timbers. The roof that covered the west half of the house is entirely gone. Part of the west wall appears to have been knocked out by force. The fire has made its way into the upstairs rooms.

Within ten minutes of Blake's arrival, it is clear that the family's shelter is saved. Thirty minutes later, only steam arises from the charred portions.

The attackers had struck when Murdoch and his son-in-law were on the water. They had chased the women from the house and carried off much of value before setting the roof ablaze. Murdoch had been within earshot and swiftly organized the defence. But it had been his decision to enter the burning structure with John Malcolm and together knock down portions of the walls and roof that had saved the rest.

He stands blackened and red-eyed beside Blake on the roof as they douse the last hot spots.

"Thank you, John. I have no other words."

"You need not thank me. Your own quick-wittedness has saved you."

"I regret most that they've stolen our muskets."

Blake nods slowly.

"A loss indeed."

He looks out toward the nearby encampment.

"No, John," Murdoch says. "It was never this tribe beside us. They are mischief-makers, but they were not among our attackers. I must doubt that these were Indians at all."

Blake grunts.

"Who then?"

"I canna tell. I canna tell."

There's nothing to do now but rebuild, the third time since their arrival here.

CHARLOTTE IS AT HER WITS' END. "You'll have to stay back from your voyage to the West Indies, John Blake. I cannot manage the children and the robbers on my own." She felt they needed help to mind the place and the children, not to mention the daily chores that if left undone would see them starve.

He was scheduled to sail in early September, a last run to the islands with a fine cargo of lumber for a fair price. Charlotte suspects his "run" down the coast has more to do with battleships and having a share in the rebellion than trade with the islands but decides the ruse he creates must be for good reason.

Not a man to miss an opportunity or to suffer the wrath of Charlotte, he turns up one day after sailing to Liverpool with a stranger on board. Blake lowers the ladder to the dory and the first one down is a boy. She cannot imagine what her husband is doing with this small creature and as they pole the dory to the shore, she looks again, focuses on the face coming toward her and wonders if maybe she is hallucinating in the late summer heat. There for all the world is young Tommy, the hapless boy whose body had been thrown overboard when he died on the ship that brought her to Jamaica. She is transfixed to this illusion when they come ashore. As triumphantly as you please, John says, "This is Jimmy, a fine lad for helping us." Then he turns to the pale-faced, skinny boy and says, "And this is Mrs. Blake."

Jimmy loses no time in making her acquaintance. He's a bold, wiry scalawag, who nods at "Missus," as he calls her while making a face at Elizabeth and poking young John in the belly. Charlotte is about to correct his behaviour when the toddlers begin to laugh at the antics of this strange half-grown man standing by their papa. "And what is it you'll do for me?" Charlotte inquires.

He is as old as thirteen and as small as nine. He had run from a London orphanage and stowed away on a ship at Wapping. He had scarcely any notion of North America never mind the Miramichi, but he knew a better world when he saw one.

Blake saw the rambunctious young refugee as a salvation of sorts when he found him on Simeon Perkins's wharf. So he offered him a home in exchange for helping his wife with the chores.

"You'll need to get into the brook and clean the filth from yourself," Charlotte demands, wondering what she can find to cover him while she scrubs the putridity from his clothes. Later, Blake teaches him how to stoke the fire and keep the embers burning for cooking while Charlotte tells him to fetch legumes from the garden and fill the water bucket for drinking at suppertime. While he darts nimbly from one chore to the next, he's entertaining the children, hiding and pouncing, pulling faces and teasing. They are delighted with his antics. He calls the baby Polly.

"Her name is Mary Ann," Charlotte says, thinking he misheard the child's name. But Jimmy ignores her.

She's wondering where she'll put him to sleep when struck with the notion that the goat and Jimmy may serve each other and the family as well. "A wigwam would be the answer," she thinks, but knowing Blake would be near to apoplexy at the very thought of such a contraption on his land, she puts her mind to fashioning a tilt that could stable a boy and a goat through winter.

Once Blake is on his way, she puts the plan to work. Poles, spruce boughs, logs and animal skins are the ingredients she needs. Jimmy is sent with an axe to fetch the poles, boughs and logs while Charlotte rummages through the parcels she carried from the Baie for the moose hide Blake had told her not to use in the cabin. It's as stiff as bark but serviceable with a good greasing of bear liver, she thinks. Finding the liver of a bear is the baffling portion of the equation—"Wioche could solve this problem"—instead she picks up the musket and takes down a fat grouse in the bush behind the cabin. She slaughters the animal and uses its liver and sinew to rub the rigid mooseskin until it's reasonably soft and pliable if somewhat bloodied and stinking. When all is ready they begin the task of hobbling the tilt together—low and small to keep the heat, she figures, while they angle the poles, slather the logs together with spruce gum, tie them with tough spindly roots and hope for the best.

When she decides the outer walls are about as good as they'll be, she fastens the moose hide to the inside walls and digs a firepit in the floor under the hole in the roof where the smoke can escape. By the time Blake returns, the tilt is ready. "It's the most primitive shelter on the Miramichi," he declares.

"There's talk of splitting the province into two parts," he tells her. "Of having our own governor."

"That may be the talk in Liverpool, John Blake, but it's another addition we'll be needing for this crowded cabin. You'll be a father again come spring."

The winter is harsh. All three children get sick. Influenza has been raging along the river, and inside the cramped tilt where the Blakes live they pass it one to the other. Charlotte nurses them with the potions John has carried up the river from Liverpool but mostly with bathing their feverish brows, keeping them warm and filling them with the blessed goat's milk that Jimmy brings with him in the morning.

This pregnancy is unlike the others. She's uncomfortable a lot of the time, her back aches, her belly takes a shape different to the other times she was with child. Charlotte's sixth sense taps away in the back of her mind like the metronome on the piano in the parlour at home. She shares her apprehension with Janet Murdoch.

"These are fearsome signs," Janet says.

"What ever do you mean by that?" Charlotte asks.

"The child may be upside down, hips first instead of head first. There's not a thing you can do about it but pray that the child will make its way to the world alive without killing you in the process."

She agrees to stay with Charlotte once the labour begins and sends John and the children to Murdoch Point, suspecting the delivery will be an agony for the eyes and ears of little ones. Jimmy insists that he stay with the women.

Her water had broken in the afternoon, two weeks before she thought it should and the contractions began immediately. By the time Janet arrives and the family departs, she feels her insides are being wrung out. She labours in such pain she tells Janet the cabin looks red. By midnight she's baying like a wounded animal. Janet is helpless save the hot linens and sympathy she offers.

"Rum, get rum," Charlotte begs when by morning she is still arched with pains that rip up her back and pummel her groin. Janet is somewhat taken aback by the request, but Jimmy is out the door and down the path to John Blake's still as though the devil himself is chasing him. He comes back with a jug of dark rum and spoons it over Charlotte's parched lips hoping some of it will slide down her throat. She feels she's being mauled when at last Janet sees a foot push its way out of the birth canal. She reaches in and grabs another slippery foot and pulls as hard as she can knowing there isn't much time now or the baby will be born dead.

"Push, Charlotte, push with all your might," she encourages while trying to turn the hips that are now presenting so the baby might slide the rest of the way through.

Charlotte is bleeding profusely, the torn flesh around the birth canal confusing Janet, who's only seen a breached birth once before. "A dead mother and a breathing infant will be no end of trouble," she tells Jimmy, who perches like an owl beside "Missus" waiting to be told what to do next.

Robert Blake is deathly still and as blue as the river when he finally makes it into the world. Janet sucks the mucus from his tiny mouth, rubs his scrawny body with her two hands and to her great relief sees him turn pink and begin to bawl. She pours an entire bucket of cold water from the brook over Charlotte's wounds while Jimmy swaddles the baby and hands him to his mother.

"You little scrapper," she says to her infant, "I'll have to teach you to lead with your head and leave your feet to come along behind."

Janet is flabbergasted. "The woman was near death just minutes ago," she tells Jimmy, "so was this child and there she is telling him what's good for him. Maybe it's the rum."

Jimmy is at Charlotte's side with his own message. "Missus, ye called me Tommy all the night. Am no Tommy, am yer boy, Jimmy." Janet tells Blake later that she thinks Charlotte is the most resilient woman she has ever known. Only a day later, she's on her feet marking his birth—1781—Robert—on the wall and taking the tally of three children in one room, a baby's cradle by her side and a boy and a goat in the tilt outside.

PEACE COMES to the river that summer by way of warring men. British soldiers who call themselves Loyalists are in retreat from the rebelling colonies in the south and settling by their dozens here on the Miramichi. The Wisharts return from the Quebec campaign and try to throw a squatter off their land but wind up living under the same roof. Even William Davidson comes back, claiming, "The river is in my blood."

"It's the prosperity that brings them," Charlotte tells her husband while they haul wood from the lot they are clearing on the south side of the Blake property.

"It's the prosperity that will start a new war," he grumbles.

Indeed their ploughs sew the seeds of a bitter hostility. This one between the old settlers and the men calling themselves Loyalists.

"That Philip Hierlihy struts about the river as though he is general of the new Loyalist army," she says.

"He's a most disgruntled man as many of the Loyalists are," Blake says. "He tells all who will listen that after such long devoted service to the King they are not awarded with tracts of land any better than we old settlers on the river."

The talk about separating Nova Scotia into two provinces picks up now. While the war to the south is not entirely finished, for the Miramichi it might as well be. They haven't seen a rebel in more than a year and the Indians have left them in peace as well. So the men have time now to plot their future—as men do, Charlotte decides.

In the meantime, Charlotte does some investigating of her own. She wants to visit the Indian camp on the other side of Murdoch's place. It draws her like a current to its hilltop clearing. Leaving the children with Jimmy one day, she wraps the braid of sweetgrass around her neck and hikes along the trail that leads to the camp. When it comes into view, she hesitates, wondering if she should have come at all. Is it nostalgia for the camp she left at the Baie that draws her here or is it to seek information about Wioche? She's still pondering her purpose when several women walk out to meet her and welcome her to the camp. They seem to know her name. Over tea and bannock they share stories about life on the river in a smattering of French and English. She tells them about her attempt to grease a moose hide without a bear's liver for the job. They share their hardships as well, but mostly they speak of the dreadful sicknesses they are suffering—measles, smallpox, white man's sicknesses. Charlotte expects that they have no immunity for the diseases and when they ask if she can help she replies, "Of course." By now she has gathered more "white man's" medicine from the supply ships, although she's not convinced their efficacy is superior to the roots and leaves she mashed and boiled at the Baie.

When she leaves the camp after promising to return with medicine, she takes a troubling tableau with her. The poverty in the camp is beyond the burden of the pioneers. The shortages, the disarray, the despair are a long way from the spiritual, highly organized camp she remembers on the Baie. The wigwams are worn out, so are the people who inhabit them. These once proud people are being beaten into retreat by the settlers who claim more and more lots of the land the Mi'kmaq once roamed freely and by the British authorities who dismiss their complaints as well as their needs. There are as many tilts as traditional wigwams at the camp, and there's refuse scattered about the grounds. Mother Earth seems to have taken a back row to the stolen pickings of war, Charlotte thinks. It's only been six years since she paddled away from the Baie—was her impression of Chief Julian's camp distorted by her own anguish when she arrived there?

She's still weaving her thoughts together on her way back to Blake Brook when she reaches Murdoch Point and decides to stop and share her concerns with Janet. No one on this river has suffered more at the hands of the Indians than Janet Murdoch, but she had said some months ago that she knew of the sickness in the camp and wanted to help.

Two days later, the two women and their assortment of apothecary jars go to the camp. Coincidentally, a woman is having a difficult labour when they arrive and when asked to help, the women look in on her and realize when they see a tiny foot at the opening of the birth canal that her baby is breech. "Upside down," Charlotte says knowingly to the woman who pulled Robert feet first into the world. Fortunately they are able to help. The baby is born. The mother survives. And Charlotte and Janet are seen as saviours, not a title they sought in coming here. Later they distribute the salves and concoctions from their jars while sipping tea made from dried berries. Wioche's name is never mentioned, but Charlotte is aware that they know about him and wonders how much they know about her.

The river news is ripe with excitement. Every ship that docks brings edicts from the King's Court in London. In early August, a paper dated 18th Day of June arrives and announces that the province is being divided.

> His Majesty having taken the same into His Royal Considera-
> tion has thought it proper that the Province of Nova Scotia
> should be divided into two parts, by drawing the line of sepa-
> ration from the Mouth of the Musquat River to it's [sic] source,
> and from thence across the Isthmus into the nearest part of
> the Bay Verte, and that the Tract of Country bounded by the
> Gulph of St. Lawrence on the East, the Province of Quebec on
> the North; the Territories of the United States on the West,
> and the Bay of Fundy on the South; should be erected into a
> Government under the Name of New Brunswick with a Civil
> Establishment suitable to it's [sic] Extent.

Another dispatch announces that Thomas Carleton is to be the governor.

Western Nova Scotia becomes New Brunswick on June 18 but it's November before Thomas Carleton arrives and takes his office as Governor at Parr Town on the Saint John River, a three-day canoe paddle from the Miramichi.

While others celebrate, Charlotte is consumed by two concerns. First, the licenses of land granted by the governor of Nova Scotia in 1777 need to be secured in the new colony. Second, the notice describing the election to be held the following year includes a voting procedure that restricts the vote to white men over the age of twenty-one who have lived in the colony for a minimum of three months and are willing to take an oath of allegiance to the British Crown. Charlotte is furious.

She'd raised her hand, or not, in decisions taken along the river to mark off the lots, to share the marshland among the settlers, for example, and presumed she'd have the right to vote on provincial issues as well.

"According to this announcement, women cannot vote for this land they have settled beside the men," she rails to her husband when he returns to the cabin.

"You'll want to be governor next," he says, then goes about the job of adding yet another addition to the cabin before winter drives them all indoors again.

It's near to freeze-up when she opens the cabin door one morning and finds a huge bearskin left on the path by the brook. Beside it, a vessel containing the bear's liver. She looks along the bank toward the Indian camp, recalls the story she shared about greasing a moose hide with the liver of a grouse because she didn't have a bear's liver for the job and thinks perhaps her angst about the pride and dignity of the Indians is unwarranted.

The snow comes early and as far as the settlers on the river can see, it's neverending. The sun seems to have left with the geese. The drifts mound up over the cabins, blanket even the tall timbers and leave an immense panorama of white interrupted only by columns of smoke curling skyward as if begging relief.

The Blakes are confined to their cramped, claustrophobic household. Charlotte uses the time to assemble the children around the hearth and teaches the older ones their letters and numbers while Jimmy entertains Robert. John, ever the provider, can hardly push the door through the heaps of snow that pile against it by night and fill in the path as fast as he digs his way to the river each day. Between them they fetch water, retrieve food buried in the pit and replenish the firewood a dozen times a day.

"We make a good team, John Blake," Charlotte tells him one evening while the family huddles around the hearth listening to his yarns, the tapping of her knitting needles and the crackling of the fire providing the acoustics to the lilt of the storyteller.

She has already marked the New Year on the wall when he first complains of a pain in his mouth. A toothache, they presume, common enough among the settlers. Within a few days the pain is intense, travelling from his upper jaw to his ear, eye, throat and pounding into the top of his head. His face is swollen, a boil on the gum beside the offending tooth is leaking pus and blood into his mouth and he is flush with fever.

They both know the tooth has got to be removed. He's not the first to have to resort to mutilating his mouth to find pain relief so after dousing himself with rum, he takes a sharpened stick and amidst howls of pain tries to dig the throbbing structure from his jaw. It doesn't budge. The children stay with Jimmy in the outer room while their Papa whacks a pointed rock into the tooth, breaking pieces away but failing to dislodge the root. Frantic with pain, he picks up a long sliver of whale bone and stabs it into the abscess and with an almighty wrench dislodges the tooth and the festering tissue it's attached to. His mouth is a mass of blood, septic fluids and ragged tissue.

She eases him onto the bed and swabs his face and mouth with cold water, hoping the fearsome pain will subside and sits by his side until he mercifully succumbs to sleep. But the night brings more fever. By morning he's vomiting blood and drooling thick green mucus, while pushing his fist into his cheek to deaden the pain in the palpitating wound.

Charlotte packs his cheek with snow; rubs ice over his brow. By midday he's delirious, muttering warnings about Indians and privateers, calling for Charlotte who's been by his side for more than twelve hours, only leaving to fetch concoctions of medicines she'd put on the fire the night before. She tries every medicinal trick she knows from boiling wintergreen leaves into tea to spooning foul-tasting elixirs into his mouth.

With each passing hour he worsens. Angry red streaks track down his neck. Watery blisters glisten on his skin. She wonders if he has the pox or has poisoned his own blood with the hacking and stabbing at the wound. He loses consciousness. Her efforts to save him are to no avail. Captain John Blake dies in the back room of the home he built on the Miramichi just before nightfall on that dreadful January day.

CHAPTER 9

The Southwest Miramichi

1785

Charlotte sits beside the still body of her husband, staring at the wall where she's marked the birthdates of her children. Dark thoughts whir like hornets. Is she cursed? A dead lover, a dead husband, and she is only thirty years old. Elizabeth is nine, John is almost eight, Polly is five and Robert three. And there's Jimmy, of course, who has kept the four little ones occupied through her vigil. She looks at her husband's ashen face—no serenity there, just the marks of his pain-filled last hours—and thinks, What am I to do with you? Then, What am I to do without you?

Finally she reaches to pick a blanket off the floor where it had fallen and gently covers him, then opens the bedroom door. Jimmy is there in a flash, the other children crowding behind him. Elizabeth hugs her as Charlotte crouches to the littler ones, John's children. In her distress, she is blunter than she means to be.

"Your father has died." Saying it out loud brings tears to her eyes, and for a moment she fears she will break down. If that happens, she doesn't know what she will do. "Let's not give in to our sadness just now. We must do something for your father first. Before night falls, we have to find a place to keep him safe until we can take him to be properly buried come spring."

Five sets of eyes look back at her solemnly.

Then Jimmy says, "Ma'am, the snow is deep out back by the tilt. Maybe we could dig into the snowbank and keep him there, safe from . . ." He doesn't want to mention the creatures they need to keep John Blake's mortal remains safe from. Charlotte manages to nod at his delicacy.

Polly begins to wail loudly, and Robert too, Elizabeth hushing them so their mother can think what to do.

"John Junior, please fetch our shovels and the pick, and come with me and Jimmy. We're going to make a proper resting spot for your father. Elizabeth, bundle up Mary Ann and Robert. It may be that they want to help too."

And thus, within an hour of John Blake's death, Charlotte leads a solemn procession of young souls now dependent entirely on her out to the deepest snowbank behind the cabin. Though she and Jimmy do the heaviest part of the work, every child has a hand in creating a nest for their father.

"We have to dig it as deep as we possibly can," Charlotte instructs them, hacking furiously at the icy layer at the bottom of a hole that is soon shoulder-height. "Jimmy, you and John go cut some spruce boughs to line his resting place."

It's nearly dark when the task is done. She leads the chilled and bedraggled children inside, instructing Elizabeth to put the kettle on and to help the younger ones thaw their feet and hands by the fire. She opens the bedroom door and stares at the still form on her marriage bed, wishing one last time for this to be a dreadful dream from which Blake, and she too, will soon wake. For a moment she is tempted to lay the new bearskin on top of the boughs at the bottom of the snowy crypt, but then more reality sets in: her husband no longer needs the warmth and her children may perish without it. Instead she shrouds him in the blanket, and with Jimmy hoisting the shoulders, she carries John Blake to be packed into the snow until spring. Nothing has ever sounded as mournful to her as the light patter falling on his blanketed form as she and Jimmy hasten to fill in his grave. Not even Pad. When Pad died, even though she was pregnant, she had no idea of the burden of children.

When they return to the house, she shrugs off her coat, shakes the snow from her skirts and gathers her children to her. Mary Ann and Robert stare up at her as though she's about to tell them a reassuring story. But what can she say to four children who are now fatherless?

"When the ice goes out of the river, we will take Papa to the cemetery. I will take care of you. We have enough to eat this winter, enough wood split. We will be warm and safe until spring is here. We will be all right, I promise."

Their upturned faces tell her she still hasn't found the answer they seek. *Your father died of a toothache and we're all alone and who knows why.* Instead, she simply says, "Come, Elizabeth, we need to get the supper started."

LATER THAT NIGHT after she's tucked all four of them, and Jimmy, into bed, she starts toward her own room, then stops at the threshold. Can she really lie down on the bed where Blake just died? Instead, she carries her diary and her lamp to the table, avoiding the chair her husband usually sat in:

I'm so stunned, I can't even find the right words to comfort the children so I've said hardly anything for fear I'll frighten them. My mind is a scramble of sadness and panic.

Death—It's so mean the way it comes in the middle of the struggle to stay alive, snatching people from my side. First Pad, then the commodore, now John, who was only fifty, and who had survived battles with the privateers and the Indians only to be felled by a toothache. They leave me alone, all of them, to provide, to try to scratch a crop out of the soil, to thatch a roof to keep the vicious weather off our heads, to bring those bloody timbers down in order to secure our claim on this place. Alone on this river that freezes up for six months of the year, locking us in solitude.

If the bleak winter ever ends, we have half-cleared lots in New Brunswick with a deed that comes from Nova Scotia. The papers Albert Plumnell brought us from Halifax may be useless in this new province. Is this my punishment for leaving my father's home? I fear these Loyalists arriving like spring geese returning to the river will take advantage of my situation now that John is dead.

So much suffering. So much loss.

Charlotte stares at the page for a minute, wanting very much to say something about her husband himself, and not her need of him. Finally she scratches out—inadequately, she feels—*You were a good man, John Blake.*

She closes the diary and goes to check on the children, who are curled up against one another and, mercifully, sound asleep.

She slumps into the chair by the hearth and there she sits, mourning, planning, wishing, and scheming through the night and all the next day, and the night and the day after that one. The children crawl in and out of her lap while Jimmy tends to the fire and the food, with Elizabeth's help. Like the smoke that lingers in layers around the hearth, the lives of those inside the cabin are suspended, drifting, waiting. At the end of the third day, Charlotte finally rises from her spot by the fire, shrugging out from under her bearskin and flicking invisible dust from her skirts. First she must get them all through this endless winter. And then she will address her plans for their future. What she absolutely cannot do any longer is sit still.

JIMMY HAS SPREAD THE WORD to the closest neighbours that John Blake is dead. The first to call is William Davidson. No one has been cordial with him since he returned to the river, accusing him, if not to his face, of abandoning the Miramichi during the bad times and returning to reap the harvest of the peace. But Charlotte has no bone to pick with him. As far as she is concerned, he built a fine business here, and when it faltered, he moved it elsewhere. When there was an opportunity to return, he took it. Having come along the river from the forks by horse-drawn sleigh to find out whether there is anything he can do for her, Davidson finds the lovely widow in full command of her children and her senses, with enough stores to last the winter and her husband safely secured until the river breaks up. Nevertheless, he vows that he'll check on her again.

Next to trek through the woods to offer their condolences are John and Janet Murdoch. As Charlotte ushers them in, she allows herself for one moment to think, What took you so long? But she can see the answer in the looks on their faces: clearly they are both concerned for her, but she's now a woman alone with four children and the Murdochs are having enough trouble feeding their own.

But that wasn't all that they were thinking. Tromping back to their own cabin after tea and bannock with Charlotte, John Murdoch says out loud what his wife has scrupled to utter so soon after Blake's death: "She'll make a good prize for another husband soon."

And as they walk, they both number on their fingers the likely candidates, as interested in Blake's land, they'd guess, as in Charlotte's fine person.

Charlotte wonders where William Wishart is but can't quite bring herself to ask Jimmy if he has seen him. But still she's surprised when after two weeks he hasn't come by, as he'd always kept a watch on her when Blake was away at sea. As the days pass, Charlotte finds it becomes easier not to think much about their situation during daylight hours, when the chores of ordinary survival take all her energies. But when the children are asleep and the fires are banked, she continues to turn the problem of securing their lives over and over in her mind and allows herself to miss the often-silent companionship of her husband.

Many days it is so cold that they cannot go outside, and so she throws herself into the task of teaching the children their lessons. Elizabeth helps with the little ones, although reading from the books Charlotte carried with her from England—Shakespearean sonnets and the poems of John Donne, and even *Clarissa*—is not to Elizabeth's liking. The lives the books describe are so foreign to her experience of the world. More weeks slip by, all of them feeling a little shipwrecked in their cabin, the woodpile depleting steadily, storms blowing around their ears for two days out of every seven.

It's the first week of March before John Murdoch returns with news. The old settlers are gathering to meet at his cabin and she needs to attend. Thirty Loyalists have been granted fifteen thousand acres of land along the river.

"Who have they been conniving with to scoop up the lots?" Charlotte asks.

"Who knows the exact truth of it," Murdoch replies. "But it's time for us to take action."

The terrain has shifted so much in recent years, and the Loyalists have made such strides and such claims, that some people are calling the old settlers such as Charlotte and the Murdochs "pre-Loyalists." This strikes the original settlers as insulting.

"It's a worrying sign that the governor of New Brunswick has taken sides," Murdoch says. "I've got Mr. Delesdernier to come hear us out and perhaps make our case. Charlotte, if you want to stay on at Blake Brook, you need to come put a word in for your claim." Charlotte has met the land agent, who has acted in claims to secure titles for other settlers, in her husband's company—John Mark Delesdernier, a Swiss who emigrated to the Miramichi shortly after she arrived. When weather permits, he does a constant circuit of the government offices in Frederick Town, Parr Town and Halifax, and he certainly understands the concerns of the settlers. He has been witness to their efforts to clear and claim the lots along the river and is known as a good land agent who frequently carries petitions to the governor. Charlotte especially likes the care the man has taken to learn the Mi'kmaq language, becoming knowledgeable about the native customs as well as their historical grievances. A rare attitude in a white man.

Jimmy wants to come with her, but she says no, she needs him to stay with the children in case she's back late: she doesn't want Elizabeth left alone to deal with keeping the fire going and feeding the children. Lacing on her fur-lined boots and donning her old fur coat, Charlotte snowshoes with Murdoch back to his place, squinting against bright sun on snow.

Charlotte is behind him when he pushes open the door to a room packed with men. When they realize the Widow Blake is among them, there's an uncomfortable silence. Then a few of them nod toward her and mutter condolences before looking to Murdoch to bring the meeting to order. Charlotte looks for Janet in the room and finds her sitting on a bench near the window. She makes her way over to sink down beside her where she won't be the pitied object of everyone's attention.

"There's a land grab going on up and down the banks of the Miramichi," Murdoch begins. "The land licences granted by the governor in Halifax are now subject to approval by Governor Carleton in Frederick Town."

"We're being done out of the land by the uppity Loyalists," says a grumpy Alexander Henderson.

"Mr. Delesdernier can help us," Murdoch says and gestures to the agent to address the crowd. "Let's hear him out and decide what we must do."

Delesdernier is stout and small, with round cheeks reddened by hard travel in freezing temperatures and a dark frock coat that has seen much patching. In order to better see them all as he speaks, he steps up on a wooden box.

"I have written a letter to Governor Carleton on your behalf," he says. "It explains that all of you in this room are the only principal and old settlers on the Miramichi River who had licences for their land from the government in Halifax."

Nods and shouts of "Too true!" greet him.

"I want to read to you the letter I have composed on your behalf," he says, drawing a folded sheet from his inside pocket:

"'In 1777, Captain Boyle of HMS *Hunter* properly qualified us as owners of the lots we occupied. Each of us had been nominated to take up one half-mile of front and to keep and hold the same until further orders from the government. Now we petition the governor to enter each of our names in the land register of New Brunswick.'"

They need little discussion to approve this wording, and after Delesdernier places ink, quill and the letter on the table, they line up to sign it. Charlotte is last, but not least, scrawling *Widow Blake* after the men's signatures.

Delesdernier promises to deliver the governor's decision to register their lots as soon as it is made.

Charlotte stays on for supper after the men leave to visit a while with Janet. The moonlight is making long shadows of the spruce trees as she makes her way back to Blake Brook. With every step she takes, her resentment and suspicion grows: it seems to her that even to John Murdoch her presence at the meeting was an afterthought. Can she trust Delesdernier or any other man to present her claim, even if she's masquerading in the name of her dead husband. The Widow Blake indeed.

When she pushes the door open she finds Jimmy sound asleep with the children. The way they loop around him reminds her suddenly of how the kittens curled into Tommy as he lay in the cattle stalls on the ship. She stokes the fire, adds another log and sits watching the flames awhile. She has to fight for her land for the sake of these children, who are her reason and her comfort. Each one brings her a different gift. Elizabeth is calm and gentle. She mothers the younger children with the sense of compassion she seems to have been born with. John Junior is something else. Like his sister Mary Ann, whose nickname, Polly, has now stuck, he's in constant motion, cleverly teasing his way into and out of trouble. She's convinced that the two of them open their eyes every morning with an adventure already in mind, often designed to bedevil her. Robert, only three, is a quiet, even studious child, who spends hours mesmerized by the fire, by the devilish activity of John and Polly, by the little chores his mother sets him. He seems happiest when he's snuggled on Charlotte's lap. "We will manage," she says out loud, as though to confirm her wavering belief.

AT MID-MORNING, the call of the whippoorwill drifts into the cabin. For weeks Charlotte has not allowed herself to wonder if word of her plight has reached the Indian camp, or whether Wioche has heard of Blake's death. When she opens the door, she steadies herself against disappointment. But it really is Wioche standing at the edge of the brook, so covered by a huge furry cloak she might have mistaken him for a bear had it not been for the whistle. She's rarely seen him to speak to him since she married John Blake, but he has never been far from her thoughts. The one benefit to being the Widow Blake is she is now free to invite him into her house. He is the one who hesitates for a moment, but shedding his cloak on the doorstep he finally follows her inside.

The children are at the table working at an arithmetic lesson Charlotte has set them. John Junior leaps up in alarm at the sight of an Indian in his father's house, and Charlotte hastens to introduce them. She knows that when it comes to Indians, he is his father's son.

"John, this is Wioche, whose people were so kind to me when I first came to the Baie. Remember the stories I've told you of the Indian camp?"

"Yes, Mum," John Junior says, and though he still doesn't

look too happy, he can't help taking a careful inventory of the man, from the leggings he wears to the tunic belted at the waist with a broad sash embroidered with porcupine quills to the long, narrow blade strapped to his thigh.

Wioche, meanwhile, is smiling at Elizabeth, who hesitantly smiles back.

"Mijooajeech," he greets her.

"That's the word for *baby*," Charlotte explains. "Wioche first met you when you were only a few hours old, Elizabeth. He is the man who made the bunting bag from rabbit fur, the one I wrapped all of you in as babies." She looks sternly at her children, who one by one come up to greet their visitor properly, even John Junior. As she and Wioche seat themselves by the fire, all cluster around her chair to stare shyly at him.

He tells her that when the camp at the Baie moved—first just to Caron Point across the channel from Alston Point—he began to spend more time travelling the Mi'kmaq district, staying mostly at Taboosimgeg up the coast. He has been by her cabin from time to time and hears news of Charlotte's family from the women she visits in the camp on the river. He doesn't have to explain to her why he hasn't stopped—Wioche was keenly aware of her husband's views on Indians. After the battle on the Lafayette, Charlotte tried very hard to change Blake's mind, but the best they could do was declare a truce on the subject. Blake never trusted the People.

Yet here Wioche sits, attempting to comfort Blake's children with tales of the Great Spirit and the place where their father watches over them. He does a better job of it than she has ever done, Charlotte thinks ruefully, remembering the immense distances the People travel to bury their dead in sacred places. She hopes none of the children will mention John Blake's temporary burial spot, and changes the subject quickly, asking for news of her friends from the Baie.

As she prepares their lunch, Wioche tells her that many people have died in an outbreak of measles. Marie's mother was one of them. Marie and André have settled in Miscou and have added two more children to their family. The Acadians are beginning to prosper again, he says, though their lives are not easy. The new English settlers treat them as though they don't belong here.

"Some of the old ones do too," Charlotte replies.

Soon the children get used to the visitor, and hours pass easily. Charlotte and Wioche talk of the new province, the struggles with the weather, the Loyalists, the migration route of the animals that has changed as more land is settled, the diminished prospects and problems of his people, who seem to be slowly giving up the fight against the settlers and the rum, accepting the inevitable, some would say, though Charlotte still admires the pride and self-sufficiency and ease with which the People once prospered here.

The afternoon slips by. Suppertime is approaching when she sends her children out to fetch the night's supply of wood, and finally shares her deepest worry with this man, her oldest and most trusted friend in this place. That she should talk to him of owning land that once belonged to all might be strange, but she needs to say it aloud to someone she knows has her interests at heart. "If we are to stay on here, Wioche, I must secure the deed. I don't think it is good enough to have the licence of land given to us by Nova Scotia. We are under a new province's governance now, and I won't feel safe until the deed is transferred. Women's rights to the land are fragile. I don't know of any woman settler who has secured a claim on her own. But I am

John Blake's widow, and surely that must count for something. It was my labour as much as his that cleared this plot: he was often away weeks at a time."

He considers her words, then says bluntly, "You must take your licence to the new governor. I've heard he's in Frederick Town now."

She's flabbergasted. "Go to Frederick Town? I wouldn't know how to find it. And if I did set off, the winter would stop me before I ever got off the river."

Wioche looks at her steadily, as if testing her resolve. "I will show you the way. There and back—it will take us ten days by snowshoe."

Since she arrived at Blake Brook, Charlotte hasn't been farther afield than Napan Bay in one direction, where the Murdochs live and the Indian camp is situated, and the forks in the other. Jimmy can take care of the children, she decides. She knows the rest of the settlers will talk—a white woman setting out alone with an Indian guide—but let them. If I come back with the deeds in my hand, they'll not use my name unkindly, she thinks.

By the time Wioche leaves in the waning light of the day, they have agreed that at dawn they will set out for Frederick Town. She will bring what provisions she can carry comfortably on her back. He will provide the snowshoes—Indian snowshoes are narrow and about as long as the distance from her waist to her feet and have mooseskin cording that makes it easier to drag the foot through the top snow rather than lifting it. "Better for long journey," Wioche says. I hope so, she thinks to herself while waving goodbye. Then she looks at her children again and wonders what she is doing: If something happens to her, their situation will be dire. No, she won't think about that. She must secure the deed.

She goes to the table, picks up her quill, opens the ink jar and begins the letter she has been thinking to write since she got up from her chair by the fire after John Blake died. She hesitates over the sheet, but only for a moment. Then her hand moves steadily.

8th March, 1785

Dearest Papa and Mama,

I send you greetings from the Miramichi River in New Brunswick where I live in a settler's cabin with my four children. You'll know some of my situation by now as I believe one Will MacCulloch carried a letter to you written by Commodore George Walker.

I am a widow, my circumstances somewhat uncertain. For that reason and because I long for news of you, I am sending this memorial. I am inquiring about the inheritance of five hundred pounds from Grandmother, kept in trust for me at your bank. Since the money is rightfully mine, I desire—in fact, need—you to forward the inheritance to me.

You can send a reply to me at Charlotte Blake, in care of Simeon Perkins, Liverpool, Nova Scotia. Trusted people will carry your reply to me.

I pray you think kindly of me and will consider your four grandchildren.

Your loving daughter,
Charlotte

She folds the letter and tucks it into the vest she will wear to Frederick Town.

—

AT SUPPERTIME, she breaks the news of the journey. This will be the first time she has been separated from any of them since they were born, and as she explains why she has to leave them for a few days, Robert climbs right into her lap.

"This is our home, the only home three of you have ever known," she says. "Your father would want me to do everything I can to secure our place here. We can't expect others to look out for our interests. It's up to me to take care of us now. You'll be all right with Jimmy while I'm gone, and if something bad happens"—her voice quakes a little—"you will run straight to the Murdochs." It's been quiet on the river these winter months. Surely they'll be safe.

After the children are asleep, she herself can't settle down to a proper rest, though she drifts and dozes for a few hours in the chair by the fire. Then she rouses herself to pack dried fish and berries, bannock, some sugar and tea into the pack she'll tie to her back, along with a couple of vessels in which to melt water for tea along the way. She layers clothing to conserve heat, finds John's beaver pelt hat to wear over her plaited hair and straps on her mooseskin boots. She's ready when a sliver of sun comes through the trees over the river, bringing Wioche sliding along on the ice with two pairs of snowshoes strung across his back. He pulls a toboggan laden with supplies.

She leans over the sleepy pile of children in the big bed to give last-minute instructions and admonishments. She makes sure to kiss each one of them and even Jimmy goodbye. "Be good," she says as she shuts the door.

Glancing toward John Blake's snowy tomb, she fervently hopes there won't be a thaw while she's away. At the river edge, she looks back to see her little family huddled together outside the cabin in their nightshirts, waving, their breaths pluming above their heads. Then she slips over the bank onto the byway of ice.

The early-morning sun ascends at their backs, casting a bronze glow on the river as they slide in unison along a trail that's been broken on the frozen waterway. They make good time to the forks and follow the left bank onto the southwest Miramichi. When Wioche suggests they stop to rest, she reckons by the sun overhead that it's been five hours since they left the cabin. She unwraps a piece of fish and a chunk of bannock while Wioche cuts pieces of ice to melt for tea. They sit on the bank of the river, grateful for the food, the sun and each other's company. After a short half-hour, they set off again.

They've put some miles behind them when the frost in the late-afternoon air starts to penetrate her clothes. Her legs are stiffening now as much from the cold as the exercise. They push ahead until the sun falls behind the trees, leaving them with only enough light to find a place to camp and gather boughs for shelter and the wood they need. Charlotte gets the fire started while Wioche deftly makes the lean-to in a semi-circle around it. She melts ice, makes tea and cooks fish and bannock for dinner. After they've eaten, they sit warming themselves by the flames, wrapped in their furs, and Wioche tells her another tale of Gluskap, this one about a porcupine and a sparrow lost in the forest. Between the porcupine's defensive quills and the sparrow's ability to fly and Gluskap's intervention in the form of a talking oak tree, the pair find their way out of their predicament.

She's enchanted with these fables, which animate shells and give language to birds and invariably have nymphlike spirits conveying magic and mirth. After he wends his way to the moral of the story, in which the sparrow and the porcupine find out that both creatures are necessary parts of creation, they prepare the fire for the long night ahead, piling it high with wood, moving their pallets of boughs closer to its edge and wrapping themselves in the extra furs and skins from the toboggan. She tucks her face inside the furry blanket and falls fast asleep before they even say goodnight.

It's still dark when she wakens. She's unbearably cold, and a heap of embers barely burns in the firepit. She thinks she may freeze to death if she can't get it blazing again. Bracing herself for the blast of even colder air as she crawls out of her fur nest, she moves as quietly as she can to the woodpile, but still wakes Wioche. He's on his feet in an instant. He teases her about being too soft for the weather, but helps her to build the fire up, shooing her under her blanket while he works. As soon as it's blazing, he crawls back under the wraps and seems to fall to sleep immediately. Still cold, Charlotte allows herself to edge nearer to him, and soon her toes and fingers warm up again and her eyes close.

For four more days, they slide along the river, bushwhack through the forest and sleep under the stars. By day and by night the threads of their two lives are woven into an unfinished tapestry of ragged edges and tangled patterns.

It's late morning on the fifth day when they see the chimneys of Frederick Town in the distance. Hauling the toboggan behind them, they slip and slide their way into the centre of the bustling town. Houses, some of them two storeys, some made of stone, line streets that seem to Charlotte to be absolutely teeming with people and horse-drawn carts. She finds herself coming to a dead stop in the road, staring around her like a person who has never seen a horse let alone the city of London; she kicks herself because in her obsession with making her claim, she hadn't thought about what she could barter here, or carry back for the children.

Wioche has remained a couple of steps behind her as they walked into town, but now he discreetly gets her attention.

"There is no place in town where we both can stay the night, Charlotte. Go to the governor and make your claim. If you get the deed, we can camp again in the woods tonight and be on our way back to your children."

It doesn't take long for them to find the governor's residence, an impressive building of imperial presence and vast fenced grounds with sentries at the gate. Wioche fades into the background as she asks one of the sentries whether the governor is in Frederick Town. When he nods, she tells him she has business to conduct and he motions her inside the grounds, pointing to the broads steps that lead to a front door flanked by columns. As she walks toward the entrance, she somewhat wryly realizes that this is the first truly imposing structure she's seen since she left England. On the doorstep, Charlotte sheds her bearskin and tidies her hair, hoping there is still a modicum of English politesse left in her comportment to aid her in her purpose. She doesn't know whether she should knock or just barge in. She tries the door, which swings open easily onto a large foyer.

A nervous-looking functionary is immediately upon her, asking her the nature of her business in this house.

"I'm seeking an audience with the governor," she tells him, putting a maximum of her old haughtiness into her tone.

She's not certain whether it's curiosity about the appearance of a woman on the threshold or luck that gets her into the antechamber. The governor is not available, but his aide, Mr. Wiltshire, will see her directly.

After a time of impatient waiting, she is ushered into the presence of a darting man with pointed features, who literally twirls his moustache when he sees her.

"The Widow Blake, sir," the functionary announces.

Eyeing her once up and down, Wiltshire immediately turns to the window, beckoning Charlotte to sit down. His patrician manner irritates her before she even begins.

"I've come for the deed to my land," she tells him abruptly. Reaching inside her pocket she produces her proof, laying it on the man's table. "This Lot Eight licence for the Miramichi, granted to John Blake in 1777, needs to be transferred to a proper deed in the province of New Brunswick."

He turns now to look at her and then her paper as she presses on.

"The land on Lot Ten has been partially cleared and crops have been planted there by John Blake and myself. It is the two—Lots Eight and Ten—I want deeds for."

"The deeds to all the lots along the river are being prepared," Wiltshire says as though to wave her off. His accent is upper crust, and he's of the age of one of the marriage prospects her mother had in mind for her. He is exactly the style of man that made running away with Pad such an appealing course of action.

"How long must I wait?"

"It is a matter that will take several months, at least, madam," he replies.

"Mr. Wiltshire, I have left my children in the care of a young boy and walked through the woods for five days to secure title to my land and I will not leave this office until I have assurance from your pen that the land is mine."

She sits very straight in the plain wooden chair and waits for his reply.

He looks at her for a long moment, taking in her patched skirts, her fur coat and mooseskin, the strands of fierce red hair that resisted her efforts to smooth it, the work-roughened hands and short nails and the intensity burning in the large blue eyes. Then he shrugs as though the matter is of no moment to him.

"I will write a memorial that I shall send to you stating that in due course you will be named the lawful owner of the land."

She continues to sit, making clear with every fibre of her being that if he wants this bedraggled settler gone, he'll have to give her the letter this instant or call the guards.

Finally, languidly, he dips his quill into the inkwell and inscribes the facts she needs on a piece of paper with the waxed seal of the governor at the top. Then he signs it himself and hands it to her. Before he can turn away again to the window, she takes her own letter from her pocket and lays it on the table. "This memorial to General Howe Taylor needs to be dispatched to England with haste. I trust you to see it goes with the first spring sailing to Bristol."

"What is General Howe Taylor to you, Widow Blake?"

"The general is my father."

He shows no surprise, but does reach for her letter. "Is your business in this office finished now?" he inquires.

As she rises from her chair, she curtsies slightly, one mooseskin-clad foot behind her as she bends a knee, and smiles, and for a moment the supercilious Mr. Wiltshire sees the young gentlewoman Charlotte Taylor once was.

SHE AND WIOCHE are well across the river and into the woods when they stop to make camp for the night, the letter folded carefully in her pocket. It isn't everything she hoped to achieve, but it is enough.

A light snow is falling. It'll be worrisome if it worsens, Charlotte thinks, but at the moment it feels like an insulator from the perishing cold. They cut extra boughs, build a lean-to and settle down together by the fire while a fat fish sizzles on the embers. Charlotte's mouth waters. Wioche also produces a large slab of cheese he has found in Frederick Town. It feels like a celebration, and she suddenly feels so overwhelming grateful to this man it brings tears to her eyes.

He nudges his shoulder into her, and a vibration dances around her chest. From the moment she laid eyes on him at the Mi'kmaq camp on the hill over Alston Point, she was bewitched by his gentle strength, his clear pride in his people, the way his kindness to her lit the dark intensity of his eyes. That was almost ten years ago, but the attraction that is making her heart race on this wintry night has never faded.

They eat hungrily, every morsel of the fish, slathering their bannock with the greasy juices that drip from its carcass, their chins shiny—Wioche laughing as Charlotte even picks the crispy bits of skin from the wooden spit. They sink their teeth into the sharp-tasting cheese, a luxury that seems impossible here in the bush. It's snowing harder now, and they each wear a mantle of white. But the fire is warm and they're utterly alone.

Wioche bumps against her playfully again, and this time she leans her head on his shoulder. At last he slips his long fingers around her chin and tilts her face to his. Then with exquisite delicacy, he covers her mouth with his lips. It's as though the fire has crawled from the pit in front of them to her groin. Her toes curl reflexively. She pulls away briefly, then buries her face in his neck. His lips graze her cheek, and she lifts her face to him. He kisses her eyelids, her nose—and this time she's the one who seeks his lips. He breaks away, only to lift her onto the bed of boughs. There's no more hesitation, no shy overtures. When he slides into her, she arches her back to bring him closer.

They lie together afterward in the ruins of their shelter like a pair of saplings intertwined. They sleepily realize they should prop up their lean-to and rebuild the fire. The wind has picked up and snow tickles their faces. But they move not at all.

A timeless interval later they waken to night and a fire that is only embers. Charlotte nurses it into blazing life again as Wioche reassembles their shelter. Then they return to the nest they'd made of furs and skins and find more warmth in each other's arms.

The trek back to Blake Brook is an unforgettable journey marked by long conversations and silent reveries as they snow-shoe through the sunlit woods, and passion spent and spent again beneath spruce boughs under the stars. A decade of longing is fulfilled; the future is unspoken.

IT'S ALMOST DUSK when they pull the toboggan up to the cabin. Wioche stays only long enough to surprise the children with candy he has found for them in Frederick Town. In the swarm of hugs and stories that greet her, Charlotte feels the grave eyes of her oldest son on her. Surely he can't realize . . . no, for John Junior, it's the thought of the Indian in the house that unsettles him. Still, she knows Wioche is wise to go, and soon.

And so she suggests that the children walk with her down to the river to wave goodbye. "Wioche has done us a service that none of you should ever forget. Because of him, we have secured our land." But she is the last to linger on the bank, watching his silhouette until it disappears around the bend of the river.

—

WHO SHOULD FIRST LIGHT bring to her cabin door the next day but William Wishart. He smiles when he sees her, as he always does: she can think of no other of the settler men who seems to appreciate her for who she is, and not who she was married to, or for the lots the Widow Blake might now own. He tells her that he and his brother had been away in Halifax and returned just a few days ago and he wants to know how he can help. Over a steaming cup of tea, she tells him of her trek to see the governor in Frederick Town and the letter she has procured.

"Charlotte, you amaze me," William says. "I think you have no match in these parts for intrepid undertakings. You put even the men to shame."

She shrugs off his praise and is uncomfortable for a moment under his gaze. She hadn't been the intrepid one. But she does need his help.

"William, we have enough stores to last until the ice melts, I'm sure, and enough seed for next summer's crops, but the planting . . . I don't know how I'll manage it. The children are awfully little, and only Jimmy really has the strength to be much help. Also . . ." She hasn't confided John Blake's temporary resting place to anyone save the Murdochs, and she is really not sure how to manage the interval between when the snow starts to melt and the ice breaks up on the river, making it possible to carry her husband safely to the burial ground. She doesn't know why talking about it makes her so uncomfortable: everyone on the river has had to deal with such harsh realities. But it's the one thing in her settler's life she feels unequal to manage.

Hearing her out, William quickly reassures her. "No reason to worry yourself, lass. I'll make a coffin for John's remains, and I'll take you and the wee children to the cemetery at Wilson's

Point for the burial. My brother and I have our sailboat, big enough to carry all of you, and John's coffin."

That matter well settled, he then shifts the conversation to spring planting. He and his brother have to clear more of their acreage, but he should be able to spare enough time to be of assistance to her.

William visits almost every day, and she has to confess she begins to look forward to seeing him. With his thoughtfulness and good humour, he is an antidote to cabin fever, another adult with whom she can discuss the challenges her little clan faces. Sometimes he is the welcome excuse to sit a while and drink tea; without Blake to help her, the days are a brutal round of endless chores.

In late March, they get a stretch of warmish weather—the maple sap is running and Charlotte has the children busy carrying brimming buckets from her short tap line to a kettle bubbling over a fire in the clearing. True to his word, William snowshoes across the river to their landing, dragging a fresh spruce coffin on sled runners. The children, who've been greedily dipping a ladle into the boiling kettle and tossing the syrup onto the snow, where it hardens into delicious candy, fall silent as they watch him struggle, sweating up the bank with his burden. Although they have never seen a coffin, they realize its purpose. Handing the big stirring stick to Elizabeth, Charlotte wipes her hands on her apron and tells the children to carry on with their task. "You, too, Jimmy," she says. The boy is clearly relieved. She just wishes she herself could stay by the fire.

AFTER THE USUAL HEAVING and threatening, the ice rises with an explosive roar one April day and is sucked down the river to the sea. The next morning, the brothers Wishart,

William and Alexander both, sail across the river to attend to Blake's coffin and his mourners. Once at Wilson's Point they quickly set to work with shovels, breaking through the thick crust of thawing topsoil, then switching to pickaxes to dig deeper. When the job is done, and the coffin lowered, rather jerkily, though Jimmy and Charlotte lend a hand as best they can with the ropes, the brothers leave her briefly with the children by the mound of fresh brown earth, a stain on the pure white snow.

It is so silent here, she thinks, so peaceful, a small clearing with a view to the river and forever. God's land. "Farewell, John Blake," she says softly. "I'll mind your children and tell them often of your deeds on this river. They will grow to know you. I will never forget you."

All of them help to fill in the grave, Charlotte urging them to hurry as dusk creeps in, mindful of the time it will take them to sail back safely to Blake Brook.

IN THE FOLLOWING WEEKS, the river is a veritable byway of passing boats bringing supplies to the ever-increasing number of settlers gobbling up the lots along the shore. The demand—and the competition—is fierce. Charlotte has few coins and nothing much to barter with; Blake traded their last cut timber for winter supplies. "Negotiating for supplies without any lumber to trade will see us starve to death by fall," Charlotte grumbles to Jimmy as they work together to clear the winter debris out of the cabin and off her cleared garden plots. "All that will be left to us is to freeze to death come winter."

Once again William Wishart comes to the rescue, and though Charlotte chastises him for ignoring his own interests in favour of hers, she is grateful when he arrives at her landing with axe and saw in his little grey dory. By the end of a week, he's cut five cord of wood, and become a fixture at her table. "You can trade some of the wood for seedlings and chickens—and maybe a cow to replace that tired old goat of yours," he teases her.

The next week, news comes that Delesdernier has failed to deliver the petition from the settlers. Apparently, he was waylaid by the demands of settlers with larger claims along the Saint John River. A new man, a Loyalist named Benjamin Marston, who was expelled from his native Massachusetts by the rebels, has been appointed by Governor Carleton as surveyor general of the King's woods. William has heard that he plans to come to the Miramichi to bring order to what he sees as an uncivilized collection of boors.

She trudges through the woods with William to a meeting of the old settlers called by John Murdoch. They decide to send yet another petition to the province, and Charlotte, who has not mentioned her hard-won letter, votes in favour. William abstains. As he accompanies her back to her cabin, he confides that he trusts none of these men to represent his interests—not Delesdernier, not Marston, maybe not even Murdoch, who has acquired more land in what William describes as "a questionable bargain with a devil not known to us." Charlotte has no idea what he's talking about. He's an odd man, she thinks, thoughtful, hard-working and honest, comfortably chatty with her, but often dead silent in public. His brother, Alexander, is the charmer of the pair, heavy-set, brown-eyed, balding, delivering his lengthy commentaries in a bubbling Scottish brogue. Not William. He keeps his own counsel, always watching, listening, calculating.

When he shows up the next day at her door, he doesn't talk of trading wood but of marriage. "You need a husband, lass, and

I need a wife," he says, and Charlotte realizes she is not the least bit surprised. She scans his face just the once, gazing for a time into his dark blue eyes, and replies just as matter-of-factly, "You make good sense."

There's no minister or even Justice of the Peace in the vicinity, but this is not an impediment. The next day, in the presence of Alexander Wishart and the Murdochs, the Murdoch children and her own, Charlotte and William pronounce themselves husband and wife. And he moves into the crowded cabin in time to start the serious business of spring.

REALIZING THAT in their long friendship he's never volunteered much about his past, she urges her new husband to talk about his family as she mends the children's clothes by lamplight. He starts with his ancestor, George Wishart, who was burned at the stake at St. Andrews as a heretic more than two hundred and thirty years ago. "He was preaching God's word," William says. "The papists feared his power to convert the Scots to his church. They plotted against him."

With history like that swirling around in his memory, she thinks, it's small wonder that one of her husband's passions is to see a Presbyterian church built on the river—in which they can be married in the eyes of God as well as man. When he moved in, she soon discovered that William possessed the only copy of a Bible she has seen since leaving Britain. He even quotes from the Book of Job from time to time when trials with the land, the logs or the Loyalists test his patience.

By summer, the river is swarming with more Loyalists, disbanded soldiers and newly arriving immigrants from Britain. Brides are snatched up at Simeon Perkins's wharf as quickly as they step off the ships. Rumour mongers spread scintillating chatter about lineage and legitimacy, which turns the river into a veritable trading post of accusations, innuendo and plotting. The fighting between the old and the new settlers is as frequent as the battles had been with the Indians and privateers, but without the fatal consequences.

"It's the marshlands they're after," Charlotte says. "We all need those lands to survive—they are the only place where you can grow a crop without having to clear the trees first." Indeed, the marshlands are like meadows, full of wild strawberries and raspberries, where the ducks and geese land in great flocks, making them easy prey for hungry settlers. One stretch of marsh is located at the forks, and the other near the Murdochs'. Between them, there isn't nearly enough to provide for a population that has increased four-fold in twenty-four months.

William sails often across the shoals to the bay and beyond to Liverpool, looking for British buyers for his cured salmon and trading the cords of wood he cuts. Unlike Blake who was gone for weeks at a time, William is rarely away for more than a night or two. He keeps the cabin well tacked together and is pleasing in the marriage bed; the children, even John Junior, are growing fond of him, though they are still restive during his nightly Bible reading. She has confided the contents of her letter to her father to William, and each of his voyages to Simeon Perkins's wharf fuels her hope that a parcel from home may be waiting there.

IN THE MEANTIME, men like Marston make it clear that their version of the New World has no place for a woman such as Charlotte. Though William does his best to protect her from the name-calling and rumours that swirl around her—the story of her winter jaunt to Frederick Town in company with a native man is the least of her transgressions—she knows that in the eyes of the newcomers on the river she is "that woman": guilty of conduct unbecoming to an Englishwoman.

Marston had posted a notice that he'd reply to settlers' questions at a meeting to be held by the dock at the marshlands on the last Sunday in July. William and Charlotte can hear his staccato voice before they've even got their dory tied up. Marston's career has been spotty at best, at least to this point. Here on the Miramichi, he's determined to maintain the integrity of the Empire. That's what he's on about—the Empire—when he notices Charlotte and William joining the crowd. Hardly skipping a beat, he announces, "Gentlemen, we have a woman in our midst."

Charlotte shoots back. "How fortunate for our deliberations."

Marston irks Charlotte on sight, with his condescension and constant fidgeting. The feeling is reciprocated.

"A married woman is the responsibility of her husband," Marston tells William Wishart, pointedly ignoring his wife.

"Away with ye," William scoffs.

"It is one thing for the Widow Blake to claim ownership of the land but quite another for a married woman to carry on as though she has the same rights as men," Marston intones.

Charlotte is steaming, and resentful that Marston is talking about her in the third person, too cowardly to address her directly. "According to you, I am expected to give up my land, my ambitions and my rights, indeed anything that I own to my present husband," she bristles. "I have secured my lots in my own stead for my children. Mr. Wishart has no issue with this. He knows as well as I how difficult and uncertain the future can be."

"But, Mrs. Wishart, as a married woman, you have no economic or legal power. Your husband is your representative and voice in public," he pronounces.

"So," she says, trying to suppress a grin, "William, my husband of only a few months, is responsible for my behaviour. Even John Blake was not responsible for my behaviour. It is ten years since that assignment has been in any person's hands but my own."

Marston says flatly, to some nodding of other male heads, "Land belongs to men, and proper women don't meddle in men's holdings."

Charlotte knows the laws of this new province, perhaps better than this newcomer does, and she is incensed by the suggestion that she should bow out of her holdings to please the sensibilities of the men in these meetings.

In the dory on the way home, she's still angry. "That I am to be satisfied to hand the land I cleared with my callused hands to another is an injustice I despised in England."

"Ach, Charlotte, pay no attention to the man."

But she can't help but feel threatened, and she swears that there is no way she will cede her status as a landowner and an independent woman to a male interloper of the likes of Marston.

When they are at home that night, and the children asleep, William tells her of the commentary Marston wrote after he was appointed sheriff, on top of being the new surveyor general. His derogatory opinion of his new charges had travelled the river faster than the wind: "Most of the people are illiterate and ignorant and much given to drunkenness. They want two things: law, to keep them in order, and gospel, to give them some better information than they seem to have and to civilize their manners, which attendance at public worship would tend to promote." Charlotte's ill opinion of their new masters is confirmed, and she is all the more determined that she and her kin will have their way.

The lots along the river are measured, altered, bought and sold. Charlotte tends her crops, and reads and rereads her letter with the governor's seal, wishing she could spit in the eye of Marston, who hunkered down safely in Harvard University, neither fighting in the colonial revolution nor enduring the hardships she and the original settlers have faced. The trail she followed to Frederick Town with Wioche is soon trampled into a thoroughfare with all the petitions moving back and forth between new and old settlers and the governor's quarters. The chaos of the times hinders William and Charlotte from registering their marriage.

The chaos in her own life prevents her from realizing she is pregnant again.

CHAPTER 10

The Miramichi

1785

*W*ith four children to feed and another expected in the New Year, William Wishart decides he cannot depend on curing salmon to support this family. It's no secret that William Davidson is amassing a fortune up at the forks with his trade in tall timbers for ship masts. The white pines preferred for such masts flourish all over the lot he and Charlotte live on, and all through the summer he brings them down, strips their bark and loads as many as his boat will carry for sale in Liverpool. He can't resist bringing home a few things for his new family, though his nature is to salt the proceeds securely away. A cauldron for cooking, a highly prized salamander—the long-handled pan with feet that can sit right over the fire. Cloth and skeins of wool, even shoes for the children and a pair of ladies' boots for Charlotte that lace halfway up her calf. The first European footwear she's owned for a decade.

She'd bargained a cow from the Murdochs, as well as a pregnant sow, both now grazing on the partially cleared lot to the west. William has built a proper shed for the goat—rather, goats. Charlotte has also procured a mate for the loyal little milk producer. They are sharing space with chickens and laying hens as well as with Jimmy, who increasingly wants to go with William to the woods and down the river to do what he calls "man's work." On the still-disputed marshlands, she has staked a piece that is producing a bountiful crop of hay that she cuts and carries in the dory for the animals.

Evenings are spent patching and sewing their clothes. This night, she takes stock of the family around her while she snips and stitches, patches and darns. The children have been spared the worst of the diseases that have swept down the river, and Charlotte likes to think it is because of the herbal remedies she learned during her first winter in the Indian camp at the bay. Not to mention her obsession with scrubbing the utensils as well as the children with soap and hot water. They've had their share of croup and influenza; measles swept through the family one winter. But for the most part, she counts her blessings for the sturdy health of her children.

She keeps Elizabeth by her side when she prepares meals, teaching her how to season the food with the precious spices John Blake brought from the West Indies, to be frugal, how to set the fire for baking, boiling or frying. When Elizabeth asks what the salamander is for, Charlotte decides to teach her how to make a favourite dish from her own childhood.

"When I was a girl your age, Cook used to make a wonderful Welsh rabbit for the family on a Sunday using just such a pan as this." Charlotte sees from the amazed look on her daughter's face that the idea of "Cook" is as mythical as the idea of angels and fairy dust. "Come, I'll show you—it has nothing whatsoever to do with rabbits. It won't be the same as Cook's. But we can make do."

She instructs Elizabeth to carry the salamander to the fire and nestle its legs right into the coals. "It needs to be red hot to make a good rabbit: the feet keep the pan high enough just to clear the flames." Elizabeth's next job is to cut the cheese in fine, even pieces so it will melt nicely as Charlotte toasts square-cut chunks of bread over the fire. "It's a tedious task, but it has to be done right. You must hold it at enough distance from the fire so that it will dry all the way through before turning slightly brown."

They mix the cheese slivers with egg, some beer from John Blake's cask and spices. "It cannot be too runny—it must stick to the toast," Charlotte instructs.

When the toast is ready, they slather the mixture over each piece and slide them onto the salamander. She tells Elizabeth to hold the end of the long handle so that she'll be a comfortable distance away from the heat. "That's the good of a salamander," she says. "You don't have to have your head over the fire." Charlotte has tender pride for this nine-year-old child whose temperament is so pleasing. Her curly black hair frames her face and her tawny-coloured skin lights up her big brown eyes as she holds the handle, concentrating intently on her job.

When the Welsh rabbit is ready, the family gathers and Charlotte makes a speech about the chef. "This fine dinner, from an old recipe straight from Cook's kitchen, was prepared in New Brunswick by the prettiest girl on the Miramichi for the pleasure of William, John, Polly, Robert and Jimmy."

When the apples are ripe, she promises her daughter, she will show her how to make a dessert that will make her the most famous cook on the river, and Elizabeth blushes. There's high spirits that night in this house full of children, all of whom are expected to learn, to survive, and take care of one another.

—

By September, Charlotte is distinctly showing, and Janet Murdoch teases her, "Maybe you'll have two babies this time." She suffers not the least nausea, the skin on her face is glowing and her hair is thick and shiny. Instead of plaiting it, as most of the women do, she leaves it loose, though sometimes it becomes so tangled and windblown she needs to rub grease through the locks to untie the knots. Her life has taken on a pattern that suits her, not withstanding the land battles she is engaged in with Marston and his crowd.

The birds begin flocking early, and she comments to William that they should expect an early winter. This prospect doesn't bother her as much as it would have even a year ago. The one benefit of the influx of settlers is that they are less isolated. There is now a store by the shoal that intends to stay open with a stock of winter essentials. Survival is a test she feels better equipped to take.

Then one day the sound of screaming carries on the river, sending all of them rushing to rescue a family whose house has burst into flames. The outcome is devastating. An infant child dead, an entire family burned out.

That night Charlotte takes time to write in her diary:

Tragedy has struck a family who only arrived a few weeks ago. They must have been looking for a new life, instead they lost one. Theirs is the real story of this river. Babies are born, fathers drown, children succumb to the pox, new settlers arrive. The coming and going is like the tide, tenacious, relentless, merciless, sorrowfully predictable in a manner that can wizen your heart.

William says they were likely in some sort of trouble

*and came here to escape it. Who hasn't come to this place
to escape where they were? I fear for the woman, Rose. Her
blurting out the truth like that—that her husband was
hiding gunpowder in the cabin—will do her no good with
her man. He steered her away from me so quickly, I'm
certain he didn't want her to say anything more. I see her
yet, sitting so straight in the boat, the keening sound
coming from her was heartbreaking. I wish we could have
been able to help them, authors of their own tragedy or not.
But there's no place to gather or to shelter a family in need.
We need so much here—a doctor, a school, a church. Rose's
words—"Get me away from this evil place"—still sting,
though it was her grief speaking.*

*This place is hard, yes, but it is spiritual at the same
time, surrounded as we are by what was here before we
came. The birds find the river every spring, the trees guard
the banks winter or summer. The stars light the night sky
and the flowers bloom despite the late frost and the driving
rain. There is a rhythm of reaping and sowing to this life, a
struggle to survive—but taught by the seasons and mindful
of the animals that stalk the forest around us, there is
abundance here as well as sorrow.*

THE NEXT DAY, Charlotte takes Elizabeth with her to visit
the Indian camp. They bring what they can—medicines to treat
white man's diseases, knitted mitts and stockings her family can
spare. They're greeted warmly, particularly by the woman
who'd given birth to the upside-down baby. Her name is
Booktawit, which means ladybird, and she had called her baby
Mimegech-k, which means butterfly. Charlotte is about to tell
Elizabeth that the name "Wioche" means pouch of skin, the

sign of the courier who brings news and medicines, but scruples suddenly about mentioning his name. If she firmly doesn't think of him, she misses him less.

While the settlers quarrel among themselves and mostly prosper, the People suffer increasing poverty and discontent. They have no immunity to fight the diseases the settlers bring and are dying off in frightful numbers.

Booktawit asks her if it is true that the Indians are going to be corralled into one part of the province, forced to leave the land they have been roaming for thousands of years. She has not heard this rumour, she says, but in her heart she knows it very well might be true. Looking around at the crowded, disorderly camp, she feels a pang of guilt about scheming to get the land for herself and arguing about how white women should have the vote when an entire nation of people are losing all they have known.

The women invite her and her daughter to drink tea by the fire, and for a time they trade stories about children and gossip along the river. The women don't complain, though it's clear that many of their men now are more interested in rum than in hunting, alcohol being even more noxious an influence here than in the settlers' tilts and cabins along the river. "Children go hungry and women cower when the men get crazed with the rum," Charlotte says, but none of the women do more than nod.

They invite her to examine the pregnant women. She tries to protest but then decides that given the fact there is no one else to help, there is maybe some knowledge she can share. For a time, the ever-attentive Elizabeth takes it all in, her round-bellied mother in intense consultation with a succession of other women in the same condition, then finds girls her age to play with.

On the way home, she asks her mother why the Indians live off by themselves. It's a question Charlotte doesn't have a ready answer for.

When they get back to the cabin, William tells her that Robert Reid, the owner of the store by the shoals, has been appointed coroner. "It's a start," she says, wondering if a newly named coroner will ask the tough questions about the fatal fire and the matter of the gunpowder.

A FEW DAYS before Christmas, Charlotte is kneading the flour for bread when her water breaks, running down her legs and forming a puddle on the floor. The last two days it felt like the baby had turned to press hard on her spine, and now for a bleak minute she remembers Robert's difficult birth.

She calls for William, as she stoops to wipe up the floor. "It's time," she says and a look of panic fleetingly crosses his features. "By my calculations I'm early," she says. "I'm hoping our baby is strong enough." She sends him to fetch Janet Murdoch and asks Elizabeth to help her gather the things she will need—clean linens, a bowl, a knife that she lays in the fire so it will be sterilized and ready to cut the cord. She hides a stash of rum in the bedclothes.

Elizabeth feels like a frightened little girl and a grown-up all at the same time as she tends her mother at Janet's side. Thankfully the birth is quick and relatively easy. The children and William are still at the supper table when the infant slides into the world. He's a tiny little morsel with a thatch of black hair and the quizzical look of the newborn. Janet summons the three other children, and William, who stands at his wife's bedside, slightly in awe, not knowing whether to reach for the child or simply gaze from a distance. "A fine laddie," he pronounces, "at least from what I can see." Charlotte laughs and hands him the swaddled bundle. "William, meet William," she says.

On Christmas Day, Charlotte leads the family in their annual rendition of "Adeste Fideles" and, holding her new baby in her arms, tells her rapt children the Christmas story. A week later, she marks 1786 on the wall just beneath her inscription of William Wishart's birth. She allows herself to spare a thought for Wioche—their trip to Frederick Town and back seems as if it exists in a whole other lifetime—and briefly wonders if his voyages this winter will bring him by the cabin. A tiny wail comes from the cradle by her bedside, young William demanding to be fed. And she is once again swept up into all-consuming motherhood, the children playing noisily around her rocking chair.

JIMMY USED TO BE her right-hand man, and he still helps with chores and is like an older brother to the children, but most days now he's back in the bush, helping William or the other men with the logging. Elizabeth has become the de facto chatelaine of this small house. On a brisk winter afternoon, with all the pomp and flourish a ten-year-old can muster, she announces the arrival of Mr. William Davidson and offers up his new title: "Northumberland County Representative to the General Assembly of New Brunswick."

Davidson has stopped by to talk to Charlotte and William about his plans for the Miramichi. But first he catches them up on news from his enterprise up past the forks. His land grant had been cut from 100,000 acres to a mere 14,450 acres in June the year before. Davidson says losing it was a blessing. Since establishing lasting ownership is predicated on clearing the land, planting a crop and settling people on it, Davidson says he's actually relieved to be free of such extensive acreage. He can now concentrate on delivering white pines for ship masts to very eager buyers from England, and work on behalf of the future of the whole region, which needs much effort if all their livelihoods are to be secure.

"The Miramichi is the most forgotten piece of land in the entire new province," he says. "The hardest life is right here on the river. And we have none of the help that has been given to the other settlements, because we're out of sight and out of mind. I mean to change that." The postwar prosperity on the river has attracted drunks, cheats and unscrupulous opportunists as well as hard-working settlers; this is not news, as Davidson well knows. Charlotte and William often sit by their fire at night, lamenting the future. Charlotte still mulls the gunpowder fire, aware that vagabonds are contributing to a new lawlessness despite there being a sheriff and a new coroner. With so many men looking to fill their pockets with profits, even the fishery is in danger of collapse. "They net out the river for fish so some are cut off entirely," Davidson exclaims. "And they take such a quantity there soon will be no fish at all."

Charlotte has always had time for Davidson, even when the others were critical of him, and in return he has always liked Charlotte's spunk. He grins as she rants about everything from the perfidies of Loyalists to the lobbying to strip women of voting rights in future elections. "The Acadians, the Micmac and I are to be left out of the vote," she complains. "I swear I will be back on that trail to Frederick Town to quarrel about this, even if I have to carry my new baby on my back."

"You have my vote, Mrs. Wishart," Davidson says, smiling at her so that his cheeks furrow in tributaries of wrinkles. "But one situation that concerns us all has eased, I am glad to report. The quarrel over who can use the marshland near the forks has been settled for the time being. The lands will be shared among the old settlers."

William and Charlotte are happily surprised. "I've been wondering if these petitions we send have any persuasive power at all," Charlotte says. "The ones I sign are not acted on. I refused to sign the one about the marshlands, fed up as I am with waiting. And now you tell me the meadow plot I took for myself is mine in law."

This gives Davidson the opening he needs to raise a delicate matter. He tells them that a petition was sent to Governor Carleton, dated January 13, protesting the old settlers' use of the marshlands and also claiming that they were usurping all the fishing on the river. The signatories described themselves as the new settlers, and among those whose names were attached were John Murdoch and Charlotte Blake.

"Are you now calling yourself a new settler, Charlotte?"

She is furious. "I did not fix my signature to that petition, Mr. Davidson. Nor did I know of its existence."

Davidson hushes her. "I can't imagine you would have, Charlotte, but you need to know how your name is being used in some quarters."

After he's gone, Charlotte tries to figure out who would forge her signature on a petition so contrary to her interests.

"I fear we now live with liars and cheats, William."

He gives her his wariest dark-eyed glance. "Maybe it's time to leave this place and find somewhere else to settle."

To leave Blake Brook? Truly that is an option Charlotte has never considered.

IN SPRING, as soon as the trail through the woods is passable, she hikes to the Indian camp with baby William tethered to her back. She hasn't been there since freeze-up. To her great surprise, she finds Wioche standing by the fire pit at the centre of the camp, as though he has been waiting for her through the four seasons that have separated them. Everyone crowds around to have a look at the boy baby—"ulbadooses," the women murmur. Charlotte finds she can't yet lift her eyes to meet his.

"Welain?" he asks.

"Yes, I am well," she replies and finally meets his glance. After the ritual tea and visit with the women, Wioche suggests they walk with the baby to the river's edge.

SETTLED ON THE BANK in a grove of scraggy pines, Wioche builds a small fire from sweetgrass and waits for the smoke to billow into smudges. She knows what will happen next and unwraps her little boy from his bunting as they sit in the sun, leaning to kiss his fat little thighs as he kicks. Wioche smiles down at the boy, then leans down to pick him up. He holds an eagle feather aloft in one hand, as he cradles the baby in the crook of his other arm, and begins the chant she knows from the bay, the same one Chief Julian sent up after Elizabeth was born. Wioche calls on the North, the East, the South and West winds, on Mother Earth and the Great Spirit to bless this child. The familiarity of the chant is comforting, but there's melancholy too, a reminder to Charlotte that the guileless days at the bay are long gone, for the Mi'kmaq, for Wioche and for the young woman who once stayed there and is now a wife, two times over, and a mother of five.

On her way back to the cabin, she's lost in reverie, the wafts of sweet-grass smoke clinging to William and her own tresses, the sound of the river gurgling in the patches of open ice near the shore. If the Great Spirit is watching over her as well, perhaps the ships arriving come spring will bring with them a response from her father.

WILLIAM HAS BEEN AWAY for an unusually long time. When he returns late one afternoon, she and Elizabeth are carrying supper to the table. She's glad to see him, and very curious about what he's been up to. But he shushes her questions. "Let's eat, my lass, and I'll tell you all about it after the children are tucked up in their beds."

True to his word, when everyone but them is safely sleeping, he stokes the fire and settles beside Charlotte in front of the hearth. "There is a place called Tabisintack," he begins. "I found it by sailing along the north side of the bay on the other side of the shoals and carrying on north where the bay runs into the ocean. You pass a collection of islands and coves that separate Tabisintack from the sea, and you think there are two rivers there, but there is only one. Funnily enough, Charlotte, the Indians call it the Taboosimgeg River, which means 'two are here.' It's an easy shore to land a boat on, and there's a point of land there that contains great marshlands for farming." He tells her the sea is teeming with fish, great sturgeons as long as six feet, and on the meadows, geese and ducks flock in such numbers they turn the earth the colour of their feathers. "I've never told you this, but I have been there two or three times now. The wind blows softly, low to the land. It's a fair place, Charlotte, away from the quarrels we know on the Miramichi."

"I've heard of this place, called Taboosimgeg . . . don't the Micmac have a camp there?"

"Yes, but there's no white men there, save for a character named Robert Beck. He once was an Irish marine, who it's said lives wild like the Indians. A story is told that he once cracked the head of an Indian, killed him on board the *Viper*."

"John Blake was on the *Viper* that day and he recounted that tale to me himself."

They sit on by the fire, dreaming aloud about what it would be like to settle on their own in such a place and end up discussing the troubles on the Miramichi, so brutally compounded by rum. It's used as wages for men's work, to trade, to warm one's innards in the cold and to bolster bravado. Charlotte wonders if she's the only woman on the river who has used it to ease birth pains. She has seen plenty of it at the Indian camp. Some men begin to crave it daily; others binge drink, even arriving inebriated at the meetings the settlers hold, making no sense at all when they speak. Fisticuffs are common now, largely due to rum-filled men acting out their anger and frustration.

Such talk leads to mention of one of the new settlers in particular, Philip Hierlihy, who is often in the middle of the fighting. Charlotte has met him at meetings, an abrasive man with intense brown eyes, a permanently furrowed brow and the bearing of a soldier. "He's not so bad when he hasn't been drinking," William says, "but rum does light a flame to him." Hierlihy is always raging about the unfair treatment that soldiers loyal to England got when they came to the Miramichi after the war. He resents the fact that the old settlers were granted lots with a half-mile frontage on the river, while the likes of Hierlihy have to settle for two-hundred-acre lots with sixty rod of frontage, about half the size. Then there is the issue of the marshlands—supposedly settled. But the new settlers are still determined to get their share of it.

More than two hundred souls are living along the river now. Whether rum-induced or not, the battle for the land is intensifying. Charlotte hopes Davidson was sincere when he said his task as representative was to bring order to the river. And the place called Tabisintack begins to play like music in her mind.

SHE'S IMAGINING the vast marshland and its bordering dark forest the next night as she sits by lamplight sewing. For weeks she's been cutting and stitching together pants for the boys and William and skirts for the girls and herself. Tonight she snips pieces of embroidered cloth from her worn-out bodices and unravels wool from ragged vests to knit new ones. The children gather around and listen to the stories she tells about what ladies in London wear and how some of them turned up on the river still wearing their fancy clothes. What a sight they made.

"Old Mrs. Cort used to dress in her best silks with beautiful plumed hats and a dainty parasol," Charlotte recounts. "Then she'd sit herself in a canoe and instruct the Indian man who worked for her family to paddle her out to meet an arriving ship." The children howl with delight at the image. "Mrs. Murdoch, our neighbour, arrived with velvet gowns, riding habits and plumed hats as well, but she soon learned it was best to leave such fine things in her trunks."

The children ask her how she used to dress before she came to the Miramichi. "Women were so painted and hidden behind all manner of costume for every occasion, Parliament finally passed a law against vanity," she tells her avid audience. "They made their skin whiter than white with powdered lead, and put red paint on their lips, and used lampblack to darken their eyelashes. Don't look at me that way, young Elizabeth. I was only fifteen years old at the time and wore no paint at all. Nanny made me write out the law into my schoolbook. Here, I'll prove it." She rises to retrieve the old notebook from her precious stack of reading materials.

"'All women whatever age, range, profession, whether virgins, maids, or widows,'" she reads aloud, "'that shall from and after such an Act, impose upon, seduce, betray into matrimony, any of His Majesty's subjects by scents, paints, cosmetic washes, artificial teeth, false hair, Spanish wool, iron stays, hoops, high-heeled shoes, bolstered hips, shall incur the penalty of the law in force against witchcraft and like misdemeanours and that the marriage, upon conviction shall stand null and void.'" The children laugh themselves silly while their usually stern mother prances about the room mimicking the ladies of London, swooshing imaginary hoops.

At bedtime, they beg for another story—their favourite tale—of Gluskap and the Boy in the Birchbark Box. "Tell us about the magic arrow," John Junior asks pleadingly. Settling them all around her chair by the fire, she begins.

"A long, long time ago, Gluskap found a couple weeping in the woods. He asked what was wrong, and they told him their disobedient son had run away because he didn't like their rules. He was only twelve winters old, and they didn't know in which direction he'd gone and were worried sick that he would meet a wild animal or other dangers and be hurt or killed. Taking pity on them, Gluskap drew a magic arrow from his quiver, nocked it to the bow, aimed it skyward and let it fly. He knew that the direction in which it fell would be the way the boy fled. For seven days, he followed the arrow, sending it skyward again and again, until he sensed he was getting close to the missing boy."

She goes on to recount the wiles of a wicked sorcerer, the moans of a pitiable old crone, the threat of a giant horned serpent and, of course, the rescue by Gluskap. Then it is time for bed. With Robert pretending to be a wicked sorcerer and Polly slithering into bed like a snake, they frighten baby William, who starts howling his little lungs out. It's another hour before the storyteller finds quiet by the hearth. And then it's her turn to ask for a story.

"William, tell me more about Tabisintack."

CHARLOTTE HAS BEEN HOPING in vain that a teacher will come to start a school on the Miramichi. When one does not materialize by the fall, she invites some of the children from nearby lots to join her own four and Jimmy in her makeshift home classroom. The older children copy sonnets and poems onto slates William has fetched from Liverpool. The younger ones learn their letters and numbers. She teaches them mostly by way of story, telling about the history of the river. And Mi'kmaq tales find their way into the mix. "You wouldn't find words such as bear, moose or Gluskap in my old nanny's school books," she quips to her husband. Even in snowstorms the settler children trek to the Wishart place on Blake Brook, and in such a manner the whole family staves off cabin fever that long winter.

In mid-May the next year, William sails away with a heavy load of logs destined for the sawmill started up by Benjamin Stymiest at Bettvin on the other side of the shoals. He likes the man, who came from New York with his wife and five children, chased out by the rebels. He's one of the few Loyalists William has time for. "He wants to get a grant for his land and he won't start the mill as a proper business until he's guaranteed ownership of the lot. But nonetheless he saws wood for many men." After William drops the load intended for lumber, he plans to take the prized white pines he cut during the winter on to Liverpool to sell to the shipbuilders.

A week goes by and William hasn't returned. Charlotte finds herself glancing up the river several times a day waiting to see him sail into sight. But there's no sign of him.

After ten days, she asks out loud, several times an hour, "Where could he be?" And soon she grows angry. "Why does he go off like this without telling me when he's coming back?" She contemplates a dozen reasons why he might be delayed, and tries them out on Jimmy, who has his own reasons to be upset with William Wishart—he wanted to go with him, not stay back with the women and children. "He's likely found a business opportunity. Or he's waiting for a ship to arrive with a special cargo—perhaps a spinning wheel, such as the one John Murdoch brought for Janet. Or maybe he's met up with his fellows from the Quebec campaign in Liverpool and they've lost track of time with their reminiscing. Or maybe he's gone up again to Tabisintack. What do you think, Jimmy?"

Jimmy doesn't know what to think, or how to answer his mistress.

When the two-week mark passes, her thoughts turn dark. "He's fallen sick and is unable to sail. Or maybe he's just run off, wanting respite from this crowded cabin. Maybe the ship is in need of repair and I worry needlessly."

She's relieved when Janet Murdoch asks her to come with her to visit the Indian camp, and on the walk there and back, Janet enumerates all the likely good reasons for the delay.

But when May turns into June, she knows something has gone terribly wrong. The children have become anxious, clinging to her as though tangled in the vibrations that are seeping out of her bones. The entire household has one eye on the river from morning to night. Polly cries in her sleep and comes into bed with her. Elizabeth tiptoes around the house as though a noise might cause them to miss the welcome sound of his return.

It is John Murdoch who finally comes to the cabin. When Charlotte opens the door to find him standing there, the crushing feeling in her chest tells her before he speaks that all the wishing and hoping and praying for the safe return of William Wishart has been for naught.

"I went myself over the shoal to Bettvin," he begins. "William had been there to the sawmill and dropped off his timber. He was last seen sailing up the north side of the bay toward open water."

She thinks, "He really was going to Tabisintack."

Murdoch continues, in his softest voice. "But he did not deliver his pine to Liverpool. For these last many weeks, the boys on the ships have been keeping an eye out for him. There's been no sign. Charlotte, we can only conclude that William is lost at sea."

He reaches for her hands, pats them, lets go. "Charlotte, I won't stop now. You see to the children, and I'll look in on you tomorrow, with Janet."

She watches his sturdy back as he strides across the clearing and into the trees. She's shocked, surely, but didn't she know this? William was not John, gone wandering for months at a time. Likely he wanted to revisit the place they had been talking about obsessively, to make sure it was a safe place to settle. He was probably going to bring her home some evidence that the fantasy was attainable, and became lost somehow on the way.

She closes her door and goes to sit by the fire. The younger children tug on her hands, trying to haul her up, asking that she go find William herself. The older ones remember all too vividly the last time this happened. She can see it in their faces, the scars of losing their provider for the second time in the space of two years. She gathers them around her and once again promises she will take care of them, that together the family will survive. But in her heart she protests: this can't be true.

That night, she lies tossing in the dark. Finally she wanders out into the main room and leans to light a taper in the fire. Then she picks up her diary:

> *Surely we are cursed. I can't bear thinking about what*
> *became of William. Did he struggle? Was it drowning? Did*
> *he cling to the remains of his ship hoping for rescue and die*
> *of exposure? Did he find the shore only to die of hunger or*
> *is he wandering yet? No, I have to believe he would have*
> *found his way. I hope it is the distant place of Tabisintack*
> *that he was seeking on his fateful journey and that his spirit*
> *will abide over the land that he sought.*
>
> *All around me brothers, fathers and sons go to sea,*
> *some never to return. Other men are killed in the felling of*
> *a tree, or suffer the mean fate of John Blake, who died for*
> *lack of a doctor. And now it is William.*

THREE MEN DEAD, twice widowed, Charlotte now has five children, two lots of land and the determination of Job to survive her latest calamity.

William Davidson comes to the cabin as soon as he hears the terrible news. "Aye, Charlotte, 'tis a trial you live. It's another husband you'll be needing and many a man on this river who'd be lucky to have ye." The thickened brogue brings the commodore to mind; this is the nearest thing to sympathy she has known and as close as a riverman can get to kindness.

But kindness won't feed her family. The very next day, Charlotte packs her husband's coins into her pocket and canoes herself up the river to the tilt of John Humphrys to buy Lot Fifty-three from him, assuring herself in such manner that she'll have enough hay to feed the livestock come winter. Then she goes home to sort out her life as a widow once again.

While people all around her assume that Charlotte is as strong and sensible as she looks—and that since widows with property are a prize possession in the colony, she'll soon have a new husband—the fact that William's body hasn't been found haunts her. And many evenings she walks down to the water to watch for his return, even though she knows he is not coming back.

AT A MEETING later that season called by Marston to try to bring peace between the Miramichi belligerents, Charlotte listens impatiently to Philip Hierlihy complaining again about the size of the lots granted to the old settlers. He's an annoying bulldog, she reckons, and with a reputation for laying about with his fists while under the influence, so that no one is willing to take him down a peg. The Widow Wishart-once-Blake feels no such compunction and tears into him. "First it's the entire river you want, Philip Hierlihy, and to be rid of us who were here first, so you puffed-up soldiers can take what you think is owed you. Now it's the size of your plots that has got you steaming. Why didn't you go to Antigonish with that brother of yours? You have no hold here. Spare me your British loyalty, your sense of entitlement and your high-handed attitude."

The other men in the room exchange amused glances while Charlotte upbraids the noisy Hierlihy. The man himself is so astounded he shuts up entirely. He's never heard a woman talk to anyone like this, much less to a former sergeant in the Prince of Wales American Regiment. Just as Charlotte had heard of him and his ways, he has heard of her, the widow who was the first woman to settle here and who by the age of thirty-two is the mother of five children from three fathers, all dead. He doesn't really know what he was expecting of "that woman," but this red-haired beauty with the trim body of a girl and the language of a logger mesmerizes him. Though he fights back, of course. It's his nature.

"What, you think you deserve these oversized lots on the river and that we should be satisfied with a grant half your size? How will the place prosper if it begins with injustice?"

The reference to justice catches her off guard and for a time she just glares at him. But it is the beginning of a conversation that carries on and off for the rest of the meeting, and indeed, when he says he will see her safely home, all during the trek back to Lot Eight from the meeting point at the marshlands.

"I don't need a man to be safe," she replied curtly but walks along the path with him anyway.

He returns to visit the next day, and she invites him for tea. As much as he irritates her, she is always fascinated by the details of a person's life, the events that influence a man's behaviour. And soon she finds herself putting the kettle on again and asking for his story.

As she guesses from his accent, he was born in Ireland and immigrated to Middletown, Connecticut, as a youngster with his family in 1753. He says they were descendants of Dermot O'Hurley, the archbishop of Cashel, who was tortured and hanged by the neck in Dublin in 1584 for refusing to embrace the Queen's religion. Charlotte contemplates the parallels in the lives of William's and Philip Hierlihy's ancestors. "Mr. Wishart's ancestor was martyred by a Scottish Queen for being Protestant," she says, "and yours was murdered by an English Queen for being Catholic, less than forty years apart. It's not unlike the turning tides of the Indians, the Acadians, the Loyalists and the old settlers over the last three decades right here in New Brunswick. Longevity seems very much attached to point of view."

And Hierlihy actually laughs with her, enjoying the interesting twists of her mind, if not the comparison with the family history of her dead husband.

She discovers he's descended from Milesian Irish Celts who, over time, altered the name O'Hurley to several variations that ultimately became Hierlihy. Their Catholic faith was altered as well. His father, Cornelius, was a lieutenant in the British Regiment when they came to Connecticut, and just two years after arriving in the New World he was killed in a battle with the French not far from this very place. Philip's older brother, Timothy, became the family patriarch, and when he married a woman from the Church of England, the entire family abandoned the Catholic faith and became Anglicans.

His stories of life in Connecticut paint a picture of a prosperous, thriving colony that dissolved into a violent crucible between those who favoured the King of England and those who wanted to become masters of their own fate. When war became unavoidable, he followed Timothy into battle with the Prince of Wales American Regiment.

He then treats her to some of the most gruesome accounts of battle she has ever heard, as if her attention has released something in him. Hiding in the woods to escape the rebels, some of the men starved, others froze to death, and their lingering cries for help still torment him. When they attacked with muskets and bayonets, sometimes they were unable to strike a killing blow. "The moaning and shrieking, the bleeding and emptying of bowels, the puking and choking—that's what men did to men. We marched and attacked and retreated and marched again week after week, year after year. The innards of men—friends and foes—stains upon your person and squelching under your boot is a sight that stays with me."

His hatred for the men who chased his family from their homestead in Connecticut is palpable. And Charlotte begins to understand his festering resentment of the sour welcome he received when he arrived on the Miramichi as a soldier who felt he had saved the land from marauding privateers.

"Your brother is said to have started a settlement in Nova Scotia. Why did you not go with him there?" Charlotte asks.

"Most of the men in the disbanded regiment were granted lots of land near Frederick Town, but my brother knew about this parcel of land in Nova Scotia and asked for the grant especially. I went with him for a time. It's a good place he has in Antigonish. But a lad I served with, Daniel Menton, knew of this Miramichi River, and said he would lay up logs for a tilt and we would prosper from the fish and the timber. I decided to come with him."

As he says his goodbyes that evening, having stayed past tea, and through all the preparations for supper, and sat down at the table with her children, she thought, No wonder he's dangerous with the rum on him. That is one lonely, and wounded, soul.

He doesn't settle for one visit, but comes the next day and the next and the one after that, till she starts assigning him chores in the garden as she can't sit still and humour his conversation.

And inside two weeks—though she knows full well that part of her attraction for Hierlihy are the lots that she owns—when he asks her to marry him, she says yes.

In early September, they stand together with Pad's daughter Elizabeth, John's children, John, Polly and Robert, and little William Wishart in front of James Horton, Justice of the Quorum for Northumberland County in the newly named Parish of Newcastle, and are duly married according to law.

When they return to the cabin, Charlotte slips the legal document in with her treasured books and marks the date on the wall. Married to Philip Hierlihy, September 11, 1787.

PHILIP'S FIRST TASK as her husband is to build another addition. A bedchamber for the girls is tacked on, making the place look like an old man's squashed top hat. New beds are built, without mattresses but laden with furs to cushion the boards and warm the children on them.

By October 1787, she is pregnant again, and the New Year is hardly begun when she discovers John Humphrys is claiming ownership of Lot Fifty-three, the very lot she bought from him just seven months earlier. She threatens to harm the man if he doesn't quit the property, and when he defies her, she sends a memorial to John O'Dell, the provincial secretary in Frederick Town, dated January 7, 1788, demanding retribution.

She capitalizes the words she wishes to emphasize, penning her blunt demand in flourishing letters that make the page look more like a work of art than an accusation. She reads it aloud to Philip before dispatching it. "I shall sign my name as Charlotte Blake since that is the name under which I made the purchase," she says.

Honourable Sir,
You have Desired me to send a Certificate of what cleared
land was on No. 53 South side of the river but the man will

not sign it for me as he means to try to get located for it
himself after the Selling of it and Giving a Deed which Sir
you have in your office which is Drawn by Mr. Ledwiny
and Signed by John Wilson Esquire.

Honourable Sir I hope you will see me testifyed in this
affair and have me Registrate for said Lot as it seems to me
that he have a mind to try to cut me out of it after I buying
of and paying for it.

Charlotte Blake

N.B. The man is John Humphrys

She's still waiting for a reply when the first Hierlihy child arrives in the midst of a howling nor'easter in June. She names him Philip, after his father, who behaves as though this is the first child who has ever been born, despite the evidence to the contrary all around him.

Jimmy, now a strapping young man, announces that he's leaving them for a job in Frederick Town the same week as Philip gets himself appointed assessor of rates and surveyor of roads for Northumberland County Middle District. Philip makes so much fuss of his new station in life that she feels like she's barely had a moment to acknowledge that Jimmy is leaving them. The morning he sets off, though, Charlotte makes him a gift of William Wishart's winter boots, and his great coat. And for a time he hugs her like the colt of a boy he once was.

Soon after, Philip is sworn in by the grand jury in the newly established premises for the Court of General Session up by the forks. Watching him, Charlotte's pride is somewhat tempered by the fact that he appears to like his new title overmuch, the status it confers more than the duty. She's been keeping him off the rum, but she can't deny that his bad temper and brawling style in public threaten the position that is so clearly dear to him.

Barely a year after Philip's birth, the second Hierlihy child arrives. Eleanor Helene raises the tally to three children under the age of four and five over the age of eight. Philip wears his large family like a badge of honour, the beginnings of his empire.

That same winter William Davidson dies from the effects of exposure after falling through the ice in the river. It's a painful loss for Charlotte. She trusted him, enjoyed his company and found comfort in the fact that he clearly approved of her non-conformist behaviour. Not so her husband, who has begun to remind her incessantly that she should behave more like the wife of a man with a position in the government.

Although Philip disapproves, she continues to go with Elizabeth, and sometimes Janet Murdoch, to the Indian camp to help the women and children. It's on the way back from the camp one spring day, with baby Eleanor tied to her mother's back—Charlotte, a little short of breath as she is pregnant again—that Elizabeth mentions that she wants to stop at Duncan Robertson's lot to deliver a parcel.

"A parcel of what?" Charlotte wants to know.

She's taken aback when Elizabeth confesses that she's made strawberry tarts for the handsome young man on Lot Five, who came to the river after serving with the 42nd Black Watch regiment in the American War. He'd recently been appointed by the government to act as the attorney on the river. Elizabeth's cheeks turn crimson when her surprised mother asks what such a gift is meant to convey to Duncan Robertson.

Charlotte can't imagine how the girl has managed to make strawberry tarts without anyone noticing. But remembering the moments she stole with Pad as a girl, she knows that a young couple can and will find a way. And here she thought fifteen-year-old Elizabeth had just been slipping away from the cabin because she wanted a rest from incessant child care. Unlike her rambunctious sister Polly, Elizabeth is shy; she's sweet with the younger children and is always an adoring daughter. It never occurred to Charlotte that she could be seeking the company of a man.

Elizabeth looks at the ground, shuffles her feet in the pine needles and says in a barely audible voice, "I want to marry Duncan." Charlotte whirls around to face her so fast, little Eleanor almost swings right out of the sling.

"Marry? You really want to marry this man?"

Charlotte stands on the bank of the river, as still as the trees all around her, confronting her first-born child, the daughter who was conceived in England and born in Nepisiguit and has been by her side for almost sixteen years. Other local girls Elizabeth's age have become wives, she knows, but she is utterly perplexed that she has missed the cues that her girl was even interested in men. Elizabeth is looking stricken and so guilty that Charlotte, finally, simply has to laugh and give her blessing. She is the last person on Earth to want to stand in the way of love, knowing how short a season it is in bloom.

The day before the nuptials, Charlotte calls her daughter to her bedchamber so they can be alone, and she twists two strands of silver into a bracelet around her delicate wrist.

"This was your father's. He wore it with the pride of a man who dared to dream of a larger future. I saved these strands for you to wear at your wedding. When you look at them, spare a thought for the father who would have smiled on your sweet face and loved you just as much as I do."

On September 22, 1791, a very pregnant Charlotte, her husband, Philip, and their brood of seven children travel to Bettvin, known to some as Bay du Vin, to witness the ceremony, performed by James Horton Esquire, now a Justice of the Peace. Charlotte's heart lurches only a little when he pronounces that "Elizabeth Willisams and Duncan Robertson, both residents of the Parish of Newcastle, are married by law."

The wall at the back of the cabin is now marked with births, deaths, and the marriage day of her first-born child.

CHAPTER II

The Miramichi

1791

For a brief time, there is one person less in the cabin, but James Hierlihy is born just before the river freezes over in November 1791. Space has become an intolerable issue at Blake Brook. Mealtime is chaotic as six children vie for their portion of stew, and the seventh one cries for his mother's breast. Bedtime is worse. They're packed in, two and three to a bed, with the infant James in a cradle. Philip has managed to find another homeless boy, Donovan, to tend the livestock. He sleeps in the shed, not the house, but they have to find him a place at the table.

Elizabeth has been coming every day to help her, treading the well-worn path from her "marriage home," as she likes to call the tilt Duncan has built on Lot Five, to the Hierlihys' collection of huts. But now she is expecting her first child, and her mother decides she has to wean herself away from her support. Elizabeth cannot be expected to tend to her brothers and sisters when she'll be feeding her own child. So Charlotte decides to seek a girl to help with the children. What's one more under her roof?

Still, when she calculates the crops she can grow that spring and the number of mouths she has to feed, the tally tells her they are on the short side of even. So they rent more land, plant more potatoes, buy more livestock. She knows of one family that sold a cow in the fall to buy eight bushels of potatoes; another traded three sheep for a half a hundredweight of flour. She doesn't want to be in that boat, and she likes to remind her husband that she is resourceful. "I once ground buds and leaves into the grain to make it stretch when the crop produced so little it might as well have failed."

But another daughter, Honnor, is born in February 1793, and life begins to feel like a constant game of stretching. A month later, Elizabeth makes Charlotte a grandmother when she gives birth to Duncan Junior.

One evening after she has visited the new mother, and spent some time on the snowshoe journey back thinking about the future her children and grandchildren now face, Charlotte tells Philip about the place William Wishart visited, about the huge meadows, the easy access to the river, the ocean teeming with fish. The fact that no one lives around there but the People in their camp, and maybe one lonely hermit. It's a place they can settle their entire family and start anew.

Philip's expression is sober as he listens to her. "It's not that the prospect is unappealing, Charlotte," he says. "And it may be what we turn our minds to achieving. But we cannot quit this land until the deeds are signed to us, or all that we've worked so hard to accumulate will be lost."

She knows he is right.

But in the meantime, she lures him on an adventure to find this Tabisintack. "If William told me right, the journey there and back will take a day, the weather being fine." Though Philip can be a hard man, he knows that now is not the time to deny a woman with so many children a little hope.

On a fine day in May, they leave their brood with Elizabeth and set out for what Philip has jokingly started to call the promised land. Going by canoe means they don't have to fear a keel getting caught in the sandbars of the shoals; they slip across them with ease and paddle along to the north side of the bay without incident. The voyage through the open water thrills Charlotte, though they stay close to shore, avoiding the swell of the sea.

JUST AFTER MIDDAY, they spot the opening to the Tabisintack River, just as William had described it. There are half a dozen islands, separated by deep water, layering the entrance to the river. Long sand dunes lick into the sea and dense seagrass covers the islands. Coves and creeks along the banks beg for exploring and fish swim in massive schools just under the surface of the water. Flocks of ducks and geese dot a huge salt marsh.

As soon as she lays her eyes on this land, Charlotte knows it is the place they must settle. She also knows, as though she's been here a hundred times before, exactly where the house will stand. The setting is magnificent: a point surrounded by water on three sides, the site for the house a half-acre back from the water, safely away from the rising tides and with a clear view to the meadow behind it and the wide-open salt marsh.

"A two-storey house," she tells Philip as he paddles them in to shore, "with proper rooms up the ladder for the children and, on the lower floor, a place to cook and sit by the hearth, and our own bedchamber." So anxious is she to put her feet on this land, she's out of the canoe too soon, sloshing in knee-deep water, nearly losing her balance.

They wander up and down the river's edge, cross the marshland to the woods, measure out the lots they will need for each of the children when they are grown. She thinks she sees sign of the Indian camp on the other side of the river but isn't certain, though the acrid scent of old fire mixes with the sharp whiff of brine in the air.

A soft wind blows low to the ground, which turns her thoughts to William. How reverently he spoke of this place. She looks out over the water and wonders if he's out there watching over her, and could possibly be happy that she's here.

Philip interrupts her reverie. "If we leave this minute, Charlotte, we can make it back to Black Brook before dark."

"It's Blake Brook," she corrects, for the thousandth time, as she reluctantly follows him back to their boat.

THE YEAR 1795 turns out to be a watershed for Charlotte. On April 15, she writes in her diary:

> I'll be forty years old this month. Hard to believe I've been here for twenty years. From wilderness to settlement, from isolation to community, from a girl to a mother of nine children and already a grandmother. And at last the new Elections Act says land-holding women can vote so I will cast my ballot with the men after all.
>
> It's ten years since I sent the memorial to Papa. Ten years of wondering—did he receive it, destroy it, misplace it? Did his reply go astray? I think of it less often now but still it prickles my soul.
>
> Philip and I plan to leave this cabin on the brook and

start again in Tabisintack as soon as we possibly can. He
has his flaws and his demons, but we are well-suited in our
mutual plan to settle a new part of this frontier. It takes
land, and lots of kin working the lots, to make the life I
have been seeking ever since I set foot on the bay. My boys
will build and plough, my girls will work beside them. The
family will set roots deep into that soil. It will be another
beginning.

THEY MAKE CLANDESTINE VISITS to Tabisintack over several seasons, mark the fields for growing, take down timbers to clear land for planting as well as for building.

On the Miramichi, the family is by no means idle. Elizabeth and Duncan have another child, Polly weds Duncan McCraw, who'd also served with the 42nd Regiment of the Black Watch, bringing another ally into the plan to settle Tabisintack. John Junior wins a position in the land assessment office of the province, another valuable placement for the success of her project, she thinks. But they are still waiting impatiently for their deeds.

Then, to her amazement, Charlotte discovers she is with child again. Elizabeth and Polly tend her at the birth, which is complicated only by Charlotte's weariness at the thought of raising another child.

But from the moment she's born, this girl child, Charlotte Mary, is a treasure to the family. The Hierlihy offspring all share their father's sandy-coloured hair and amber eyes. But this new baby has hair the colour of strawberries mixed with sunshine and eyes so blue they startle the onlooker. When Charlotte gazes at her, and her nine brothers and sisters, she feels a surge of pride. Five boys: John Junior, the serious older brother; Robert, trying desperately to be as useful as John; William, sweet-faced and gentle; Philip, the relentless organizer of everything from the children's chores to games of pirates down by the shore; James, the image of his ambitious, hot-headed father. And five girls: the beautiful and reliable Elizabeth; rambunctious Polly with auburn hair like her mother's; Eleanor, the enigma, who is kind and stubbornly self-sufficient at once; Honnor who toddles in hot pursuit of the others; and now Charlotte Mary, a wee colleen with the look of the Irish all over her.

Charlotte is still staying close to the cabin, tired out by her labour and enchanted by the new baby, when she sees a canoe on the river. Wioche. She beckons him to land, carrying the baby down to greet him. "You'll have a cup of strong, black tea with us," she insists. What she means is it is high time he became a visitor to the Hierlihy cabin.

"Wioche, we want to settle at Tabisintack," she tells him after she has settled him by the hearth with the promised cup. As was the scene so long ago now, her littlest ones cluster by her chair, peeking solemnly at the handsome Indian their mother seems on such good terms with.

"We call that place Taboosimgeg," he replies. "It's a good place, where wood, fish, marsh, game and wind come to Mother Earth."

When she asks if it is near where he lives, he tells her there are three Indian camps at Taboosimgeg, one directly across river from where she and Philip paddled the canoe to the shore. "I saw you there once," he says.

She's flabbergasted. "You saw me there? Why didn't I see you?"

"You nearly fell into the water when you climbed out of the boat."

She laughs. She had forgotten how well the People know the bush, sniff out the scents, observe the changes.

Philip arrives home just then and can't help but scowl as she introduces the Indian, even though in the tales of her life she's shared with him, he knows that Wioche has been a true friend to her and her children.

That evening, Philip comes home staggering with drink from yet another settlers' meeting, bloodied and cursing a man called William Donald. Charlotte throws cold water from the brook over his beaten face and gives him the sharpest edge of her tongue. "You're the shame of this family with your bad temper and volatile behaviour. You can't tell me that William Donald was the one to pick this fight."

She's startled when John Junior and Robert take Philip's side, mulishly staring at her as though her anger is unreasonable. "Don't look at me, my sons. This isn't the first time your father has been the instigator of fisticuffs. But if he values his family, I hope it will be the last."

Later she wonders whether the visit from Wioche has anything to do with Philip's lapse. But she still won't attend the Court of General Session in August when the trial of Philip Hierlihy is convened. Again, the older boys take his part. "They goad him and humiliate him into these quarrels," John Junior argues, and Charlotte reads something in his eyes that dares her to ask him why. Is he implying that she is the cause? That Philip is defending her honour? Things have really come to a sorry pass along the river if that is true, though she knows that in some people's minds her strong will, and many husbands, has made her notorious.

"Many other men exhibit the same behaviour, Mother. And you can't doubt that he wants the best for this family," John insists. But she won't go, and when the court finds Philip guilty and fines him ten shillings and costs, Charlotte refuses to speak to him for a week.

Meanwhile, the government continues to delay the official stamping of the 1777 deeds. "It's like waiting for a storm," Charlotte growls, knowing other men on the river are poised like snakes, waiting to strike at their lots if the deeds are denied. But the waiting goes on. So does the uneasiness, so do the hostilities.

The New Year brings the settlers together in the solidarity that comes with sadness. John Murdoch has been suffering for more than two years with horribly painful sores in his mouth. On January 11, in an agony his family can hardly bear to watch, he dies and Janet is left a widow.

"At least her children are mostly grown, and surely they'll take care of her," Charlotte confides to Philip on the way back to the cabin, where it feels like all they do now is wait—like hostages—for the decision from the capital about Miramichi Lots Eight, Nine and Ten.

IT'S MARCH 4, 1798, before word comes that a runner has arrived with the deeds from Frederick Town. The old settlers gather at the Hendersons' place to meet the courier; and there is an eerie silence as the names are called and the packets are delivered. To John Blake Junior, Lot Eight, settled by John Blake Senior, now deceased—161 acres. To Philip Hierlihy for service in the Prince of Wales American Regiment during the American Revolution, Lot Nine—160 acres. To Charlotte Hierlihy, widow of John Blake, Lot Ten—154 acres. Now it is official. She is a landowner in her own right.

The lots for her sons-in-law, Duncan Robertson and Duncan McCraw, are yet to be deeded. Leaving a lot without the security of a deed is tantamount to giving it away to any number of poachers lurking along the river. The time is not yet right for her whole clan to move.

Two days later, Philip is due back in court. He has been accused yet again of fighting, this time the more serious charge of assault and battery, but he is remanded and asked to return in August. Charlotte is determined to get him out of here, to Tabisintack, a move she thinks will calm his temper or at least keep him away from the river ruffians she now blames for his troubles. The quarrelling and physical fighting and lawlessness have increased exponentially. New settlers are arriving weekly; the judiciary cannot keep up with the charges. She worries about her own older boys, who are now twenty-one, seventeen and thirteen, getting involved in a fracas that could cost them their lives. She can hardly wait to escape.

The river, once a proud artery running through pristine land, which challenged the humans who came here, is bleeding from the wounds made by wild men, becoming the byway to stripped forests and ugly lives. Their departure for Tabisintack can't come too soon.

That summer, when they go again to Tabisintack, they discover the elusive Beck wandering the shores. Beck tells Philip he owns a lot on the south side of the river he'll sell for fifteen British pounds. Philip snatches up the offer immediately and has the deed transferred to his own name, thanks to Duncan's quick action in his position as attorney.

With that legal toehold, Philip decides that it's safe to clear the plot where the house will stand, leaving a shelter of trees around it. The boys hand-hue the wood for the two-storey structure of Charlotte's dreams. They dig a cellar for dry goods, line it with stones they haul from the fields and pack mud mixed with straw around the base and between the stones to make a rock-hard wall.

They only stay a few days at a time, sleeping in makeshift shelters and coaxing the plan into being. Charlotte plants a garden in the meadow and asks Wioche, when he visits, how they can drain the salt marsh for more farmland. She knows the Acadians have created such plots, but Wioche pleads ignorance. And Charlotte is a little ashamed: why should he collaborate so directly in her taming of the land?

They return to Blake Brook exhausted and exhilarated, and then they do double duty, taking care of the lots on the Miramichi.

As the log walls rise on her new home, they chink the spaces between the timbers with seaweed and pieces of birchbark, a lesson Charlotte learned from the Mi'kmaq. Then they cover the outside walls with more bark.

And, as it turns out once Beck is gone, they are not the only white folks in this place they have started to refer to as The Point. One afternoon while the boys are hammering the second floor into place and Charlotte is pulling weeds and rocks from the garden plot, helped more or less by James, Eleanor, Honnor and Charlotte Mary, two men walk up to where they are working and introduce themselves. David Savoy and Jacques Breaux live down shore, on the other side of the saltwater marsh, and tell Charlotte, in accents that make it clear they are Acadians, that they abandoned the Miramichi in 1790.

They are offspring of Acadians originally from a place called Shepody, who were chased out in the expulsion, fled to the Baie de Chaleur and finally returned to Negowack. She knows the place. It's an Indian word meaning "improperly situated," on the north side of Miramichi Bay. But it's the mention of her bay that catches her.

"I lived there when I arrived here in 1775," she offers. It turns out they know all about her: they heard about the redheaded Englishwoman who came to the bay with Commodore Walker.

She wants to know what they have heard, and who they know on the bay—the Landrys?

"Bien sur," says Savoy, a square-shouldered, black-haired man who manages to be handsome despite the gap between his two front teeth. "That's how we heard about you."

"And do you know Wioche, a Micmac from around there? His family has marriage ties with the Landrys."

"Mais oui," Breaux chimes in.

This vast wilderness isn't so isolated after all, she thinks, wondering why it is that she's hardly ever left her homestead on the river while others, such as the Acadians and the Indians, move about and stay in contact.

Breaux continues. "My father is Anselme Breaux. David's mother is Anselme's sister, so we are cousins. Do you not know the Breaux families in Negowack?"

She has to admit that she does not.

"Surely you know Otho Robichaud, known as Sieur?"

She knows the name, but her world till now hasn't reached beyond Napan Bay in one direction and the forks in the other.

Their story holds her attention for much of the afternoon. The deprivation their families suffered, the struggle to survive, and their deft way of recounting some forty-three years of family history, reminding her of the way André Landry told tales around the fire at the camp on the bay. Time has flown by, her garden work neglected, and finally she glances at her untidy plot as a sign that she must get back to work.

Her neighbours take the hint. But before they go, they offer her a little more detail about the place she has now chosen to settle.

"My father and his brother Victor passed three winters here hunting and trapping before moving to Negowack where they started a new settlement," Breaux says. "It is a good place. You will be happy here."

She says goodbye, entreating them to return to visit again, and they are away toward the river when Savoy calls back to her. "Madame, did the man who came to the bay looking for you, a Monsieur MacCulloch, did he ever find you?"

"Will MacCulloch?" An image flashes into her mind—the dashing Will staging his audacious plan to keep her in the Mi'kmaq camp while the *Hanley* sailed for Britain.

The children crowd around as their confident, hard-talking mother suddenly looks as though she's about to dissolve in front of their eyes. "Who is Will MacCulloch, Mother?" Eleanor asks.

"Come back," Charlotte calls, already running toward them. "What do you know of Mr. MacCulloch?"

"All I know is he was asking after you," says Savoy. "But I'll ask les gens when next I go to the Baie."

She thanks him and waves as they head off again. She's perspiring in the cool afternoon air, her face flushed. And her thoughts are hectic: When was Will here? Is this somehow connected to the memorial I sent to Papa?

As soon as David and Jacques are out of earshot, the children start asking questions.

"Mama, why do the men speak like that?" Eleanor, now a big girl of nine, asks.

Realizing how small their world has been on the Miramichi where English settlers and the Mi'kmaq have been their only acquaintances, Charlotte explains that David and Jacques are

French, Acadians actually, whose families have been here for a very long time. Philip asks when they came here. "Before the British. But they were sent away." All three want to know why, so while Charlotte digs into the earth and the children pull on the weeds, ripping out the roots, she tells them the story, as she knows it, about the Acadians.

"They were the first to come here from Europe, from a country called France. But their government ignored them, left them to find their way, even though they were very loyal to their country and their Catholic religion. I met some Acadians when I lived with the People at the Baie de Chaleur, where Wioche also lived. They're kind people, hard-working and very clever about surviving in the woods. When they were abandoned here by their homeland, they learned from the Indians, made clothes from the pelts of bear, beaver, otter, fox and marten. I was told that the early Acadian settlers loved the colour red and used to get garments from the British and cut them up, unravel them, spin them and weave strips of the red into their clothes.

"They had interesting customs too. They weren't allowed to marry until the girl could weave and the boy could make a set of wheels. During the long winters they told stories, drank home-made wine and cider and kept warm by the fire. They were wonderful farmers too, and other settlers that came after envied them for it.

"But then there was war between Britain and France and when the British won, they sent all the Acadians away to punish them for not helping the British. And the British settlers took over their farms."

"Where were they sent?" James wants to know.

"It was a terrible time. They had no quarrel with anyone but were made to suffer. Families were separated, children lost their parents, husbands lost their wives and many died on the way to a place in the south, a French territory called Louisiana. Some refused to go and hid with the Indians. Many began to find their way back here about the same time that I arrived from England."

She smiles when she says, "I feel they are the same today as they were a hundred years ago. They still sing and tell stories and help one another. There's a lot to learn from the Acadians. They made dykes to hold back the tidal waters and protect their farms and dug ditches to drain the marshlands. Maybe those two men we met can teach us how to do that with the saltwater marshlands here."

Back at the cabin on the Miramichi a few days later, after the children are all in bed, Charlotte reaches for her diary:

If Will was here looking for me, then my father surely was informed of my whereabouts. He must have my memorial by now, but there's been no reply. If Papa was told of my condition—a runaway girl with child by a black man in the wilderness of the New World—he would surely have disowned me. Perhaps Will came here with the merchant marines and simply was curious as to what had happened to me. On the other hand, he was to carry a message to my father from the commodore. Could my father have entrusted his reply to Will to bring to me?

It is my father's thoughts I seek this night. The birth of ten babies, scraping a life out of this land to keep them alive, struggling to get title to what's rightfully mine have been my preoccupation; the years passing by, from one harvest, newborn and catastrophe to another. Has he

forgotten me? Is he still alive? Is my long-suffering mother
still living?

They would both hate this place, think it uncivilized,
primitive. My children wrapped in beaver pelts and my own
skirts made of deer hide—that would bring on the vapours
for Mother. But would Papa see it that way? I can skin a
deer, dry fish for winter, haul wood like a man, make tea
from wildberries; these are not the skills of a gentlewoman.
I am truly not the daughter they tried to raise.

But I find I am of an age now where I long for news of
them. I long to tell them my news. They cannot alter my
course now; time and distance have made their demands of
me impotent. But, God help me, I wish to hear their names
from the lips of one who has seen them. Perhaps Will has
left tidings. Maybe that will be revealed to me when I see
Mssrs. Savoy and Breaux again at The Point.

PHILIP AND CHARLOTTE set a time for the move: the fifteenth of September 1798, after the harvest is in. The planning and factoring, the rejigging and packing for the move to The Point turn into a logistical nightmare. Two critical decisions have to be made: who will go to The Point come fall and who will stay back to guard Lots Eight, Nine and Ten. Also, how are they going to move the livestock?

Lot Five was officially granted to Elizabeth and Duncan on May 4. The pair and their children will travel with them and take a lot in Tabisintack, but need to return to the Miramichi before winter and stay there until their lot can be sold. The prospect of this separation from her mother, possibly for all of the long winter, sends Elizabeth into heart-rending tears. Charlotte is amazed by what a sentimental woman her first-born has become.

John Blake will stay behind to protect the ownership of the three family lots on the Miramichi but will take a lot at The Point as well and begin clearing it that fall in order to claim ownership. Polly and Duncan McCraw will also take a lot, but they too must stay behind on Lot Seven until it is sold.

That leaves seven children, only two of them over the age of ten, and Charlotte and Philip as the first occupants of the house at The Point for the winter, but the entire clan will make the trip to settle them in.

The next item to calculate is the livestock. David Savoy is turning out to be a veritable font of information. He has suggested that moving the animals is not wise as the loss of animals en route—a very distinct possibility, given their means of transport—would be grave. He suggests that they leave the livestock with John, who can slaughter them just before freeze-up and transport the carcasses to The Point. Come spring they can get all the livestock they need. "Laying hens and goats for milking can be had for the winter and the trail from Negowack is well tramped for pulling a wagon," Savoy says. Although prejudice toward the French hangs on among many settlers, Charlotte accepts David's advice with alacrity.

They've decided that they will have to travel overland, a daunting prospect. But none of the clan owns horses or a wagon. Then Chief John Julian comes to the rescue—she suspects Wioche has had something to do with it. She'd always known that Francis Julian's brother was chief of the Mi'kmaq hereabouts, and that he lived in a well-appointed camp by the forks, but she has never laid eyes on him in all the years she has lived at Blake Brook. He arrives to see her one fine late-August morning, and for a moment Charlotte thinks it is Francis Julian come all the way from the bay.

Chief John is the image of his brother—as dignified and as tall, his bronzed and angular face wrinkled with age, as she assumes Francis Julian's would now be. Even though his power in this region is greatly diminished, he is the owner of a sturdy wagon and a team of horses. And he has an offer for the Englishwoman who takes the time to visit the women at one of his camps. In exchange for half of the hay she will harvest from her share of the local marshland, he will loan her a driver, his horses and wagon for the move. Since they will only need enough hay to feed the livestock until November, she tells him he's welcome to half and whatever else is left after her eldest son slaughters their animals.

On the morning of September 15, dories assemble at the landing on Blake Brook to ferry their household goods to the north side of the river where they will be packed on the wagon. The loading is a sight to behold. Tables, chairs, beds and quilts; moosehide sacks of clothing, bear skins and pelts of every sort. Hearth utensils clatter along beside earthen pots that in turn bump against the prized salamander and Philip's beer barrels. Perched on the top of the heap is Charlotte's spinning wheel, which William Wishart had promised to procure and Philip has finally delivered.

By the time the wagon is loaded, Philip is both impatient and worried. "The horses will be dead before they can haul that cargo to The Point or we'll be dead from waiting for them."

Before the wagon pulls away to begin its two-day trek over the barely broken trail to Tabisintack, Chief Julian has a last word of advice for John and Robert, who are going to share the driving chores. Then he beckons to Charlotte. "Go safely to Taboosimgeg," he says. "The Great Spirit will watch over you." She thanks him for his kindness, and he slaps the hip of the horse and says, "Siawasi." The wagon, with the better part of their worldly goods, lurches away into the trees.

As Charlotte climbs into the dory to row back across the river, Philip wryly comments, "Well, Mrs. Hierlihy, we have the French fixing the livestock at one end and the Indians fixing the wagon at the other. It's a fine pair of breeds you choose."

She replies tartly, "We would be nowhere without such friends, as you know, and others around these parts are ignorant on this subject." Then she turns her head toward the far shore, leaving her husband chuckling at her feistiness. When they land, Charlotte takes up the task of organizing the loading of the two dories and two canoes that will ferry the family to its new home.

She carries her own most precious items tied in a cotton scarf: the pins and combs, the sketch of the garden at home rolled carefully into a tube, the braid of sweetgrass now as dry as tinder and her diary and her precious books.

The departure is noisy, chaotic, joyful—fourteen of them, children, husbands and wives, crammed into four boats, paddle down the Miramichi bound for the new land. It takes six hours by water before the Blakes, Wisharts and Hierlihys are relocated at The Point. The Robertsons and McCraws are also part of the convoy that brilliant fall day. They arrive in the late afternoon and together begin the mission that has been Charlotte and Philip's dream—to settle Tabisintack.

It's two more nights and days before the wagon arrives like some great ship, its mast askew, sailing out of the woods and mooring its awkward, top-heavy load at The Point. All hands are employed in the off-loading. Even the little girls—Honnor now five and Charlotte Mary only three—carry parcels into the house. The bedchambers are readied, the dry cellar is stocked, the hearth is lit, and by suppertime, the family has gathered around the old table enjoying a homecoming feast. There are boiled lobsters (pulled out of the ocean right in front of their dock) and baked salmon, potatoes and string beans. And three apple-crumble pies that Elizabeth has baked. Philip opens a keg of beer for the men, Charlotte is so happy she fills a flagon for herself and her two grown daughters. After supper they all spill out to walking through the ripening garden, across the meadow to the saltwater marsh and down to the river's edge to watch the sun set over their new lives.

Before going to sleep that night, Charlotte takes the oil lamp to the wall beside the hearth and carves *Home, 1798* into the log wall. Then she goes to her bedchamber, the first room she and Philip have slept in without a child beside them. As she falls asleep, she thinks, now that we've truly settled this place it is finally time to pen our petition to the governor for title to our land.

THEY ALL MUST HURRY to the rhythm of autumn as it ticks down to winter. Before he heads back to the river, John treks with Robert to Negowack to fetch the laying hens and a pair of milking goats. Charlotte directs her small army to bring in the harvest. The cellar is filling with the fruits of the summer's labour. She kneels in the potato patch, gathering the potatoes she has spaded out of the dark damp earth, keeping an eye on the direction David and Jacques came from, wanting their report about Will; vexed by the notion that there is a message she may have missed.

Philip fishes mere yards off the shore, hauling in vast quantities of salmon and cod for drying, salting and storing. When it rains, they find the leaks in the roof and chink the holes again. The wind is something they all have to get used to. It seems to blow constantly, sometimes like a whisper, close to the land. Other times it roars out of the northeast or the northwest with such force, she tells the men to examine the beams of the house to make sure it's sturdy enough to withstand these powerful blows. They'll be much harder indeed when they are pushing a blizzard's worth of snow.

At the first opportunity, she rows across the river to the Indian camp and asks after Wioche. He is travelling the district, the women tell her. She knows he moves from camp to camp all the way from the Baie de Chaleur to the southern tip of Mi'kmaq territory at Kouchibouguac, but she decides this is as good a time as any to make proper acquaintance with the women at the camp. They already know her name and, seemingly, every aspect of the family's arrival at The Point. She's invited to consult on the health of the pregnant women here— clearly Wioche is not the only one to have heralded her arrival. She feels like a bit of a sham as a midwife, but she knows her advice on hygiene—a sterilized knife for cutting the cord, and boiled linens for stanching the woman's bleeding—is sound. She also has great sympathy for any woman who has survived a difficult labour, knowing how close every woman comes to death as she brings new life into the world.

In return, the women offer her advice about the climate here, which is especially harsh in winter, with punishing storms blowing straight off the Atlantic. She also asks the women to explain to her the origins of the name Taboosimgeg. The eldest among them, Akkie, says, "You must sit awhile to hear this story, Miss Charlotte." And the other women laugh. Charlotte laughs too, expectantly. Akkie's full name, it turns out, is Aktapaak, which means midnight, and it is obvious that she has seen many moons. Her back is bent, she has only a single prominent front tooth left and her hands are so gnarled they look like tree roots. Akkie settles a blanket around her shoulders and tucks her moccasined feet under her deerskin skirts. Then she pats the ground beside her, motioning for Charlotte to sit, and begins her tale.

"There are two stories about the origins of the name Taboosimgeg," she says. "One from a legend, and the other from a mistake. The legend says that two chiefs fought to the death on this river—right over there by that rock that pokes above the tide." Akkie points. "Before the Europeans came, the Iroquois Chief Gwetej attacked the Mi'kmaq chief." As she describes the mortal combat, she gestures up the river in the direction the Iroquois came, mimics their war whoops and swings an imaginary axe, to the delight of her audience. "The head of the Iroquois chief was split in half and the rock is the spirit where he died."

Akkie, exhausted, gestures to a younger woman to tell Charlotte the other, much less gruesome story. "When you paddle here from the ocean, you think you see two rivers," she says. "One is only a cove, but at first you are fooled. So we call it 'taboosimgeg' because two are there."

After cups and cups of tea and stories about the children, she bids them farewell and promises to visit again. "The water between us is narrow and easy to cross—in both directions," she tells them, making it clear that she too expects visitors. But it turns out that this is the last contact they'll have before spring.

WINTER CATCHES THEM completely by surprise. It isn't even All Saints' Day, the settlers' usual measure of the end of fall, when the temperature plummets, the ground freezes and fierce cold grips The Point. It comes so fast John hasn't arrived with the slaughtered meat from the Miramichi. It begins with a nor'easter.

At the outset, she knows it will be a three-day storm, nor'easters always are. But the intensity of this one, the sound of the rising wind and the groaning in the trees is frightful. Hours pass uneasily as they huddle close to the hearth, watching the smoke draft backward from the chimney, feeling the house shudder in the fury of the storm.

At last, the wind dies away as if whining about the demise of its strength. Philip and the boys struggle through drifts to the shore and find that the boats are destroyed, bits of slats strewn over the slabs of ice already lining the beach. What's more, the rising tides, swelled by the northeast wind, have ripped chunks of the shoreline clean away. The embankment is gashed with gaping wounds; shredded pine trees have been cleaved from their lacerated roots and seagrass-covered hunks of earth and rocks as big as a child have been tossed along the frozen beach.

Charlotte opens the hatch to the dry cellar to find the entire harvest floating in frigid, muddy water. The first order of business is to try to retrieve the soaked stores of food. Man, woman and child pitch in to carry the soggy stockpile to the hearth—the dried fish and berries, the potatoes, turnips and corn—until the whole main floor is covered with drying vegetables. The fish and berries are better frozen, Philip decides, and are buried outside in the snow. Partway through the rescue mission, Charlotte beats a path through the snow to the shed where the hens and goats are housed, wondering if they have survived the storm. Miraculously, they are tucked into the hay and still alive. She scatters extra meal and returns to the fray.

When Charlotte takes stock that first night, she knows rations are going to be meagre until John turns up with the meat.

But John doesn't arrive. And winter doesn't let up. It snows and blows relentlessly. The roof fails to keep the winter out; the planks are pulling apart and leaving gaps for snow to billow down on the children in their beds. They're grateful for Charlotte's hoarded surplus of animal skins, and tack them over the holes in the roof. The entire first winter at The Point is one of patching, calculating, stretching their supplies and trying to stay warm.

Month after month they endure endless blizzards, two more nor'easters and winds that start to play on their minds. The moaning of the creaking timbers and eerie whistling of the wind feel like harbingers of doom to Charlotte. The children can rarely get outside, she's got cabin fever, and Philip is unrelieved of his bad temper. By February, they are reduced to bannock and tea, and salted, dried, then frozen fish cooked over the fire. The hens have ceased to lay and the goats don't let down their milk, husbanding their energies to stay alive in the cold.

Every day, one or the other of them wonders aloud why John has not managed to find a way to get the slaughtered meat to them. Charlotte grows angry with him, irrationally: on some level she knows that the Miramichi must be suffering the same siege.

Then, as quickly as it caught them by surprise when it struck, winter quits The Point in early April. A week goes by with no snow.

On one bright morning, Charlotte walks out her front door, lifts her face up to the sky and exclaims, "There's heat in that sun!"

Spring surges onto The Point, melting the snowbanks, budding the trees and warming their bones. All of them go outside at every excuse and soak up the sun like survivors. The ice in the river cracks and heaves in its springtime dance and is quickly washed out to sea.

But as much as the weather is shining upon the family, they are still desperately hungry. Charlotte is just about to lead a march to Negowack in search of food they can buy with their coin when she sees a sight nothing short of redemption. Two canoes are paddling around the bend in the river and in them are Elizabeth and Duncan, Polly and Duncan McCraw, and John Blake. They beach their boats and tumble straight into the arms of their hungry, pale, emaciated kin.

Parcels of salted meat, dried apples, fresh bread and a hefty jug of rum are opened before they're even back at the house. Settled at the table, they all eat until they're full, sharing stories about the brutal winter. Elizabeth sits with tears running down her face at the sight of them. "I worried all winter! We couldn't move because of the storms on the river, but we knew they would be hitting you worse!" Several times John prepared to travel by foot, bringing what he could, but he would have to abandon the plan when yet another stormy blast hit the river. When the ice broke up in the Miramichi just yesterday, they packed all the food that would fit in two canoes and came to the rescue.

Elizabeth is very firm on one subject, despite her tears. She, for one, is not going to stay on the Miramichi for another anxious winter. Before the impromptu feast is cleared away, and the rest of the supplies are hauled into the larder, they've agreed that whether the lots are sold on the Miramichi this season or not, Elizabeth, Duncan and their children, along with the very pregnant Polly and her Duncan, will come live at The Point. The only one of her children who wants to stay on at Blake Brook is John, who says he will look after all of their interests there. His mother suspects it has something to do with a settler's daughter he has been courting, but she doesn't press the issue.

—

THAT SUMMER, young Robert beats his oldest brother to the altar and marries Ann Jamieson from the Miramichi, and brings her to live at The Point. Charlotte applies every ounce of fierce will to planning for the winter. They plant aiming for a surplus. They breed livestock looking to grow a herd. Not willing to put her faith in the dry cellar, Charlotte herself digs a pit in the ground on the south side of the house near the river. Come fall she buries her potatoes, turnip, carrots, squash, corn in layers of dry sand and insulates them with hay from the meadow.

They now know what to expect, and they'll all face it together. It's the only way they'll survive, let alone prosper.

CHAPTER 12

The Point

1802

*T*he mystery around Will MacCulloch remains unsolved. Neither David Savoy nor Jacques Breaux can find any further trace of him, or of anyone who seems to have encountered MacCulloch after he stopped at the Baie de Chaleur. By the fire of an evening, Charlotte occasionally finds herself daydreaming scenes of reunion and forgiveness with her father, and then kicks herself for being so foolish. Never in her life has she worried about such things. The thing she loved most from the moment she stepped off the commodore's boat was that here you could make your life and not inherit it or have to accept your place in it.

In the four years since Charlotte's family had passed their first winter in Tabisintack, other settlers had built homesteads too. Twenty families in all, counting the farms and homesteads inland along the river. She lobbies the province to send a teacher to the new settlement and, as is her wont, makes a few enemies in the process. Though she knows that you can catch more flies with honey than vinegar, she can't help but accuse the neighbours who won't sign her petitions of neglecting their children's future. She has always been bothered that her own children, schooled at home, have only the most rudimentary reading and writing skills. But it is the next generation, her grandchildren, she fights for now. At the supper table, she's known to grumble: "In Frederick Town, they have a grammar school where they teach reading, writing and arithmetic and book-keeping too. Now they even have a college, which students from other areas attend. But children from here will never gain admittance because they haven't got the proper foundation."

Philip thinks she's gone a little cracked on the subject, and takes every opportunity to point out that their own "ill-schooled" children are doing very well for themselves.

And even in this new settlement, people outside the family gossip about the way she dares to presume that her husband's land is her own. Tongues also wag about her keeping company with an Indian. Her son William has made her a beautiful birch-bark canoe, under the careful direction of Wioche, and very occasionally the matriarch of The Point can be seen on the river, loitering of an afternoon, clearly in conversation with a man of the People, who paddles in the stern.

There's tension, too, between Charlotte and her husband, who loves her tough fibre as long as it is pointed in a direction he favours, but who finds himself uncomfortable with his nonconforming wife as the settlement grows around them. When he tells her there are traditions to be honoured, she replies, "It's one thing to preserve useful customs, but, Philip, many of these so-called honourable traditions are suffocating the aspirations of people who want to build this province."

In response, he employs that dismissive air she dislikes so much. "Charlotte, I fought for King and country. Don't be talking such nonsense to me. If I believed that cant, I would have fought for the other side and stayed in America."

"But look how long we have to wait to get land grants or law enforcement. It's as though the British officials in Frederick Town think we're not worthy of their precious time."

Surely he will agree with her here, as he is always anxious about their security. But his only response is, "All in due course."

Charlotte isn't through with him yet. "We were isolated on the Miramichi, bound by the river and the woods. Then you Loyalists arrived and saw this land as your own castle. Look at the men appointed in Frederick Town. They serve tea and scones to one another and know nothing about the way we have to live. The fine Anglicans of Britain have decided that Methodists and Baptists cannot even solemnize marriages here, though Anglican ministers don't deign to rough it with us in the bush. Acadians can't vote because they're Catholic. And the Indians have a school, but we don't because the governor thinks they are heathens who need to be civilized. Now, other settlers are saying that land-owning women such as me are to be disenfranchised again because we're too delicate to know what government is about—after tilling the punishing soil, bearing your children and filling the pot on the hearth."

The children trade knowing looks behind their parents' backs during these disputes, but not one of them would openly argue with Charlotte. They've been schooled in her views on everything from noxious British tradition to Mi'kmaq legend.

LATE IN THE WINTER of 1802, the family hears that a man called Dugald Campbell has been appointed to survey the province. Her two sons-in-law know him, and served with him in the 42nd Regiment. His first report has brought home to the government that there's not ten miles of road fit for wheeled carriage in the entire province. Outside of Frederick Town and the renamed Saint John (the union of Parr Town and Carleton, and the largest city in the province), the byways are nothing more than tramped paths made by settlers' feet and horses' hooves, and not all that many horses at that. Along the Miramichi, the trees have been cut so far back on the lots that hauling the wood to the river and then shipping it to the point of trade has become a time-consuming and costly proposition. Something has to be done to bring order to New Brunswick. The rebel colonies to the south are flourishing in trade, schooling and goods while New Brunswick is floundering.

In Charlotte's own home, they are kept going by a hodge-podge of income—Philip's pittance as a disbanded soldier, his meagre salary from the government office in Newcastle where he charts roads that he doubts will ever be built, cash money or barter from the wood the young men cut and carry down the river for sale. If they concentrated on clearing more land, they might make more money, but Charlotte's sons love the life of the river. Both John and Robert have joined crews that assemble logs in massive booms and steer them from the forks to Miramichi Bay. The job is dangerous and daring, as tides and weather both threaten to shift the heavy booms and swamp the men who run them. They spend much of the season from spring thaw to freeze-up on the Miramichi, and the rest logging. The farming and the fighting for a school are left mostly to Charlotte.

That April the ice breaks up early, and the boys—rather, the young men, since John is now twenty-five, Robert is twenty-one and William is sixteen—are eager to quit the confines of their mother's household and head back to the lots on the river. Philip is just as anxious to quit the confines of the household and head to Newcastle, where he can collect his soldier's half-pay and attend a meeting Dugald Campbell is holding to discuss the province's roads and trade.

Charlotte, who once might have asked to be taken along, is relieved to have a few days on her own with the little ones for her ritualistic turning of the soil, which she's begun to think of as her annual bargaining with the earth to give forth come fall. So on one unseasonably fine morning in April, the sun beating down and shooting sparks of light off the slurry of ice still floating in the river, she and the children go down to the landing to see the boys and their father away in the new dory William built over the winter. Even Akkie over at the Indian camp waves as the foursome row by, heading out to the open sea. Fourteen-year-old Philip watches after them till they've disappeared from view, clearly disappointed that his father wouldn't take him along to Newcastle and that he's been left to provide muscle for his mother. "They'll be over the shoals and past Black Brook by midday," he says when he straggles back up to join her in the garden plot. "Blake Brook," Charlotte says with a sigh.

They need to take advantage of the day to air the linens and blankets, Charlotte decides, and the bearskins as well. And so for a time she and her five helpers shuttle in and out of the house spreading bedding over bushes and hanging linens from the long clothesline. Then she takes Philip and his spade and Charlotte Mary, now five years old, to the garden, Philip will dig and she will pull the withered stalks, which the little girl with gather up in her bucket and carry to the compost heap.

The wind, always lowing at The Point, comes up at midday. "It's from the northwest," Charlotte says. "Papa and the boys, they'll be fairly flying to the mouth of Miramichi. But then they'll have to make the turn, put their shoulders to the oars and fight the wind."

No sooner are the words out of her mouth than the strangest piece of weather she has ever seen swoops down on The Point. Purple clouds drop so close to the ground, she thinks she can reach up and touch them. The birds fall quiet, and the geese on the marsh take flight in great honking waves to the woods. The wind turns fierce, swirling their bedclothes into the air, and pushing Charlotte Mary halfway across the garden patch, her mother running to grab her up in her arms. The other children reach for the flying blankets and bearskins, chasing some pieces right down to the water's edge.

Then, just as suddenly, the sun slides out from under the black mass overhead and the squall blows off The Point. Within minutes, the birds are back pecking at the overturned soil in the garden. As she sets her littlest girl down, Charlotte murmurs, "The earth got a good sweeping today."

They don't expect Philip back until the next day. So it is a surprise to see a dory just like William's coming toward shore late in the afternoon. Philip runs down to the landing, shading his eyes to see what he can make out, then shouts back, "Look, Mama, they're carrying something." She can make out just three heads in the boat, and a bundle propped between them.

"What in the name of God is going on?" Charlotte drops the blanket she's been folding and runs toward the shore.

She stops at the bottom of the landing, her feet refusing to move, her legs wobbling like seaweed. It's John, Robert and a thoroughly battered William, and between them the body of Philip Hierlihy, blue with cold.

Her skirts get wet as she helps her sons carry her husband

from the boat and lay him on the shore. "Philip, run and get something to cover your father, please," she says and sinks down to take his hand in her work-roughened clasp.

John looms above her, and she finds she can't even pose the question. It's clear Philip's been drowned.

"We were at Oak Point," he blurts out. "And a wicked blow came out of the northwest. We tried to turn the dory toward shore, but the wash from under the cliffs beat us back and then ice chunks from the melt smashed onto the dory, overturned us. The cold knocked the breath right out of us, but Robert and I managed to cling to the dory, got it turned upright again and crawled back in."

She's in no hurry to hear the end of the story, and shushes him briefly as Philip runs back with a coverlet that she spreads carefully over her husband. William sits down heavily beside her, and puts a clumsy arm over her shoulders. She briefly brushes his bruised cheek with a kiss, and his clothes are still soaking. She sends a questioning look in John's direction.

"William was dashed into the cliffs and managed to scramble to shore, but Philip was in the water. When we got to him it was as if he was frozen by the sea—he wasn't breathing, though I never saw his head go down. Then the squall stopped, but it lasted too long for Philip."

All of them now sit down beside their mother and Philip Hierlihy as the sun begins to set over the clearing, casting long shadows from the forest. And finally Charlotte finds her voice. "John, get your brothers to help you carry him to the house. And go and build a coffin."

She sits vigil beside him all night long as he rests on a bench in the main room, a candle flickering by his feet. She studies his face, traces the wrinkles at the corners of his eyes and smoothes his tangled and sandy-grey hair. At one point in the dark hours, Charlotte carries a lamp to the chest in their bed-chamber to root in his trunk. Before dawn, while the family sleeps around her, she strips off each salt-stained article of clothing and washes him from head to toe, and then dresses him again in his old uniform, carefully folded away all the years of their marriage.

The next day, Charlotte Taylor Blake Hierlihy once again has to bury a husband. This time in the Catholic churchyard at Bartibog. "He began his life as a Catholic," she says, "and he can be buried as one."

On the boatride back from the graveyard, Charlotte pays scant attention to her surroundings, or even the deep knot of sadness lodged under her breastbone, or the faint sense of gratitude she feels that at least the sea gave back this husband for a proper burial. She's lost in worry about how she'll man-age. Philip was forty-seven years old, the same age as Charlotte. Five of her ten children are under the age of fifteen. The lots they have settled on at The Point still have no deeds. For all his faults, she trusted him to look after the family business. If the plan they dreamed of is to be realized, she has her work cut out for her.

THE NEXT WINTER, The Point at the mouth of the Tabisintack River is recognized as a settlement by the province and awarded its own court and officers of law. Among those who report for duty to the Court of Sessions in March 1803 are John Blake, now the commissioner and surveyor of roads, William Wishart, appointed constable, and Duncan Robertson, assessor and overseer of roads. On a visit to Philip's grave at Bartibog, Charlotte actually finds herself addressing his marker to tell him this news. "The boys have learned from you," she whispers. "I'll make sure that Philip and James also follow in your footsteps."

ONE DAY THAT MAY, while Charlotte is weeding the first pea and bean shoots in her garden, she sees the sails of a ship out beyond the islands. A trading vessel, perhaps. But why has it turned in to this shore rather than sailing on to the port at Miramichi Bay? The ship drops anchor, a skiff is lowered and a lone man climbs down into it and rows himself toward shore. She can only see the back of him as he approaches, a stranger with curly fair hair poking out from under his hat. Then the boat swings around to her landing, and the stranger calls out to her where she stands leaning on her hoe. "Hey you, wi the reid heid." To the astonished Charlotte, it's like the past, the present and the future rolled into one.

"Will MacCulloch, I cannot believe my eyes," she shouts as he approaches.

"Aye, lassie, you're a bonnie sight for this lad as well. I've been searchin' these shores for yer pretty face."

"The years have not dimmed your blarney or your brogue," she says, and before she knows it he is giving her an enormous hug, swirling her around in a circle so big her feet fly out from under her. She breaks free, then self-consciously tucks her straying red hair back into the untidy knot at the back of her neck. "Let me look at you, Will. I should have known you even with your back to the shore by those curly locks of yours."

He has some age upon him, and his clothing bespeaks a man of substance, but the boyish grin is just the same. "I nae forgot you, bonnie Charlotte, and would ha' stayed on these shores had I thought you'd be my ain woman."

Settled at the table with a huge pot of tea in front of them, and biscuits made by young Eleanor, they catch up on their lives. He's a captain now in the merchant marines and plies the waters of trading centres in Spain, Portugal and France. Life has been good to the rascal she knew. The only time the twinkle leaves his eye is when he tells her that, just as she's had three husbands, he has had three wives. Two died in childbirth, and a third of tuberculosis. He has five sons, though he jokes that none of them is quite so handsome as the original. Presently he lives with the two boys still in short pants in a fine house in Bristol, where a housekeeper looks after them when he's away at sea.

Charlotte waits until the first burst of reminiscence is over before letting him know just how much she'd been thinking of him these last five years. "When we first came to The Point to clear land for our house, I met two Acadians with family on the Baie. I understand you were back in these parts some years ago."

He looks bemused. "Twasn't me, Charlotte. I have not set foot on these shores since the last day I saw you—running off to the Indian camp."

"But I heard word that a man named MacCulloch was asking for me," she insists.

"Ay, lassie, I guess when you put it like that, it was me for sure. Near to ten years ago, I asked a marine who was sailing to Nepisiguit to seek information about ye. But his only news was that you'd moved away."

He falls silent and looks once again a little troubled.

"Well, you've found me now, Will. Why were you bothering to look?"

"The lovely Charlotte," he replies softly, though she has an inclination that what's coming has nothing to do with her charms. "The shipping company I toil for has a renewed interest in Nepisiguit, and seeing as how I had spent time here, asked me to return to take a good look about. Ye've been on my mind, Charlotte, so I decided to take the chance to find ye and know what has become of the girl who preferred this wild country to England."

"Just for auld lang syne, is it? Did you ever meet my father, Will, when you went back? I believe you carried a letter to him from George Walker."

"I did. Charlotte . . ." Will leans forward to take one of her hands as she leans back, out of reach. "In the end, I became quite a friend to your father. He was nay too happy with yer bolt from the family. Never accepted it, really. He wasn't a bad man, you know. And in the end he was helpful to me. He just didn't know what to do with a daughter who broke with all the conventions."

"Do you know if he got the letter I sent him? It's almost twenty years ago now, and I never received an answer."

"Ay, Charlotte, he did. Your father was going to reply—he always said he was going to reply. I told him he should, but he did nae tell me that he'd done so. Did you nae receive one from him?"

"No, I never did—though I watched for it, hoped to receive it. All these many years I have wondered what my father was thinking; if he wished to see me, to know what became of his only daughter. He once said he would disown me if I disobeyed him. That I did. I have never wanted to go back. But I suppose over the years I began to hope there would be some contact."

Will's bright blue eyes soften. "Well, Charlotte, I'm here to tell you that it will never happen now. Your maither died, it must be ten years ago now. And your faither, well he had some business reversals. He loaned me money on some ventures when I was first improving my station in life, Charlotte, and so when he got himself into difficulties, I was of some aid to him. He died two years ago, this fall."

Before she can respond, Will pulls a packet from his pocket and hands it to her. She opens it to find fifty pounds in ten-pound notes and a smaller item wrapped in brown paper. "That's yer maither's wedding ring, I saved it for ye. Even thought some day I may give ye the token as my ain wife."

She has to laugh. "Will, you are incorrigible. Listen to you and the way you talk. I tell you one thing for certain, I will never marry again. Three times a widow is enough for this woman, no matter how tough people think I may be."

He is serious again. "Charlotte, your faither told me about your inheritance. I believe he was meaning to send it, just as he was meaning to write to you . . . but then his financial troubles destroyed his capital. This is all that was left for you. When he knew he was dying, he asked me to make sure you got it." Will can't quite meet her eye.

When she walks him back down to the landing, and watches him as he rows away from her toward his ship, she suddenly wonders whether Will's gift really came from her father or out of his own pocket.

IN 1810, the surveyor Dugald Campbell finally files his last report, and the province announces The Great Tabisintack Land Grant. The Great Tabisintack Land Grab, Charlotte jokes, but at last the lots she and her children own on and around The Point are protected by law.

Relations among the settlers reach a new low, as land greed works on friends and even family like a horrible yeast. To qualify for the land grant, each settler has to make a set number of improvements to his lot, knowing that his vigilant neighbours may challenge his claim if he fails, in their view, to meet the requirements. David Savoy tries to get title to a lot surveyed for his cousin Charles Breaux. Two of Charlotte's sons sign Savoy's petition and vouch for his claim that no improvements have been made on the lot in question. He isn't successful, and relations are ruined with his friend. Charlotte is shocked by such behaviour, but scandalizes her neighbours when she makes a case for her ownership of the glebe, a lot the land grant has set aside for a church. She's been growing hay for her animals on that lot, a claim better than any other as far as she is concerned. But she too loses.

The Point and surrounding area is also unsettled by rumours of a new war between America and England. The Americans make several sorties into both Upper and Lower Canada and, though they are thwarted, there's talk that the Indians are helping the Yankees, and tensions between the settlers and the Mi'kmaq camps also rise.

And there are changes brewing in Charlotte's house. Eleanor marries the disputatious David Savoy on November 11, 1810, and moves down shore. Then Charlotte Mary, only fourteen, marries Benjamin Stymiest Jr., and together they move to a lot farther up the Tabisintack River. They name the place Stymiest Millstream, and Benjamin starts a small sawmill. Charlotte's two-storey house now feels empty, with only herself and Honnor rattling around in it. Unmarried, William, who lives in his own tiny cabin some hundreds of yards away from the main house, is there every night at the supper table.

ON NIGHTS when she finds herself lying sleepless and lonely in the pre-dawn hours, the one thing Charlotte has always been able to find comfort in is her sense that she's been a good mother, and grandmother too. She knows that her outspokenness has sometimes made it difficult for her children, her boys in particular, who have had to defend her to the point of fistfights in the taverns. And that others look askance at the amount of land her family has accumulated, and the fact that Charlotte is a woman who never scruples to fight for her property rights. But the fact that a state of peace mostly reigns in a clan with children from four fathers, and that many days more than one of her adult children come to call, she regards as the pinnacle achievement of her life.

It's a nasty shock to Charlotte when her oldest son upsets her sense of family solidarity, first by selling half his share of Lot Eight on the Miramichi, the lot he inherited from his father, to his brother Robert without mentioning the plan to her. When she tries to bring it up with him, after finding the news out from Robert, he refuses to be repentant. "The land is still in the family, Mother. What's your concern? In my view, Robert needed a toehold on the river."

But then, after a lengthy stay on the Miramichi, he returns to The Point to "inform" her, as he puts it, that he has been married to Catherine Doe, the settler's daughter, for two years now.

Charlotte can't take it in. Why hadn't he told her? Had he kept it a secret from them all, and why did he feel the need?

"I'm telling you now, because Catherine has just made me a father. We have a baby girl."

This is too much for his mother, who embarrasses herself by bursting into tears at this news.

"Why in heaven's name wouldn't you let me know such news in advance, John?"

All he will say is that he has his own life to live, and he wants the freedom to make his own choices. They part on uneasy terms, Charlotte deeply, desperately hurt, though her tears soon dry and her blunt tongue lets him know how he has disappointed her.

Six months later, on September 18, 1811, the five Hierlihy offspring suddenly sell Lot Nine, the land that was granted to their father under the auspices of the province of New Brunswick in 1798. Charlotte is truly stunned. She'd worked so hard to get that land and saw it as part of the family's collective holdings. Worse, she knows her children know her wishes in this matter. It's within their rights to sell the lot, but why would they do it without at least consulting her? What's going on among these grown children of hers?

Little did she realize that one of them was about to declare open war directly upon her. On February 19, 1812—without even trying to raise the issue with his mother—John Blake writes to the Honourable Martin Hunter, president of His Majesty's Council and commander in chief of the province of New Brunswick, and claims that Lot Ten on the Miramichi is rightfully his. His father, John Blake Sr., was the first settler on the Miramichi, he writes, and had a quantity of land to the extent of 550 acres. In his view, he has been defrauded of the land owing to the remarriages of his mother, Charlotte Blake-Wishart-Hierlihy. He makes a pointed argument that women do not hold title to land in New Brunswick. If widowed, they are allowed one-third of the property. Everything else is to be granted to the sons. "The sons of John Blake have been deprived of what is their right."

In closing he writes, "By way of making up for the loss which your Memorialist has sustained in consequence of this transaction of the said Mother's and for his assistance in support of a wife and children, your Memorialist would beg leave to apply for a portion of the vacant lands on the River Nappin."

There's no way his mother won't find out about this, and though John tries to paint his letter in the best light when next he sees her—simply as a lever he was trying to exert to get the land he has his eye upon—Charlotte will have none of it. "What do you really aim for," she demands. "You sold your father's Lot Eight. The other on Lot Ten is none of your inheritance, and by using me in your games, you may undo my ownership, John. What is it that you have against me?"

This is too much for John, who explodes. "Mother, you want everything your way. You want to know everything. You want to direct everything, as if all of us must dance to the plans you have in your head forever. I want to stand on my own feet, as the son of John Blake, who was on the Miramichi before you were even in this country. Sometimes I get sick of having to carry the weight of you around, Mother, you and your contrary ways and your softness for Indians and your constant planning and scheming."

When he storms out of her house at The Point to head back to the river, Charlotte is not entirely certain whether she will see him again—or even whether she wants to.

THE FRACTURE in her family hurts her bitterly, try as she might to hide it. When the long winter of 1812 starts to ease in March, she desperately needs a break from her brooding. And she decides that she will ask Wioche to take her back to Baie de Chaleur, which she has not seen since the day she climbed into Blake's canoe carrying Elizabeth and paddled away from George Walker's trading post.

She keeps a watch on the Indian camp for Wioche's return:

most winters he stays in other camps of the People. Then one morning, standing in the snow-covered garden, she sees him across the water. But what is he doing? He's got a toboggan with some great item loaded onto it. As he draws near to her shore, she is utterly amazed to see her old trunk. Hauling it up the bank, Wioche explains. "Marie left it with me when she and André moved to Caraquet. I kept it for many years at the Baie, and this trip I thought I would bring it back to you."

The plaque with the name Charlotte Howe Taylor, which gave her identity away to Commodore Walker, is still in place. The pale lining has survived the decades untouched, a poignant reminder of the silk dresses and embroidered bodices that once filled it. She stoops to idly run her hands through the pockets along the side of the chest, and her fingers encounter a little packet, wrapped in a bit of cloth—a tiny package of seeds, forgotten all these years. She stares at them, then looks up at Wioche. "These are seeds Pad and I brought from the garden in England to scatter about the home we thought we would have. I wonder if they will still grow."

They carry the trunk to the house, where Charlotte finds a place for it in her bedchamber. In it, she decides, she will store her family's history: the deeds, her diary, the records of the house, the children, the men she has married—the chest will tell the story of this New World, good and bad.

And then she asks Wioche if he will take her to the Baie.

"We should wait till the ice breaks up, and we could paddle there," he replies.

But Charlotte can't bear to wait that long.

TWO WEEKS LATER, they set out along the still-frozen river, Honnor waving from the landing, maybe a little worried that her mother is setting off on such a long jaunt with an Indian man. She and Wioche have stolen many half-days together over the years but have never repeated a journey the like of their trip to Frederick Town, through the bush and under the stars. She's fifty-seven years old now, her red hair streaked with grey and her face lined, the once-girlish freckles paler now. But her sea-blue eyes still sparkle. In the presence of Wioche, she does not feel her age.

He falls silent as she tells him about John Blake's letter, then comments soberly, "What would make John behave this way? There must be something more to it than greed for land."

They trek a little farther, Charlotte for the very first time mulling her innocence in the matter.

Then Wioche says, "My people, too, feel cheated. Ten years have passed since land was granted to Mi'kmaq, but we still have no rights to own our lands. And with the way the world is now, I fear that we have no choice but to own our land, or lose everything."

The provincial authorities reserved fourteen tracts of land for the People, but kept the title with the Crown, which means that the Indians can live on their lands but cannot own them. What's more, the tracts have never been surveyed, so the Indians have no official means to prevent encroachments. Some Indian lands have already been put up for public auction. And her own lot, as described on the deed, actually contains a small portion of Indian land. She is not blameless, not in the least.

Wioche says what is obvious to both of them. "The People cannot survive with no land, no hunting, no fishing." Then, as they stop to rest a little, the harmony of these virgin woods soothes both their souls, and he lets the matter drop. After a while of sitting companionably, watching sun sparkle on the ice, as the breeze ruffles the branches over their heads, she asks, "Do you notice the wind? Even during the calm of a summer day it's always blowing. When we moved to The Point, there were so many trees around, it felt to me like the wind was sneaking through them, trying to blow us away. Now that The Point is bare, the wind blows incessantly over the shore and the meadow. Even when it is a sweet wind, I notice it. Do you?"

"Charlotte, these are messages to you from the Great Spirit. Mother Earth takes care of you because you pay attention to them."

"To my mind, the messages are not always all that kind," Charlotte laughs. Then she ventures what she is really trying to ask. "William Wishart died near The Point, I'm certain of that. Is it his spirit in that wind? Or is it truly something else?"

Wioche lets the question drift. He sees her in a light others don't, but still wonders what it is she seeks. "Charlotte, don't worry about your quarrel with John. I'm sure it will come right with time. You must be patient."

The tramp through the woods is easy on this centuries-old Indian trail. When the sun drops behind the trees, Wioche says, "There's a Mi'kmaq camp nearby. We can stay there."

Charlotte looks at him, much the same man he was when she was twenty. "Let's make camp right here," she suggests, pointing to a patch of high ground where the snow has already melted, a clearing in a stand of towering pines.

Spruce boughs for their bed, wood for a fire, pine branches for shelter. A fish cooked over the fire for their supper, tea in companionable silence. She is the one to take him by the hand and lead him to their shelter. And as they embrace, she feels she has known no greater peace that lying with this man under the fading light of day, and then again as the stars come out.

Before noon the next day, they walk out of the tunnel that is the Nepisiguit River, onto the shores of the harbour that opens out into the Baie de Chaleur. The salt water is flash-frozen in icy green waves, and the view takes her breath away. Except for the trees and the bay itself, the place is entirely changed. There are cabins all along the shore, as well as large two-storey houses that sit in cleared farm fields.

"I don't think we should trust the ice to carry us, Charlotte," Wioche says, and so she impatiently trudges beside him as they snowshoe around the bay.

At Alston Point, there's hardly a trace of Walker's old compound, and the local settlement is already encroaching on the land where his fishery once stood. The land is marked for lots all the way from the old Mi'kmaq camp to here. Long docks have been constructed in the harbour to accommodate the ships that arrive for the lumber. They aren't alone on the beach, and the sound of hammers and sawing and the clip-clop of horses on the nearby path all speak of the changes thirty-six years have wrought.

Turning to look out to sea, Charlotte surveys giant icebergs, some of them pushed up by the tide that still ebbs and flows under the frozen surface, and strands them like great white palaces next to the shore.

The sun is plunging toward the treetops, painting those palaces with brilliant orange streaks, by the time they walk up the hill to the old Mi'kmaq camp. There's hardly a sign that anyone ever lived here. The bush has reclaimed the site; even the fire pit has given its ashes back to the earth. A few dilapidated wooden structures are still standing, including her old tilt. They have to dislodge the door from the turf where it has sunk and tear back the branches that have grown across the threshold to get inside. Charlotte is overwhelmed with memories: her first nights staying with the Indians she'd been taught to fear, her labour with Elizabeth, learning to dry fish, gather berries and herbs . . . all the ways of the People that have protected her ever since. The faint scent of soot fills her nostrils, bringing back the inferno she created in the midst of a blizzard. She can think of no place she would rather be at this moment as together they sweep out dead leaves and branches, lay a new bed of spruce boughs and lie down for the night.

On the return tramp to Tabisintack, Charlotte is acutely aware of the contradictions stalking her. The land she covets is the land the Mi'kmaq have lost. The settlers, who came with hope for a new life, now live with the versions of the propriety at least some of them fled. The province makes progress for white settlers, with crushing consequences for the original inhabitants. Even the lots her family own at The Point encroach on reserved Indian land. But she decides to set the remorse that pricks her conscience aside for another time and take what pleasure this day still offers.

It's turned into April, the month the Mi'kmaq call "Unadumooe-goos," egg-laying month, when the birds return to nest and hatch their young. Charlotte decides it's time for her to hatch some new plans of her own. When she and Wioche sleep together for a last time under the heavens that night, she has decided on a course of action that will either settle the quarrelling in her family or send an arrow into the heart of the clan.

When she arrives home, she immediately writes to the governor in Frederick Town:

To all people to whom these presents shall come, I Charlotte Hierlihy do send greeting. Know ye, That I, said

Charlotte Hierlihy, widow of Tabisintack in the county of Northumberland and Province of New Brunswick for and in consideration of the love and good will and affection and also five shillings to me in hand Paid the receipt whereof I hereby acknowledge, which I have and do bear towards my loving son William Wishart of the same parish and county, have given and granted unto the same William Wishart, his heirs, executors or Administrators all that tract or parcel of land laying on the south side of the river Miramichi (being Lot No. Ten) county and province aforesaid of which (before the signing of these presents) I have delivered him the said William Wishart the aforesaid land, to have and to hold, in Fee simple to his heirs, executors or administrators from henceforth as his and their proper right, absolutely without any manner of condition. In witness whereof I have hereunto put my hand and seal the Sixth day of April 1812.

The next day she hitches up the wagon and rides with Honnor into Newcastle to have the letter witnessed by the Justice of the Peace.

In the presence of Alexr. Allan, Northumberland County. Be it remembered that on the Sixth Day of April in the year of our Lord 1812, Personally appeared before me Alexr. Allan Esquire one of his Majesty's Justices of the Peace in and for the said county. Charlotte Hierlihy the within named Grantor who declared that she signed, sealed and delivered the within written instrument for the purposes therein mentioned. Alexr. Allan J.P. Newcastle (to wit).

When they get back to The Point, she sends for John Blake before she tells her other sons and daughters, or even the intended recipient, what she has decided.

It's awkward between them, but she is glad when he comes.

"I want to talk to you about Lot Ten, John."

He makes as though to rise from her table, but she reaches for his arm and holds him still.

"That lot was cleared by William Wishart, John. It rightfully belongs not to you, or even to me, but to your half-brother William. I've deeded it over to him. If you have quarrel with this decision, make it known to me now. Otherwise, I won't hear another word of it."

He stares at the table a long time, before he lifts his head to meet her eye. "No, Mother. You'll hear no complaint from me."

And Charlotte is pleased in the weeks and months that follow to see that the jealousy and resentments that had been brewing among her children seem to have eased. That fall, John Blake, his wife, Catherine, and their three children move permanently to his lot on The Point, and most Sundays the young Blake family joins Charlotte for dinner.

CHAPTER 13

The Point

1814

*T*wo years pass, peacefully, after Charlotte's fight with her oldest son. Though the renewed war with the United States rages in Upper and Lower Canada, none of its guns are fired on the Miramichi or at Tabisintack.

On a bright mid-September afternoon, Charlotte is at the end of the house closest to the river, admiring the abundance of hollyhocks—planted from the seeds that spent thirty-seven years in her trunk. They didn't all germinate, of course, but slender stalks now lean like drunken soldiers against the wall of the house in sweet, nostalgic blooms of pink, yellow and purple— just like the ones in the garden sketch she'd carried with her from England.

Absent-mindedly she rubs at an ache in her left arm, wondering what's she has lifted to strain it, but then shooting pain comes, numbing the arm and then clamping her jaw in a vise. She stands still for a moment trying to understand whether she should sit down where she is, or try for the house, when a crushing weight grips her chest. She can't catch her breath. She looks around for help. William is in the far field with horse and wagon, bringing in the sheaves of wheat. She cannot shout or even wave her arms, not that he'd see her or hear her from the distance. She slowly sinks to her knees clutching her chest. Her eyes won't focus. Her stomach begins to heave. She's still on her knees trying to pull air into her lungs past the intense pain when Honnor, and then William, are suddenly standing over her.

As luck would have it, the only doctor in northeastern New Brunswick, the kindly Dr. Bell, is less than half a mile away. He's on his regular autumn rounds to see patients in Miscou, Nepisiguit, Tabisintack, Newcastle and Chatham before returning for the winter to Frederick Town. On this leg, he's staying with Eleanor and her husband, David Savoy.

"Mother, I'm going to fetch the doctor. I don't think we should move you until he sees you. Do you think if Honnor gets a blanket from the house and sits with you, you'll be all right till I can get back?"

Charlotte nods. As Honnor runs for the house, William hops on to his horse's bare back and gallops off to the Savoys, returning as quickly as he can with Dr. Bell behind him, and Eleanor and David in breathless chase.

The skin on Charlotte's face seems transparent, her breath raspy and intermittent.

"It's a heart seizure," the doctor pronounces. "It's all right to move her to the house—but go gently now."

Once she's laid on her bed, the doctor administers a dose of foxglove elixir.

"Now Mrs. H., you must rest until you are feeling better, and a little longer than that. I don't want you leaving this bed until I say that you may."

Her chest is still as tight as though a bear were sitting on it, and she makes no protest, but she gets a shock when she overhears the doctor talking to William and Honnor in the front room, "If she survives until morning, she'll likely be out of danger. We can only wait and see." If she survives? He clearly doesn't know Charlotte.

Her children stand vigil, fetching water, making tea, imploring her to lie still. Once the suffocating pain has passed, she is impatient with the fuss and tells them to be off and do the work that has to be done while there's still light to see the fields. Honnor is not to be put off so easily. "Mother, the doctor told us that it'll be four or five days until he knows how badly your heart has been damaged, and he wants you in bed the whole time. So I'm staying put right here." And she settles herself in a chair by the bedside, staring sternly at her mother, until Charlotte gives up complaining and realizes just how tired she feels.

Word passes quickly throughout the settlement that Charlotte is stricken. She is thoroughly surprised by the response to her illness from people she has worked with, fought with, schemed against and sometimes ignored.

"You'd think it was a wake," Polly quips at the continuing stream of visitors, causing Charlotte to laugh. The women bring soup and fresh-baked bread. The men offer to help William with the harvest even though they need to get their own fields cut. The daughters of the fledgling community are sent by their mothers to do chores for Charlotte after completing their own at home. And the women from the Indian camp come every day with their medicinal concoctions and their loving concern.

Her sons leave their logging on the Miramichi as soon as they hear and paddle with dispatch to The Point. When she sees John, Robert, Philip and James all rushing through her bedroom door, she prefers not to admit to the flood of emotions that their presence brings, especially John's. Instead she gruffly says, "What are all of you doing here? I'll be back in the fields in no time and you should be back on the river earning your keep."

When they aren't hovering over her, Charlotte's offspring take long walks around the property to worry out of her earshot. Honnor, an introspective young woman, twenty-one years old and not yet married, is clearly frightened by the prospect of being alone in the house if her mother has another attack. William, still unmarried himself, decides that the best plan is for him to return to live at the family house until Charlotte is stronger.

They aren't the only ones contemplating the consequences of another heart attack. The incident has left more than a scar on Charlotte's heart muscle. Her days in bed have forced her to think to a future further away than the next harvest, the next lot of land. In her diary, she writes:

> If I had died, what would I leave behind after this lifetime of struggle? I have ten children from four fathers and have barely avoided the toxic consequences of one son thinking he's being done out of his share. There is calm in the family now. Each son has his own lot of land and the support of nine siblings. But when I die there will be this lot of mine to be taken. It is the finest lot at The Point, in fact in all of Tabisintack. My daughters are softer creatures than I am, and wrapped up in their own children's lives. One of my sons will need to take on the role of patriarch when I go. Some would say John, but I'm uncertain of him. There's a small bitter streak in him, and I'm not sure how to gainsay it.

The next January, she writes another letter that eventually

she will send to the governor of the province.

Northumberland County

*Know all men by these presents that I Charlotte Hierlihy of
Tabisintack in said county, widow have in consideration
of being maintained decently the remainder of my natural
life as well as for the natural affection and esteem I have for
my son William do grant, bargain and convey alienate and
confirm and these presents to my said son William Wishart
of Tabisintack in said county have granted bargained
conveyed alienated and confirmed all and singular my
lands as well as land as mine that is granted to me in my
own name on the grant of certain lands to John Blake and
others at Tabisintack aforesaid by refirince had to said grant
will more fully appear. To have and to hold all the properties
commodities and privileges either on law or Equity in my
name belonging or appertaining and I Charlotte Taylor for
myself, my heirs and assigns will the said granted and conveyed presents over warrant and spend to the sire of my son
William Wishart his heirs and assigns against the claim of
all men forever in witness where of I have unto these
presents at my grant and at the same time applied my seal
at Tabisintack in said county this ___ day of January in the
year of our Lord one thousand eight hundred and fourteen
and in the 54th year of the reign of our Lord the King*

Charlotte Hierlihy

She leaves it undated, though she presumes she may need to
fill it in sooner rather than later. Then she folds the parchment

and stores it in her trunk leaving the signing and sealing to the time of her choosing when her holdings would be transferred to William.

IT'S NOT AS THOUGH Charlotte is ever alone with William and Honnor. By now she's surrounded by two dozen grandchildren, sixteen of them belonging to Elizabeth. The noise and continual fuss they bring to her hearth are a source of joy she had never imagined. She wants them to know the history of this place where they run endlessly chasing cows, exasperating the men who are cutting the hay, and plucking raspberries as they please. One day, helping William dig a pit by the river for winter storage, they find the tip of a treasure in the upturned earth and after they dig it out, they drag it back to the house to ask their Grandmother what they've found. She gathers them together and tells them the story of the ancient Indian kettle, the same story Marie once told her.

"They didn't have iron pots for cooking," she begins. "Crafting a wooden kettle like this took a long time and a lot of work." Using the marks on the kettle, she explains that they first had to find the stump of a big tree. It needed to be a tree that had already fallen over, as they didn't have the tools to cut so large a tree down, and it had to be close to the camp because they didn't have a means to carry the stump a long distance. They would use stone axes to cut a hole in the top of the stump. Then they'd make a fire in the hole. Once the stump was burned about four inches deep, they'd put out the fire and use sharpened bones and stones to hollow out the charred wood. They did that again and again until the kettle was deep.

"Now I'll tell you how they cooked in this big kettle. They couldn't put it on the open fire or it would burn! It was made of wood, after all. So instead they put flat rocks in the fire and left them there until they were red-hot. They put water in the kettle along with whatever they wanted to cook. Then they would pick up the hot rocks with sticks and drop them into the water to make it boil. Other stones were kept in the fire and when the ones in the kettle lost their heat, they'd be replaced with hot rocks from the fire. They kept doing that until the meat or fish was cooked the way they liked it."

The children, of course, want to cook something in the big kettle. And as is their grandmother's habit, she immediately falls in with a plan, leading a procession down to the shore, instructing them to fetch flat rocks, collect wood for the fire and coax a nice fat fish from the water. Once the fire is blazing, she places the rocks in the fire—"You've brought me enough to cook a whale," she teases them—and sets them to cleaning the fish while the rocks heat. By the time the filets are cut into chunks and the kettle has been scrubbed out—"Be ever so careful not to hurt the ancient thing," she warns—the rocks are red hot and the experiment begins. They pour fresh water into the kettle, plop the fish in and watch their grandmother use two sticks to lift the rocks, one by one, and drop them in. They are delighted by the great sizzle and hiss and stand as close as they dare to the steam, watching the fish slowly turn opaque and finally white. The experiment is complete.

"So, children, how many rocks does it take to cook a fish."

"Fifteen," they shout in unison.

THERE ARE PLENTY of hands to do the chores and the pantry is never empty. She marks her sixtieth birthday with a sense of calm and, after the harvest is in, she takes the winter months to sew and spend time with the books she's read so many times she thinks she can recite them. The bitter cold settles in her bones more than it used to so she stays closer to the fire. Her diary shows its age as well, the leather binding so cracked she has to be careful how she opens it.

> They're all around me—the children and their children. Elizabeth is nearly as old as her father was when he died. She and I began this journey together, and she's at my side yet, as much a sister as my first-born child. John Blake is the age his father was when I met him at the Baie. He has his likeness and his good sense and his occasional irrational temper, but things are comfortable between us now. Polly, the rascally, auburn-haired beauty who got her name from a boy who turned up on a boat one day; she works right along side her husband, Duncan, as hard as he does. Robert is already thirty-five years old, trying to be on the river logging and here at The Point farming all at once. He says he'll go south to a place called Richibucto next. I would prefer that he stay here, but he seeks opportunity wherever it is to be found.
>
> William, your namesake is as kind and gentle a son as a woman could pray for. And, Philip, you'd maybe be pleased to know it's the Loyalists who are all taking the posts in this province. Your five children have grown and prospered, as you said they must.
>
> I remember it all while I sit by the fire this night. The wind whispers along the shore and the moon casts its silver light across the meadow. The squeezing in my breast, the spasm in my throat, are not from my heart malady but rather from the ache of what is lost and the size of what is gained . . .

Honnor shakes her shoulder gently. "Mama, you've fallen asleep in your chair. Come away to bed." Charlotte closes her diary and carries the lamp to her room.

THE YEAR 1816 is known as the year without summer, the year the ice never fully leaves the rivers. In 1818, James Hierlihy is married to Louiza Urquhart, the granddaughter of Reverend John Urquhart, who started the first Presbyterian church on the Miramichi in 1804. Her grandmother, Margaret Milligan, is apparently a relative of John Quincy Adams, who according to the river gossip is being groomed to become president of the United States. The nuptials are the talk of the settlement.

In the years that follow, the Miramichi is transformed from a lawless, struggling, mostly forgotten outpost to a centre of commerce, with a new shipbuilding company started by Joseph Cunard, a postal system, a ferry service, a stagecoach that connects Frederick Town to Nepisiguit, and a steamboat service that links Halifax to Quebec. Although drunken brawling and duels—particularly between sailors weighing anchor on the Miramichi after long weeks at sea and the rowdier settlers along the closest shores—continue to be commonplace, Newcastle becomes a major trading town in the province. The new prosperity spills over to Tabisintack, where the Blake, Wishart and Hierlihy families reap the benefits of improved transportation for the lumber they cut and the fish they catch.

In 1822, Honnor, twenty-nine, marries John Murray, a local farmer who is as quiet and unassuming as she is. William, who is farming his own lot as well as Charlotte's, continues to live with his mother, though she's had no more heart trouble. Her life has become very pleasing to her, at last.

She and Wioche slip the canoe into the water on sunny afternoons to paddle along the Tabisintack River. "There goes Mrs. H and the Indian," people comment as they float by, themselves part of the local colour now. They explore the coves and caves along the river, stop to walk in the meadows, in perpetual conversation. As Charlotte has found peace, Wioche's world has become bleaker. He fears the People will become extinct at the hands of those who came to the New World in the name of greed.

This is harsh, and maybe accurate, but it hurts her nonetheless. "The Acadians didn't come with greed in their hearts, Wioche. Nor did I. I wanted a life of my own. And look what I got: five decades of hard labour! And an oldest son who almost broke my heart by wanting the same thing." They thoroughly debate with each other—she in the safety of a knowledgeable soulmate and he in a search for hope.

THE SUMMER OF 1825 is hot and drought-ridden. By August, there's not been a drop of rain, the crops are wilting, the wells are running dry. Even the animals' behaviour is bizarre. The moose vanish, so do the deer.

Halfway into autumn, the air is still scorching hot, the marsh sun-baked and cracked, the bog grass crisped to an unearthly yellow. In September, forest fires rage in the south, and Government House in Frederick Town burns to the ground. By early October, the fires reach the Miramichi.

Even in Tabisintack, the air is so hot, it's like breathing embers; the woods are burning only an hour away from The Point. Strangers arrive with reports Charlotte can hardly believe. A refugee from Frederick Town says the fire came so fast, it turned everything in its path to cinders. "Giant flames shot into heaven like an artillery barrage. The town looks like there's been a volcanic eruption. The livestock were mad with fear and running amok through the streets. People were falling to their knees praying for deliverance."

She and William are up before dawn on October 7 trying to soak everything they can with water when an explosion booms in the distance. Then another one, and a third. The sky is black with ash. Hot coals blow in a violent wind onto The Point. Cinders hiss when they hit the water. Smoke that has been hovering in the distance for days suddenly smothers them with thick soot.

By mid-afternoon, the river people start arriving with frightful tales. People in Newcastle have drowned trying to find respite in the water, or have been burned alive in their beds, or crushed by collapsing, blazing timbers. They describe the noise of the fire whooshing, exploding, rumbling incessantly; the sky dark as night, save the immense sheets of flame illuminating the heavens.

Through the night and all the next day, more survivors stagger to the shore. One chronicler, Robert Cooney, who had arrived on the Miramichi the year before to work at the newly established newspaper wrote, "The character of the scene was such that all it required to complete a picture of the General Judgment was the blast of a Trumpet, the voice of the Archangel and the resurrection of the Dead."

The fire burns all around them and finally runs itself into the sea, steaming to an end. It does not touch The Point.

The destruction along the Miramichi River is enormous. Newcastle is in ruins. Of two hundred houses, only twelve remain standing and those are severely damaged. Chatham, across the river from Newcastle, is spared. Ships anchored between the two towns are burned to crisps; others farther downstream are dashed into the rocks by hurricane winds fed by the heat. Of two thousand settlers, three hundred people are dead, six hundred buildings are destroyed and eight hundred and seventy-five cattle lost. Black heaps of ashes along the roadside turn out to be the remains of inhabitants. Most of the wildlife has perished. Salmon, bass and trout have suffocated and float bloated in the river.

Later Charlotte hears that it was five separate forest fires, started by drought and driven together by the wind, that collided in apocalyptic proportions. They consumed everything but a few tracts of land from Frederick Town to the Baie de Chaleur—four million acres of the best lumber in New Brunswick. When she realizes the magnitude of the destruction, Charlotte is humbled by their own escape. For as long as they live, they will never forget the Great Miramichi Fire.

That night when all is quiet on The Point, she picks up her diary:

> *The blackened earth is cooling now. This fire—is it man-made or God-delivered? There have been many here on this land, the Micmac, the Acadians, the French and the British. They've come from England, Scotland, Ireland, France and beyond, carrying their histories and quarrels and dreams. They've brought the religions denied them in the countries they fled, traditions they share with the people they meet, their sweat and determination to tame this wild land and make a future for their children. There's a piece of every-place else here—language, customs, traits, even recipes. My own hearth could be described as Acadian, British and Micmac!*

> *There are those who see this land as nothing more than*
> *a piece of turf to own and rule and gain riches from. But*
> *for the most part, the people here are yoked to the sea, the*
> *tall trees and wild rivers, the plentiful fish and the flower-*
> *ing meadows.*
>
> *The aftermath of the fire will be the test for everyone.*

AS IT TURNS OUT, the Great Miramichi fire is a turning point for the people of New Brunswick. Faced with near ruin, they put their ploughs into the soil and till their way to prosperity. The shipbuilding industry is resurrected on the Miramichi. Enterprising young men with business plans for plants to pack and sell fish, create jobs. And the forests, their floors now fertile with post-fire ash, begin to grow again.

At The Point, the confounding mix of tragedy and blessedness is just the way life is, Charlotte thinks. Elizabeth's Duncan drowns in the Tabisintack River, leaving her a widow with six of her sixteen children still under the age of twelve. The next year, Philip Hierlihy is married to Jane Lewis. Jane signs the marriage certificate with an X, which causes her new mother-in-law to complain once more about the lack of schools in the settlement. Her own daughters often select an X over the signatures she taught them.

Charlotte, now seventy-five, longs to see the sights her children exclaim about. But she's tired more often than not. Even her sharp tongue has mellowed some. When William announces his betrothal to Elizabeth Johnston in June, she is actually pleased there will be a new chatelaine in her fine house. The marriage is set for November 22, and while others fuss with the cooking, she secretly makes plans for one last move.

CHAPTER 14

The Millstream

1830

A convoy of canoes paddles upriver on a particularly stunning autumn day in October 1830. James and William take the lead, with their mother, weakened by her failing heart, wrapped in blankets and cushioned in the middle of the canoe with a huge black bearskin. Her trunk is strapped to the second canoe, and draws curious glances from those on the shore, many of them her extended family.

When they round The Point, she looks out over the cultivated fields, the house in which she's lived for thirty-two years and the water that nearly surrounds it. She can't resist a glance to the open sea and spares a thought for William Wishart. She leans forward to tap his namesake on the shoulder and says, "I'd like for it now to be known as Wishart's Point." He nods his agreement, smiling back at her.

There are some rapids to be ridden about a mile before Stymiest Millstream, and as bad luck would have it, they catch the third canoe, dumping both James and Philip and all the contents into the drink. The water level is low, so the two are quickly up on their feet again, chasing baskets of clothing and the knickknacks that swirl around them on the current then snag on the rocks. "My frocks will be stiff with the brine," Charlotte says. "But a bit of soap and water and a good breeze will make them right again."

It takes all morning to paddle the ten miles to Stymiest Millstream, but Charlotte Mary is standing on the dock waiting when the entourage arrives as if she knows exactly when to expect them. She adores this renegade mother of hers, and is continually surprised and always amused by her stubborn refusal to kowtow to anyone. At thirty-nine, she is the youngest daughter, has a house full of children and welcomes the opportunity for them to learn at the knee of their grandmother. But she too is wondering what has propelled Charlotte to leave her beloved Point and come to the head of the tide on the river to live with them.

They off-load the canoes, laying the soggy bundles out to dry on the lawn, and settle Charlotte into her new quarters.

Despite the constant chatter of children and the hum of Benjamin's sawmill, Charlotte tells her daughter soon after arriving, "The wind from the Point blows itself out some on its way through the woods. I find it peaceful here."

She's only been in her daughter's house for a day when a canoe slips into the stream from the opposite bank and a man deftly strokes his way across the water. Wioche tells them the Indian camp on the opposite shore became his permanent home during the summer months. "I'm an old man now and cannot walk the Mi'kmaq district," he jokes. But he can paddle a canoe and that's what he and Charlotte do every day that the weather is fine.

"Not far, mind you," Charlotte Mary tells her siblings. "Just a ways upriver and back. That pouch he carries—it has dried blueberry leaves in it. They make tea from the leaves and claim it eases the pain in their joints."

They ply the waters like two ancient historians, their hair snowy white, hers fastened in a knot on top of her head, his tied in two plaits that fall over his shoulders, their faces tawny and weathered by the years of facing the elements, their eyes crinkled but sparkling yet.

"I wonder what they talk about," Charlotte Mary muses each time the pair set out for their paddle.

IN THE DAYS after she arrives, Charlotte looks everywhere for the tattered old diary she's kept since her nanny taught her the alphabet. She empties the trunk, where she usually kept it. Then she wonders whether it was in the canoe that tipped. She shakes out every item that survived the drenching—the dresses that have already been washed, the box with her brushes and combs—and then once more goes through the bag she had carried on her lap. But she knows, even while she rummages through her belongings, that her words are likely at the bottom of the Tabisintack River.

She sends word to William, who scours the house at Wishart's Point to no avail. The family, duty bound to try to find the lost diary, send out the grandchildren to check the shores and scavenge the muddy river bottom. But they know before putting their paddles in the water that the precious old book is gone. Charlotte turns her thoughts to tasks that will camouflage her loss.

She spends time with Elizabeth, who has never really recovered from losing Duncan. She makes regular visits to Wishart's

Point, paddling down the river with Wioche for visits with William and his wife. But mostly she burrows in at Stymiest Millstream, and daydreams about her men, her children, her grandchildren, the ties that bind. The mighty forests and wild waters that stole her heart from the moment she encountered them, the fields she's cleared and cultivated, the gardens that feed her flock, all tied to the story of her long pioneering life.

She remembers the trials too. The fights with the Loyalists on the Miramichi, the storm that wrecked nearly everything the first winter they spent at The Point. And she relishes recalling her attempts to outwit her adversaries—the journey she and Wioche made to Frederick Town to secure the deed to John Blake's lot, the tumbledown shed she built with Jimmy to house a goat so that Elizabeth would have milk. The tally of her life comes out in her favour, she decides. But she has no respite from losses.

She is seventy-seven when her oldest son takes sick and dies. And for a time the loss of John defeats her. In all the years of brewing potions to nurse them through illnesses or waiting for them to return from the perils of logging, or the sea, or the hunt, she's never lost one of them, never even come close. There's something perverse about a mother mourning a child.

The family makes a floating procession down the river, through the sea and into the bay at the Miramichi and over the shoals to the burial ground, where John Blake is laid to rest next to his father. The very next day Robert and John's widow, Catherine, sell part of Lot Eight to the county. It was their father's original 1777 Nova Scotia land grant. The deed names it as Black Brook. "It's Blake Brook," Charlotte complains, knowing it's futile. The name is as lost as the man it was named for and his first-born son.

On the way back from the funeral, when they pass Burnt Church, the grandchildren in her canoe ask Charlotte how it came to have such a name. And Charlotte begins a story that isn't finished until after the journey's end.

"It used to be called Eskinwobudich, the Indian word for lookout. Long before I came here, when I was still a little girl in England, the village was attacked by British soldiers who wanted to be rid of the Indians and the Acadians both. They burned everything, including a stone church, the first church on the river. Afterwards, people started calling the place Burnt Church." The children want to know why the soldiers did this. "Didn't they like them?" Charlotte Mary's youngest asks. Her grandmother says, "In my old trunk, I have a letter written by the colonel who directed the attack. John Blake, grandfather to some of you, was one of the soldiers in that raid and came upon the account written and brought it to me to read for him. He was a good man, John Blake, but he had some trouble with his letters."

Back at home, the youngsters pester her to read them the colonel's letter, and Charlotte retrieves it, fragile and sepia with age. It's much too long to retain a child's attention, so she scans it quickly, then selects a passage from the conclusion of Colonel Murray's account. "This was written on the twenty-fourth of September, 1758," she tells them:

> *In the Evening of the 17th in Obedience to your Instructions*
> *embarked the Troops, having two Days hunted all around*
> *Us for the Indians and Acadians to no purpose, we however*
> *destroyed their Provisions, Wigwams and Houses, the*
> *Church which was a very handsome one built with Stone,*
> *did not escape. We took Numbers of Cattle, Hogs and*

Sheep, and Three Hogsheads of Beaver Skins, and I am persuaded there is not now a French Man in the River Miramichi, and it will be our fault if they are ever allowed to settle there again, as it will always be in the Power of two or three Armed vessels capable of going over the Barr, to render them miserable should they attempt it.

Her assembled grandchildren are mesmerized. And little Benjamin knows just what to ask next: "Did the Indians and Acadians really go away? Uncle David is Acadian. Wioche is an Indian." Charlotte tries to explain the history, fully aware of her own complicity in displacing both Acadian and Indian. Her whole life here, it seems, has been lived in the knowledge that everything she wished to secure for her family helped to undo the security of her friends.

The children never tire of their grandmother's stories. When they walk with her in the winter, she tells them how the snow sparkles because of millions of crystals with different surfaces that reflect the light from the sun or the moon. And in spring she teaches them the lessons of planting. "Look, the buds on the poplars are near to bursting. When the new leaves are as big as a squirrel's ear, that's the time to plant the corn."

When little Benjamin swings from an apple tree in full bloom, snapping the branch from the trunk, she reminds him, "There will be no apples on that branch come fall. You need to choose a branch that'll hold you, so you'll have food in the winter."

Inevitably they ask her why she left her mother and father and came across the ocean.

"There was trouble in Britain at that time," she says earnestly. "My father said there would be fewer opportunities for young men. People were angry and worrying. But the talk about the New World across the ocean was exciting. So this is where I wanted to be." She's explained herself this way to the children so many times by now she nearly believes it herself. The midnight flight from her home and the calamitous stop in the West Indies are foggy memories, overwritten with the passage of time.

She tells them about the kind of home she grew up in. "When I was a child, I was never allowed to go any place without my nurse. She was always with me. I remember my home, a very lovely stone house with a stone wall all around it and beautiful flowers and shade trees. I can still picture them in my memory. There was a sketch of the garden that I brought with me, but I fear it is lost now. Maybe it went into the river with my diary."

SHE'S MORE THAN EIGHTY when she decides it's time to retrieve the letter long stored in her old trunk. She dates it September 3, 1836. Then she asks the Justice of the Peace, William Ferguson, and her son James to be the witnesses when she signs, seals and delivers her will to deed all of her lands to William Wishart. No one argues. In fact, the only one who is surprised is Charlotte herself, when fall turns to winter then spring and she is still with them.

She celebrates her eighty-fifth birthday at Wishart's Point, and an enormous crowd of well-wishers descends to honour the woman who was truly the beginning. More than seventy grandchildren, eight of them named Charlotte, and all of her grown sons and daughters but John, dead now for eight years, fete the woman who has played such an influential role in their lives. Most of the inhabitants of the now-flourishing Tabisintack settlement come to pay homage to "old Mrs. H." The Mi'kmaq send woven baskets, a braid of sweetgrass and a fox pelt hat to keep her warm. They sing the most popular song in this settlement of Scot descendants, and when the end of the chorus— "We'll drink a cup of kindness yet for auld lang syne"—lifts up over The Point, Charlotte lets her gaze drift to the sea. The wind whispers through her white hair, pulling it out of the combs and blowing the strands over her face. It's the last time she ever sees The Point.

THE WINTER takes its toll on her. Wioche, as old as she is, slides across the frozen river to sit with her by the fire while the storms outside nearly bury the cabin with snow. By the time spring announces itself, she isn't able to leave her bed for his visits. "Tell me a story," she asks Wioche. He begins, as he always does, with the creation myth, the one she loves best, about Gitchi Manitou sending Gluskap to Earth. About him digging holes to make valleys and piling the dirt to make mountains. As often as not, Charlotte is sleeping before the story ends.

On an early morning, April 25, 1841, when the sun is casting its glow along the river and the earth is bursting with blossoms, Charlotte Mary carries the strong black tea her mother prefers for breakfast into the bedchamber and finds her lying, eyes open, chest still. Charlotte Taylor Blake Wishart Hierlihy, the indomitable and daring matriarch, is dead.

A SERVICE IS ARRANGED for the cemetery in Tabisintack, on a grassy plain that stands watch above the river and looks out over Wishart's Point. While Charlotte Mary and her family go ahead to the cemetery, three canoes line up at the Stymiest shore. Led by Wioche, Mi'kmaq women, wailing and chanting, gather the earthly remains of their friend, wrap her in their finest blankets and lay her in the canoe on a bed of otter skins. Then they turn to the south, the direction of woman, and give thanks to the creator for the life and good deeds of Charlotte Taylor.

"Nisgam wi la lin ugjit ula gelusit e'pit—Great Spirit, thank you for this good woman."

Wioche paddles the canoe that carries Charlotte down the river. The women paddle on either side, chanting mournfully all the way to the cemetery where they deliver their beloved Charlotte to her descendants.

The Indians linger by the shore, as the family gathers around the grave, listening to the eulogy, the gospel reading and the singing. "Oh God, our help in ages past," the mourners sing. "Time, like an ever rolling stream, bears all its sons away; they fly, forgotten, as a dream dies at the opening day."

After the last shovelful of earth is tamped into the grave, they drift away, on foot, by buggy, in boats and canoes.

The old Mi'kmaq man sits on the hill. From here he can see the mound of fresh brown earth that covers the new grave; to the east, the homestead at Wishart's Point, now bathed in evening light; to the northwest, the sparkling river he plied so many times with Charlotte. From here he can feel the coastal winds that stirred her soul, and see the land she tried to tame.

Night settles in and birdsong announces vespers. Wioche stays there watching, remembering, making his farewell to the woman he has always loved, the impetuous and beautiful Charlotte Taylor. He's still there when the moon rises and turns him into a silhouette. In the still of the night, the only sound that breaks the quiet is the song of the whippoorwill, a long, mournful call that echoes along the river, across the treetops, up to the heavens, calling, calling, again and again.

CHARLOTTE TAYLOR'S ROOTS were firmly planted in Tabusintac by the time she died. More than seventy grandchildren, eight of them called Charlotte, carried her pioneering style and her story to the next generation. Ten years after she died, on April 26, 1851, her son and heir William Wishart also passed away. Today, more than two thousand of her descendants gather every five years at Tabusintac's Old Home Week.

I first attempted to write Charlotte's story as a straightforward non-fiction account. I wanted to contribute to the early history of New Brunswick, as well as to augment the sparse chronicles of the women pioneers of that time. But even as I was researching, I also was caught up in the vivid reimagining of Charlotte's life and frustrated by the missing links—I could not find out for certain how she wound up on the Miramichi or confirm the elusive relationship her descendants claim she had with a First Nations man. So I finally decided that my ancestor would have encouraged me to take liberties, crafting fictional bridges and scenes between the known facts in a historical reconstruction of her life.

. We do know the names of her husbands, her children and her grandchildren—although no record was found for her marriage to William Wishart, nor a birth certificate for the child born during that marriage, William. Details about her neighbours on the Miramichi and Commodore George Walker are from archival data. So are the re-creations of the battles with the American patriots and the Indians, events such as the Great Miramichi Fire, and the petitions and land claims she sent to the government.

We also know that she left England with her lover, a man called Willisams, who was previously in the employ of her father's household staff. But that is all we know about him.

Walker's men, in particular Will MacCulloch, are fictional, inspired by tales of the real men who served in the Royal Marines and Royal Navy at that time.

As for Wioche, there are facts known about her bond with the Mi'kmaq. She was a midwife to the women; she trekked to Fredericton with an aboriginal man; when she died, the Mi'kmaq carried her to a canoe and paddled her to the cemetery in Tabusintac. But the story repeated by almost all of her descendants, about her lifelong relationship with a Mi'kmaq man, remained elusive despite my combing of record offices and searching for letters. To unravel this puzzle, I went to Gilbert Sewell, the Mi'kmaq storyteller in Big Cove, New Brunswick. He began at the end by telling me that if the Mi'kmaq took her to the burial ground, she would most certainly have held a special place in the band and would likely have been adopted by them. The question was when and why.

That required an examination of how Charlotte got to the Miramichi in the first place. Although there is no archival evidence documenting her arrival in the New World, there are two stories that circulate among her descendants. One has her landing at Miscou Island in northern New Brunswick, after her lover drowned in the sea when their landing craft tipped between the ship and the shore. The other is that she went to the West Indies and that her lover died of yellow fever shortly after they arrived. I chose the latter version, partly because it would have been unlikely for a British ship to make a landing at Miscou in 1775. But mostly because of the story—widely believed by her descendants but unproven—that Mr. Willisams was a black man whose ancestors came to England from the West Indies.

How she got to British North America from the West Indies was another puzzle. I chose her route by weighing the odds. John Blake plied the waters between the West Indies and the Miramichi and he worked with Commodore George Walker, who ran the only trading outpost in the vast northeast. Walker also sailed to the West Indies on trading missions. By examining the shipping schedules between May and October 1775, and the log of John Blake's travels in the spring, summer and fall of that year—and then adding in the fact that Charlotte's first child, Elizabeth, was born before that year was out—I surmised that her shepherd must have been George Walker. As a consequence, she would have begun her life in British North America at Alston Point. I also guessed that she would have sought the company of women for the birth of her child, and since there were no European women at Walker's compound, the women she turned to would have been Mi'kmaq. Given her savvy about wilderness survival by the time she married Blake, I assumed she found shelter with the Mi'kmaq, who were friends of Walker's and lived at a camp near Alston Point.

Was it possible that the Mi'kmaq man she trekked to Fredericton with was someone she met at Alston Point? Gilbert Sewell thinks so. He told me that the chief's appointed traveller would have covered the Mi'kmaq district that included the Miramichi, and that his name would have been Wioche. The Wioche of this book, however, is a fictional character.

Charlotte's progeny today—my generation of great-great-great-grandchildren—include writers and journalists, teachers and lawyers, doctors and farmers, bank executives and fishers, judges and Cabinet ministers, along with a few convicted felons. I imagine that Charlotte, the woman who turned her back on England at the tender age of twenty, would have been either proud of or intrigued by all of us, just as all of us are deeply intrigued by her.

ACKNOWLEDGMENTS

WRITING THE STORY of Charlotte Taylor was a fascinating and frustrating voyage into archives, family stories and history books. I am indebted to many who assisted me in my quest to get as close as possible to the *veritas* in the life of this intrepid, wily woman.

First, my thanks to Anne Collins, editor, publisher and mentor, whose reputation for turning raw prose into readable story is unparalleled. And to my agent, Michael Levine, for making sure my manuscript landed in such capable hands.

Many of Charlotte's descendants were helpful in this odyssey. From snowshoeing with me to try out the method Charlotte used in her 1776 trek, to taking me "up river" and "down shore" by boat to test drive her terrain, Mylie and Loraine Wishart and Bertha Wishart were wonderfully supportive and a fount of information. I am also grateful to Mary Lynn Smith, who is the keeper of the key to the *Life and Times of Charlotte*

Taylor (www3.bc.sympatico.ca/charlotte_taylor). Her meticulous research was invaluable to me.

Gilbert Sewell, the Mi'kmaq storyteller, was patient with my many questions and generous with his time. The braid of sweetgrass he gave me hung over my computer for the two years it took to shape the story I wanted to tell.

I am also indebted to Mary Wolfe, Donna Clinch and Margaret McKay, who despite hordes of mosquitoes and boggy terrain tramped through cemeteries with me searching for clues. And to Barry MacKenzie, for guiding me to the precise spot where Charlotte and John Blake lived on the Miramichi. He takes no credit for the bear we encountered on the way.

I also want to thank Doug Young, Mary Ann Rogers, Antony Marcil, Doady Armstrong and Susan Shalala, who works in the New Brunswick Archives in Fredericton, for their help with the research for this book.

My thanks go to botanist David Appleton for his advice on the survival rate of a packet of seeds tucked away in a trunk for decades, to sailing expert Peter Cowern, to food historian Liz Driver and to Pat Allen, whose careful reconstruction of the travels of Commodore George Walker was very useful. And I am grateful to Olga Davis, whose sharp eye deciphered the scrawl of Charlotte's two-hundred-year-old letters.

In a special category of thanks all their own are those who encouraged me to take on this project and gave me their unwavering support: Cynthia Good, Ernest Hillen, W.J. Hogan and Charlotte's great-great-great-great-grandchildren, my own three treasures, Heather, Peter and Anna. Thank you one and all.

BOOKS, PAPERS AND ARCHIVES

Allen, Patricia. "Commodore George Walker at Alston Point, Nepisiguit: 1768–1777" (New Brunswick Manuscripts in Archeology, 2003).

Arbuckle, Doreen Menzies. *The Northwest Miramichi* (Ottawa: Western
Printers Ltd. 1978).

Biggar, Mitch. "The Revolutionary War" at *www.geocities.com/Heartland/
Ranch/9002/war.htm.*

Branch, Kimberly. "Charlotte: Mother of Tabusintac" (University of
New Brunswick, term paper, 1995).

Cooney, Robert. "A Comprehensive History of the Northern Part of
the Province of New Brunswick" (Joseph Howe, 1832), found in
Esther Clark Wright's *The Miramichi* (Sackville: Tribune Press,
1945).

Daigle, Jean, ed., *The Acadians of the Maritimes* (Centre D'Etudes
Acadiennes, Université de Moncton, 1982).

Denys, Nicolas. *The Native People of Acadia* (retold by Ian Maxwell,
1993) (Champlain Society, 1908).

————. *The Description and Natural History of the Coasts of North America* (retold by Ian Maxwell, 1993) (Champlain Society, 1908).

Foxe, John. *Foxe's Book of Martyrs.* Edited by William Byron Forbush. Chapter 15 George Wishart at *www.ccel.org/f/foxe/martyrs.*

Fraser, James. *By Favourable Winds: A History of Chatham, New Brunswick* (Town of Chatham, 1975).

Fraser, James A. *Loggieville: Child of Miramichi* (Fredericton, 1973).

Frink, Tim. *New Brunswick: A Short History* (Stonington Books, 1997).

Ganong, William F. "The History of Caraquet and Pokemouche." Reprinted from *Acadiensis* at *http://ahcn.net?histoire/ganong/neguac-bc.htm.*

————. "The History of Neguac and Burnt Church." Reprinted from *Acadiensis* at *http://ahcn.net?histoire/ganong/neguac-bc.htm.*

————. "A Monograph of Historic Sites in the Province of New Brunswick" (*Transactions of the Royal Society of Canada*, Section II, 1899).

————. "Gamaliel Smethurst's Narrative of his Journey from Nepisiguit to Fort Cumberland" (*New Brunswick Historical Society Collections*, 1905).

————. "The History of Tabusintac" (*Acadiensis*, vol. VII, no 4, October 1907, p. 314–331).

————and Richard Denys. "Sieur de Fronsac and his settlement in Northern New Brunswick" (*New Brunswick Historical Society Collection*, no 7, 1907).

————. "The Official Account of the Destruction of Burnt Church" (*New Brunswick Historical Society Collections*, no 9, 1914, p. 301–307).

————. Ganong Papers (New Brunswick Museum).

Gibbon, Mary. *Miscou Island: Vulnerability and the Generations* (Mary Gibbon, 2001).

Givan, Fredrica. "Breaux and Savoy, Acadian Settlers at Tabusintac" at *http://archiver.rootsweb.com/th/read/Acadian-Cajun/1998–11/0911594515.*

Gray, Charlotte. *The Museum Called Canada: 25 Rooms of Wonder* (Toronto: Random House Canada, 2004).

Klein, Kim. "A 'Petticoat Polity' Women Voters in New Brunswick Before Confederation" (*Acadiensis*, xxvi, Autumn, 1996, pp. 71–75).

Larracey, E.W. *The First Hundred* (Moncton Publishing Company, 1970).

Long, J. *Voyages and Travels of an Indian Interpreter and Trader.* Originally published in London, England, 1791. Reprinted by Coles Publishing Company Toronto, 1971.

LeClercq, Father Chrestien. *New Relation of Gaspesia With the Customs and Religion of the Gaspesian Indians.* Translated and edited by William F. Ganong (Toronto: Champlain Society, 1910).

Macmillan, Cyrus. *Gloosekaps's Country and other Indian Tales* (Toronto: Oxford University Press, 1967).

MacNaughton, Katherine Flora Cameron. *The Development of the Theory and Practice of Education in New Brunswick 1784–1900* (University of New Brunswick, 1947).

MacNutt, W.S. *New Brunswick: A History: 1784–1867* (Toronto: Macmillan of Canada, 1963).

Maillet, Antonine. *Pelagie: The Return to Acadie* (Toronto: Doubleday, 1982).

Manny, Louise. "Scenes of an Earlier Day." Records of Northumberland County New Brunswick, 1935.

Paul, Daniel N. *We Were Not the Savages* (Black Point, Nova Scotia: Fernwood Publishing, 2000).

Piesse, G.W.S. "The Art of Perfumery (1879)" at *www.saponifier.com*.

Provincial Archives of New Brunswick: Deeds, letters and petitions. Fredericton.

Rand, Rev. S.T. *Micmac Grammar* (Truro, Nova Scotia: Specialty Printers, 1999).

Raymond, W.O. *The Marston Diaries: Benjamin Marston at Halifax, Shelburne and Miramichi* at *http://ultratext.hil.unb.ca/Texts/Marston/articles/Shelburne_notes.html*.

Raymond, W.O. *The North Shore: Incidents in the Early History of Eastern and Northern New Brunswick* (New Brunswick Historical Society, Collections).

Robertson, J. Logie. *The Poetical Works of Robert Burns* (Toronto: Oxford University Press, 1896).

Running Wolf, Michael and Clark Smith, Patricia. *On the Trail of Elder Brother: Glous'gap Stories of the Micmac Indians* (New York: Persea Books, 2000).

Savoy, Gail. *A History of Tabusintac, N.B.* (Tabusintac: Tabusintac Centennial Memorial Library, 2005).

Stymiest, Carl. *Down by the Old Mill Stream: A Stymiest Chronicle* (Victoria: Trafford, 2001).

Taylor, Jonathan. "Light Fittings in Georgian and Early Victorian Interiors" (*The Building Conservation Directory*, 1998).

Theriault, Fidele. *George Walker et son Etablissement a Nipisiguit* (New Brunswick Archives, 1999).

The Canadian Indian: Quebec and Atlantic Provinces. Indian and Northern Affairs (Ottawa, 1973).

"The Church in New Brunswick: An Early History" at *www. knightsofcolumbus-renous.ca/church_history/miramichi.html*.

The Diary of Simeon Perkins (Toronto: Greenwood Press, reprint, 1969).

The Diary of Simeon Perkins, 1766–1780, 1797–1803, 1804–1812 (Champlain Society).

The Winslow Papers CD Archives, volume 1 at *http://personal.nbnet.nb.ca/halew/Winslow.html*.

Voices United: The Hymn and Worship Book of the United Church of Canada (The United Church Publishing House, 1996).

Waugh, Alec. *The Sugar Islands* (New York: Farrar Strauss, 1949).

———. *A Family of Islands: A History of the West Indies* (New York: Doubleday, 1964).

Webster, J. Clarence. *Historical Guide to New Brunswick* (New Brunswick Government Bureau of Information and Tourist Travel, 1947).

Wilson, James. "Narrative of a Voyage from Dublin to Quebec, In North America" at *http://ist.uwaterloo.ca/~marj/genealogy/voyages/dublin1817.html.*

WEB SITES

Acadian History Time Line
 http://users.andara.com/-grose/acadianh.html
Cargo Ship Mayflower
 www.americanrevolution.org/may4.html
Chronology of the Abolition of Slavery
 www.blackhistoricalmuseum.com/chronology.htm
Food Time Line
 www.foodtimeline.org/foodpuddings.html
Hearth to Hearth: Hunting the Welsh Rabbit
 www.journalofantiques.com/hearthmay.htm
Order in Council Establishing New Brunswick
 http://webhome.idirect.com/-cpwalsh/nb/acts/ukoic1784.htm
The Importance of Food in Eighteenth-Century Louisbourg
 http://fortress.uccb.ns.ca/behind/food.html.
The Life and Times of Charlotte Taylor by Mary Lynn Smith
 www3.bc.sympatico.ca/charlotte_taylor
The Micmac Creation Story
 www.indigenouspeople.net/crmicmac.htm
The Mi'kmaq. Nova Scotia Museum
 http://museum.giv.ns.ca/arch/infos/mikmaq1.htm
The Stymiest Family History
 www.wizardsrealmcentral.com/stymiest/id20.html